SMITH'S GUIDE TO HABEAS CORPUS RELIEF FOR STATE PRISONERS UNDER 28 U.S.C. §2254

By Zachary A. Smith

Complete with Example Pleadings of Everything From the Initial Habeas Corpus Petition to a Petition for a Writ of Certiorari

First Edition, February 2011

ISBN 978-0-9842716-8-9
Published by Allen & Allen Semiotics, Inc.
Long Beach, CA

TABLE OF CONTENTS

TABLE OF CONTENTS

DISCLAIMER

This book is not an alternative to professional assistance by an attorney. This book does not provide licensed, professional legal advice. Its author is not a lawyer. Its text is for informational purposes only. The material contained herein is not intended to substitute for professional assistance by an attorney. Never disregard professional legal advice, and never delay in seeking it or hiring an attorney to represent you because of anything you read in this book. It is the responsibility of you, the reader, to seek out and secure legal advice on how to proceed within the federal judicial system.

The information in this book has been carefully researched, and all efforts have been made to ensure accuracy. The author and publisher assume no responsibility for any injuries suffered or damages or losses incurred during, or as a result of, the application of the information presented here. All information should be carefully studied and clearly understood before taking any action based on the contents of this book. The reader assumes full responsibility for the consequences of his or her own actions, filing, and strategic decisions.

INTRODUCTION

For the last fifteen years, I've studied and practiced law. I am not an attorney. I just played one in prison. That doesn't mean the legal battles I've fought for others and myself were not real. Still, after many victories and many more defeats, I remain incarcerated, like you.

On June 29, 1995, I was arrested and charged with first-degree murder and armed criminal action. I was nineteen years old and didn't know anything about the law. While in the county jail, I began reading all the law books I could get my hands on. I obtained a job in the prison law library after my first conviction. Some people would say that I took to law like a fish to water. I ate, slept, and breathed law day and night, until I got my conviction overturned.

After being convicted a second time on retrial, I went back to studying and practicing law. It became apparent that there were no books written specifically for prisoners to help them attack their convictions in the federal courts. I therefore decided to write this book.

In the following pages I've laid out the process, step by step, for attacking your conviction in the federal courts via habeas corpus relief under 28 U.S.C. §2254. At the end of each chapter, I've provided example petitions, motions, form letters, certificates of appealability, notices of appeal, motions for leave to proceed in forma pauperis, appellate briefs, petitions for a writ of certiorari, and more. There is no other book available that includes examples of everything you'll be required to prepare and file to litigate your federal habeas corpus petition.

It is my intent for this book to prove an invaluable resource guide for you, and for every other prisoner in the United States fighting for their freedom or the freedom of others. Good luck in your future endeavors.

Sincerely,

Z.A. Smith

Z. A. Smith

Note: A percentage of the net proceeds from the sale of this book will be given to non-profit organizations dedicated to helping prisoners and fighting for our rights.

1. OVERVIEW OF FEDERAL HABEAS CORPUS REVIEW

TIMELINESS OF PETITION FOR HABEAS CORPUS RELIEF

A prisoner's petition for a writ of habeas corpus is considered filed on the day the prisoner delivers it to prison authorities, which includes dropping the petition in a prison mailbox. *Houston v. Lack, 487 U.S. 266, 270-74, 108 S.Ct. 2379 (1988)*.

A petitioner must overcome several procedural barriers before a court will review the merits of a petition for a writ of habeas corpus. As Justice O'Connor noted in *Daniels v. United States*, "Procedural barriers, such as statutes of limitations and rules concerning procedural default and exhaustion of remedies, operate to limit access to review on the merits of a constitutional claim." *532 U.S. 374, 381, 121 S.Ct. 1578 (2001)*; see also *United States v. Olano, 507 U.S. 725, 731, 113 S.Ct. 1770 (1993)*.

In general, a state prisoner seeking habeas corpus relief pursuant to 28 U.S.C. §2254 must comply with the statute of limitations period set forth therein, which provides:

(d)(1) A 1-year period of limitation shall apply to an application for a writ of habeas corpus by a person in custody pursuant to the judgment of a state court. The limitation period shall run from the latest of --

(A) the date on which the judgment became final by the conclusion of direct review or the expiration of the time for seeking such review;

(B) the date on which the impediment to filing an application created by state action in violation of the Constitution or laws of the United States is removed, if the applicant was prevented from filing such state action;

(C) the date on which the constitutional right was initially recognized by the Supreme Court, if the right has been newly recognized by the Supreme Court and made retroactively applicable to cases on collateral review; or

(D) the date on which the factual predicate of the claim or claims presented could have been discovered through the exercise of due diligence.

The statute of limitations is tolled for any period of time in which a properly filed petition for post-conviction relief is pending before the state courts. See *28 U.S.C. §2244(d)(2)*, which provides:

> (d)(2) The time during which a properly filed application for state post-conviction or other collateral review with respect to the pertinent judgment or claim is pending shall not be counted toward any period of limitation under this subsection.

The time during which a properly filed application for state post-conviction or other collateral review with respect to the pertinent judgment or claim is pending shall not be counted toward the AEDPA statute of limitations. *28 U.S.C. §2244(d)(2)*. The statute of limitations is not tolled during the interval between the date on which a judgment becomes final and the date on which the petitioner files his first state collateral challenge because there is no case "pending." Once a petitioner commences state collateral proceedings, a state habeas petition is "pending" during a full round of review in the state courts, including the time between a lower court decision and the filing of a new petition in a higher court, as long as the intervals between the filing of those petitions are "reasonable." *Carey V. Saffold, 536 U.S. 214-222-224, 122 S.Ct. 2134 (2002).*

The United Sates Supreme Court held in *Artuz v. Bennett, 531 U.S. 4, 121 S.Ct. 361, 363-365 (2000)* that an application for post-conviction or other collateral review is "properly filed" when its delivery and acceptance are in compliance with the applicable laws and rules governing filings, e.g., requirements concerning the form of the document, the court and office in which it must be lodged, payment of filing fee, and applicable time limits upon its delivery.

The Supreme Court has further held: "A litigant seeking equitable tolling bears the burden of establishing two elements: (1) that he has been pursuing his rights diligently, and (2) that some extraordinary circumstances stood in his way." *Pace v. Diguglielmo, 544 U.S. 408, 418, 125 S.Ct. 1807 (2005).*

In *Lawrence v. Florida, 549 U.S. 327, 336, 127 S.Ct. 1079 (2007)*, the Court held that the tolling provision under §2244(d)(2), which stated that the one-year limitations period under §2244(d)(1) for filing a federal habeas petition was tolled while an application for state post-conviction or other collateral review was pending, did not toll the limitations period during the pendency of the inmate's petition for certiorari seeking review of the denial of state post-conviction relief. Nor was the inmate entitled to equitable tolling, assuming that equitable tolling was available; legal confusion did not warrant equitable tolling, as the law was sufficiently clear that tolling under §2244(d)(2) was not available while a certiorari petition was pending, nor was equitable tolling warranted based on counsel's miscalculation of the limitations period.

Read naturally, the text of 28 U.S.C. §2244(d)(2) must mean that the statute of limitations is tolled only while state courts review a state post-conviction application. A state post-conviction application "remains pending" until the application has achieved final resolution through the state's post-conviction procedures. The United States Supreme Court is not a part of a state's post-conviction procedures. State review ends when the state courts have finally resolved an application for state post-conviction relief. After the state's highest court has issued its mandate or denied review, no other state avenues for relief remain open, and an application for state post-conviction relief no longer exists. All that remains is a separate certiorari petition pending before a federal court. The application for state post-conviction review is therefore not "pending" after the state court's post-conviction review is complete, and §2244(d)(2) does not toll the one-year limitations period during the pendency of a petition for certiorari.

You should exercise caution when putting off filing your federal habeas corpus petition to pursue other state remedies in an attempt to exhaust your claims. Take the time to do the legal research; find case law from your federal circuit that specifically states the state post-conviction applications you want to file will actually toll the one-year time limitation for filing a habeas corpus petition. You may also address your questions to a public defender appointed to represent you on a direct appeal, or on post-conviction relief.

STANDARD FOR HABEAS CORPUS REVIEW

28 U.S.C. §2254

(a) The Supreme Court, a Justice thereof, a circuit judge, or a district court shall entertain an application for a writ of habeas corpus on behalf of a person in custody pursuant to the judgment of a State court only on the ground that he is in custody in violation of the Constitution or laws or treaties of the United States.

(b)

    (1) An application for a writ of habeas corpus on behalf of a person in custody pursuant to the judgment of a State court shall not be granted unless it appears that --

        (A) the applicant has exhausted the remedies available in the courts of the State; or

        (B)

            (i) there is an absence of available state corrective process; or

            (ii) circumstances exist that render such process ineffective to protect the rights of the applicant.

    (2) An application for a writ of habeas corpus may be denied on the merits, notwithstanding the failure of the applicant to exhaust the remedies available in the courts of the State.

    (3) A State shall not be deemed to have waived the exhaustion requirement or be estopped from reliance upon the requirement unless the State, through counsel, expressly waives the requirement.

(c) An applicant shall not be deemed to have exhausted the remedies available in the courts of the state, within the meaning of this section, if he has the right under the law of the state to raise, by any available procedure, the question presented.

(d) An application for a writ of habeas corpus on behalf of a person in custody pursuant to the judgment of a State court shall not be granted with respect to any claim that was adjudicated on the merits in State court proceedings unless the adjudication of the claim --

(1) resulted in a decision that was contrary to, or involved an unreasonable application of, clearly established Federal law, as determined by the Supreme Court of the United States; or

(2) resulted in a decision that was based on an unreasonable determination of the facts in light of the evidence presented in the State court proceeding.

(e)

(1) In a proceeding instituted by an application for a writ of habeas corpus by a person in custody pursuant to the judgment of a State court, a determination of a factual issue made by a State court shall be presumed to be correct. The applicant shall have the burden of rebutting the presumption of correctness by clear and convincing evidence.

(2) If the applicant has failed to develop the factual basis of a claim in State court proceedings, the court shall not hold an evidentiary hearing on the claim unless the applicant shows that --

(A) the claim relies on--
(i) a new rule of constitutional law, made retroactive to cases on collateral review by the Supreme Court, that was previously unavailable; or
(ii) a factual predicate that could not have been previously discovered through the exercise of due diligence; and

(B) the facts underlying the claim would be sufficient to establish by clear and convincing evidence that but for constitutional error, no reasonable fact finder would have found the applicant guilty of the underlying offense.

(f) If the applicant challenges the sufficiency of the evidence adduced in such State court proceeding to support the State court's determination of a factual issue made therein, the applicant, if able, shall produce that part of the record pertinent to a determination of the sufficiency of the evidence to support such determination. If the applicant, because of indigency or other reason is unable to produce such part of the record, then the State shall produce such part of the record and the Federal court shall direct the State to do so by order directed to an appropriate State official. If the State cannot provide such pertinent part of the record, then the court shall determine under the existing facts and circumstances what weight shall be given to the State court's factual determination.

(g) A copy of the official records of the State court, duly certified by the clerk of such court to be a true and correct copy of a finding, judicial opinion, or other reliable written indicia showing such a factual determination by the state court shall be admissible in the Federal court proceeding.

(h) Except as provided in section 408 of the Controlled Substances Act, in all proceedings brought under this section, and any subsequent proceedings on review, the court may appoint counsel for an applicant who is or becomes financially unable to afford counsel, except as provided by a rule promulgated by the Supreme Court pursuant to statutory authority. Appointment of counsel under this section shall be governed by section 3006A of Title 18.

(i) The ineffectiveness or incompetence of counsel during Federal or State collateral post-conviction proceedings shall not be a ground for relief in a proceeding arising under section 2254.

For a better understanding of §2254(d)(1) and its application by the federal court, read *Williams (Terry) v. Taylor, 529 U.S. 362 (2000)*.

EXHAUSTION REQUIREMENT

State prisoners seeking relief under §2254 must satisfy specific and precise procedural standards. Among these procedural prerequisites is a requirement that the petitioner "has exhausted the remedies available in the court of the state" before seeking relief in federal court. *28 U.S.C. §2254(b)*. §2254's exhaustion requirement calls for total exhaustion of all available state remedies. Thus, a habeas petitioner "shall not be deemed to have exhausted the remedies available in the courts of the state, within the meaning of this section, if he has the right under the law to raise, by any available procedure, the question presented." *28 U.S.C. §2254(c)*. In instances where a state prisoner has failed to exhaust the legal remedies available to him in the state courts, federal courts typically will refuse to entertain a petition for habeas corpus.

In *O'Sullivan v. Boerckel, 526 U.S. 838, 119 S.Ct. 1728 (1999)*, the United States Supreme Court explained the habeas exhaustion requirement as follows. "Because the exhaustion doctrine is designed to give the state courts a full and fair opportunity to resolve federal constitutional claims before those claims are presented to the federal courts ... state prisoners must give the state courts one full opportunity to resolve any constitutional issues by invoking one complete round of the State's established appellate review process" before filing for federal habeas relief. *Id. at 845*. Exhaustion requires that a prisoner "fairly present" the substance of each federal constitutional claim to the state court before seeking federal habeas relief. *Id. at 844*.

In most states, "one complete round" ordinarily means that each §2254 claim must have been presented in an appeal to the court of appeals of that state, and then in a petition for further review to the supreme court of that state if the court of appeals rules against the petitioner. However, some states, like Missouri, only require prisoners to present the legal issue to the state's court of appeals in order to exhaust it at the state level. The Missouri Supreme Court determined that since seeking review from that court is discretionary, presenting legal issues to them through an application to transfer is not required in order to meet the exhaustion requirement.

Your state may be similar, but you should do research to be sure, because if a habeas claim has not been presented on the merits all the way through your state's appellate review process and you are now barred from such presentation, the claim is "procedurally defaulted," not unexhausted. In such a case, when a claim is procedurally defaulted, you are barred from raising the issue in federal court unless you can show cause and prejudice for the procedural default.

It is in your best interest to fully and in a timely manner exhaust all your state remedies in state court when the opportunity is available. If your legal issue is barred on state procedural grounds, it will be procedurally defaulted in federal court.

PROCEDURAL DEFAULT

The procedural default doctrine, which, like the exhaustion doctrine, is grounded in principles of comity, federalism, and judicial efficiency (*Dretke v. Haley, 541 U.S. 386, 124 S.Ct. 1847, 1851-52 [2004]*) normally will preclude a federal court from reaching the merits of a habeas claim when either (1) that claim was presented to the state courts and the state court ruling against the petitioner rests on adequate and independent state-law procedural grounds, or (2) the claim was not presented to the state courts and it is clear that those courts would now hold the claim procedurally barred. *Coleman v. Thompson, 501 U.S. 722, 111 S.Ct. 2546, 2557 & n.1 (1991).* Thus, when the habeas petitioner has failed to fairly present to the state courts the claim on which he seeks relief in federal court and the opportunity to raise that claim in state court has passed, the petitioner has procedurally defaulted that claim. *Boerckel, 526 U.S. at 853-54, 119 S.Ct. at 1736.*

The procedural default doctrine does not impose an absolute bar to federal relief, however. "It provides only a strong prudential reason, grounded in 'considerations of comity and concerns for the orderly administration of justice,' not to pass upon a defaulted constitutional claim presented for federal habeas corpus review." *Haley, 124 S.Ct. at 1852.* The doctrine is therefore subject to equitable exceptions. *Id.* A procedural default will bar a federal court from granting relief on a habeas claim unless the petitioner demonstrates cause for the default and prejudice resulting therefrom, *Wainwright v. Sykes, 433 U.S. 72, 87-88, 97 S.Ct. 2497 (1977),* or, alternatively, he convinces the court that a miscarriage of justice would result if his claim were not entertained on the merits. *Murray v. Carrier, 477 U.S. 478, 495-96, 106 S.Ct. 2639 (1986).* See also *Edwards v. Carpenter, 529 U.S. 446, 451, 120 S.Ct. 1587 (2000).*

To establish cause for his default, a petitioner ordinarily must show that some external impediment blocked him from asserting his federal claim in state court. *Carrier, 477 U.S. at 488, 492, 106 S.Ct. at 2645, 2648.* To establish prejudice, he "must shoulder the burden of showing, not merely that the errors at his trial created a *possibility* of prejudice, but that they worked to his *actual* and substantial disadvantage, infecting his entire trial with error of constitutional dimensions." *United States v. Frady, 456 U.S. 152, 170, 102 S.Ct. 1584, 1586 (1982).*

If the petitioner cannot show cause and prejudice but instead seeks to overcome his procedural default by establishing the prospect of a miscarriage of justice, then he must demonstrate that he is actually innocent of the crime for which he was convicted -- that is, he must convince the court that no reasonable juror would have found him guilty but for the errors allegedly committed by the state. *Schlup v. Delo, 513 U.S. 298, 327-29, 115 S.Ct. 851, 867-68 (1995).*

2. PETITION FOR WRIT OF HABEAS CORPUS

PREPARATION OF PETITION

Upon written request, any United States federal district court will send you a packet to prepare your petition for a writ of habeas corpus. An example letter and copy of the packet -- with instructions for preparing your petition -- are included at the end of this chapter. I've also included a petition, filed by an attorney, to refer to when preparing your own petition.

Some states have more than one district court, so you'll have to determine which district you're incarcerated in and file your petition with the appropriate court. For example, in Missouri there is a Southern, Eastern, and Western district. To be sure; when you write to request a writ packet, ask the clerk of your state's United States district court which district you're incarcerated in. Most public defenders will give you §2254 forms and the address of the district court to file them in once your state remedies are exhausted.

There is no legal knowledge required to prepare your habeas corpus petition. As you'll see from the example petition at the end of this chapter, you just have to answer the questions, then state all grounds that were exhausted in state court and the facts supporting them. You are not required to argue or cite law. You'll get a chance to do that in your traverse. The traverse is your reply to the State's response to the court's order to show cause why a writ of habeas corpus should not be granted.

PROCEEDING *IN FORMA PAUPERIS*

The filing fee required for your petition is $5. If you cannot pay the fee, you may ask to proceed *in forma pauperis* (as a poor person). You will receive the forms to do that with your habeas corpus packet. You'll also have to submit a certified printout of your inmate account, showing that you do not have the $5 to pay the filing fee. If the total of the deposits your account received during the period immediately preceding your petition's filing date exceeds $500.00, you must pay the filing fee. In other words, you must have received less than $500.00 in a six month period prior to filing your petition. See instructions and sample forms at the end of this chapter.

MAILING PETITION

Once you've completed the petition, and either enclose an institutional check for the $5 filing fee or file *in forma pauperis*, your petition is considered filed the date it's dropped into the institutional mailbox. The envelope may be sealed because it is legal mail. The filing fee must accompany your petition unless you're filing as a poor person. You only have to send the court one original petition, but do keep a copy for yourself, too.

After the court receives your petition, you will receive a notice of the filing. At that time, the court will order the respondent to show cause why a writ of habeas corpus should not be issued. In habeas corpus cases, the respondent is the warden of the prison you are incarcerated in, and will be represented by the attorney general's office of the state you're incarcerated in. The State's response will be discussed in the next chapter.

EXAMPLE FORM LETTER REQUESTING HABEAS CORPUS PACKET

September 23, 2010

United States District Court
400 E. 9th Street
Kansas City, MO 64106

Dear Clerk:

I'd like to request a packet for filing a petition for a writ of habeas corpus under §2254 please. Thank you for your time and assistance.

Respectfully,

Z.A.Smith

Zachary Smith
#521163- 4C-243
CRCC
1115 East Pence Road
Cameron, MO 64429

EXAMPLE LETTER IN RESPONSE FROM DISTRICT COURT

UNITED STATES DISTRICT COURT
WESTERN DISTRICT OF MISSOURI
Office of the Clerk

Ann Thompson
Court Executive

REPLY TO:
400 East 9ᵗʰ Street, Room 1510
Kansas City, MO 64106

September 30, 2010

Zachary Smith
#521163 - 4C-243
CRCC
1115 East Pence Road
Cameron, MO 64429

Dear Mr. Smith:

In response to your letter, enclosed is a complete set of federal habeas corpus forms for filing a petition pursuant to 28 U.S.C. § 2254.

Sincerely,

J.K. Carter
Pro Se Staff Attorney

BLANK PETITION FOR WRIT OF HABEAS CORPUS PACKET

Petition for Relief from a Conviction or Sentence
By a Person in State Custody

(Petition Under 28 U.S.C. § 2254 for a Writ of Habeas Corpus)

Instructions

1. To use this form, you must be a person who is currently serving a sentence under a judgment against you in a state court. You are asking for relief from the conviction or the sentence. This form is your petition for relief.

2. You may also use this form to challenge a state judgment that imposed a sentence to be served in the future, but you must fill in the name of the state where the judgment was entered. If you want to challenge a <u>federal</u> judgment that imposed a sentence to be served in the future, you should file a motion under 28 U.S.C. § 2255 in the federal court that entered the judgment.

3. Make sure the form is typed or neatly written.

4. You must tell the truth and sign the form. If you make a false statement of a material fact, you may be prosecuted for perjury.

5. Answer all the questions. You do not need to cite law. You may submit additional pages if necessary. If you do not fill out the form properly, you will be asked to submit additional or correct information. If you want to submit a brief or arguments, you must submit them in a separate memorandum.

6. You must pay the fee of $5. If the fee is paid, your petition will be filed. If you cannot pay the fee, you may ask to proceed <u>in forma pauperis</u> (as a poor person). To do that, you must fill out the enclosed <u>in forma pauperis</u> forms. Also, you must submit a certificate signed by an officer at the institution where you are confined showing the amount of money that the institution is holding for you. If the total of the deposits into your account during the period immediately preceding the date you file your petition exceeds $500.00, you must pay the filing fee.

7. In this petition, you may challenge the judgment entered by only one court. If you want to challenge a judgment entered by a different court (either in the same state or in different states), you must file a separate petition.

8. When you have completed the form, send the original (keep one copy for your records) to the Clerk of the United States District Court at this address:

> Clerk, United States District Court
> for the Western District of Missouri
> 400 E Ninth St
> Kansas City, MO 64106

9. <u>CAUTION</u>: You must include in this petition <u>all</u> the grounds for relief from the conviction or sentence that you challenge. And you must state the facts that support each ground. If you fail to set forth all the grounds in this petition, you may be barred from presenting additional grounds at a later date.

10. <u>CAPITAL CASES</u>: If you are under a sentence of death, you are entitled to the assistance of counsel and should request the appointment of counsel.

Note: 13 single-sided pages to follow without headers or page numbers

PETITION UNDER 28 U.S.C. § 2254 FOR WRIT OF HABEAS CORPUS BY A PERSON IN STATE CUSTODY

United States District Court	District
Name (under which you were convicted):	**Docket or Case No:**
Place of Confinement :	**Prisoner No.:**
Petitioner **V.** (<u>include</u> the name under which you were convicted)	**Respondent** (Authorized person having custody of Petitioner)
The Attorney General of the State of :	

PETITION

1. (a) Name and location of court that entered the judgment of conviction you are challenging:_____
_____
_____
_____

    (b) Criminal docket or case number (if you know): _____

2. (a) Date of the judgment of conviction (if you know):_____

    (b) Date of sentencing:_____

3. Length of sentence:_____

4. In this case, were you convicted on more than one count or of more than one crime?   Yes__ No

5. Identify all crimes of which you were convicted and sentenced in this case:_____
_____
_____
_____
_____

6. (a) What was your plea? (Check one)
      (1) Not guilty ____   (3) Nolo Contendere (no contest)____

      (2) Guilty ____   (4) Insanity plea ____

   (b) If you entered a guilty plea to one count or charge and a not guilty plea to another count or charge, what did you plead guilty to and what did you plead not guilty to?_____

_____

_____

_____

_____

   (c) If you went to trial, what kind of trial did you have? (check one)

         Jury____   Judge only ____

7. Did you testify at a pretrial hearing , trial, or a post-trial hearing?

         Yes ____   No ____

8. Did you appeal from the judgment of conviction?

         Yes ____   No ____

9. If you did appeal, answer the following:

(a) Name of court:_____

(b) Docket or case number (if you know):_____

(c) Result:_____

(d) Date of result (if you know):_____

(e) Citation to the case (if you know):_____

(f) Grounds raised:_____

_____

_____

_____

_____

(g) Did you seek further review by a higher state court?   Yes____   No____

   If "Yes," answer the following:

   (1) Name of court:_____

   (2) Docket or case number (if you know):_____

   (3) Result:_____

   (4) Date of result (if you know):_____

(5) Citation of the case (if you know):_____

(6) Grounds raised:_____

_____

_____

_____

_____

_____

(h) Did you file a petition for certiorari in the United States Supreme Court? Yes ___ No ___
If "Yes," answer the following:

(1) Docket or case number (if you know):_____

(2) Result:_____

(3) Date of result (if you know):_____

(4) Citation to the case (if you know):_____

10. Other than the direct appeals listed above, have you previously filed any other petition, application or motions concerning this judgement of conviction in any state court?

Yes ___   No ___

11.   If your answer to Question 10 was "YES," give the following information:

(a) (1) Name of court:_____

(2) Docket or case number (if you know):_____

(3) Date of filing (if you know):_____

(4) Nature of the proceeding:_____

(5) Grounds raised:_____

_____

_____

_____

_____

_____

(6) Did you receive a hearing where evidence was given on your petition, application, or motion?
Yes ___   No ___

(7) Result: _____

(8) Date of result (if you know): _____

(b) If you filed any second petition, application, or motion, give the same information:

(1) Name of court:_____

(2) Docket of case number (if you know):_____

(3) Date of filing (if you know):_____

(4) Nature of the proceeding:_____

(5) Grounds raised:_____
_____
_____
_____
_____
_____

(6) Did you receive a hearing where evidence was given on your petition, application, or motion?
Yes ___   No ___

(7) Result: _____

(8) Date of Result (if you know): _____

(c) If you file any third petition, application, or motion, give the same information:

(1) Name of court:_____

(2) Docket of case number (if you know):_____

(3) Date of filing (if you know):_____

(4) Nature of the proceeding:_____

(5) Grounds raised:_____
_____
_____
_____
_____
_____

(6) Did you receive a hearing where evidence was given on your petition, application, or motion?

Yes   ___   No ___

(7) Result:_____

(8) Date of result (if you know): _____

(d) Did you appeal to the highest state court having jurisdiction over the action taken on your petition, application, or motion?

(1) First petition: Yes ___   No ___
(2) Second petition   Yes ___   No ___
(3) Third petition   Yes ___   No ___

(e) If you did not appeal to the highest state court having jurisdiction, explain why you did not:_____
_____
_____
_____

12. For this petition, state every ground on which you claim that you are being held in violation of the Constitution, laws, or treaties of the United States. Attach additional pages if you have more than four grounds. State the <u>facts</u> supporting each ground.

<u>CAUTION</u>: To proceed in the federal court, you must ordinarily first exhaust (use up) your available state court remedies on each ground on which you request action by the federal court. Also, if you fail to set forth all the grounds in this petition, you may be barred from presenting additional grounds at a later date.

GROUND ONE:_____
_____
_____

(a) Supporting facts (Do not argue or cite law. Just state the specific facts that support your claim):
_____
_____
_____
_____
_____
_____
_____
_____

(b) If you did not exhaust your state remedies on Ground One, explain why:_____
_____
_____
_____

(c) **Direct Appeal of Ground One**:

    (1) If you appealed from the judgment of conviction, did your raise this issue?
        Yes ___   No ___

    (2) If you did <u>not</u> raise this issue in your direct appeal, explain why?_____
_____
_____

(d) **Post-Conviction Proceedings**:

    (1) Did you raise this issue through a post-conviction motion or petition for habeas corpus in a state trial court?   Yes ___   No ___

    (2) If your answer to Question (d)(1) is "Yes," state:

        Type of motion or petition:_____

        Name and location of the court where the motion or petition was filed:_____
_____

Docket or case number (if you know):_____

Date of the court's decision:_____

Result (attach a copy of the court's opinion or order, if available):_____

_____

(3) Did you receive a hearing on your motion or petition?
   Yes ___   No ___

(4) Did you appeal from the denial of your motion or petition?
   Yes ___   No ___

(5) If your answer to Question (d)(4) is "Yes," did you raise this issue in the appeal?
   Yes ___   No ___

(6) If your answer to Question (d)(4) is "Yes," state

   Name and location of the court where the appeal was filed:_____

   _____

   Docket or case number (if you know):_____

   Date of the court's decision:_____

   Result (attach a copy of the court's opinion or order if available)_____

   _____

   (7) If your answer to Question (d)(4) or Questions (d)(5) is "No", explain why you did not raise this
issue:_____

_____

(e) **Other Remedies**: Describe any other procedures (such as habeas corpus, administrative remedies, etc)
that you have used to exhaust your state remedies on Ground One:_____

_____

_____

GROUND TWO:_____

_____

_____

(a) Supporting facts (Do not argue or cite law. Just state the specific facts that support your claim):

_____

_____

_____

_____

_____

_____

_____

(b) If you did not exhaust your state remedies on Ground Two, explain why:_____

_____

_____

_____

(c) **Direct Appeal of Ground Two**:

      (1) If you appealed from the judgment of conviction, did you raise this issue?
         Yes ___   No ___

      (2) If you did <u>not</u> raise this issue in your direct appeal, explain why?_____

_____

_____

(d) **Post-Conviction Proceedings**:

      (1) Did you raise this issue through a post-conviction motion or petition for habeas corpus in a state trial court?
         Yes ___   No ___

      (2) If your answer to Question (d)(1) is "Yes," state:

         Type of motion or petition:_____

         Name and location of the court where the motion or petition was filed:_____

_____

         Docket or case number (if you know):_____

         Date of the court's decision:_____

         Result (attach a copy of the court's opinion or order, if available):_____

_____

      (3) Did you receive a hearing on your motion or petition?
         Yes ___   No ___

      (4) Did you appeal from the denial of your motion or petition?
         Yes ___   No ___

      (5) If your answer to Question (d)(4) is "Yes," did you raise this issue in the appeal?
         Yes ___   No ___

      (6) If your answer to Question (d)(4) is "Yes," state:

         Name and location of the court where the appeal was filed:_____

_____

         Docket or case number (if you know):_____

         Date of the court's decision:_____

         Results (attach a copy of the court's opinion or order if available)_____

_____

(7) If your answer to Question (d)(4) or Questions (d)(5) is "No," explain why you did not raise this issue:_____

_____

(e) **Other Remedies:** Describe any other procedures (such as habeas corpus, administrative remedies, etc) that you have used to exhaust your state remedies on Ground Two:_____

_____

_____

GROUND THREE:_____

_____

_____

(a) Supporting facts (Do not argue or cite law. Just state the specific facts that support your claim):

_____

_____

_____

_____

_____

_____

(b) If you did not exhaust your state remedies on Ground Three, explain why:_____

_____

_____

_____

(c) **Direct Appeal of Ground Three:**

(1) If you appealed from the judgment of conviction, did you raise this issue?
Yes ___   No ___

(2) If you did <u>not</u> raise this issue in your direct appeal, explain why?_____

_____

_____

(d) **Post-Conviction Proceedings:**

(1) Did you raise this issue through a post-conviction motion or petition for habeas corpus in a state trial court?
Yes ____   No____

(2) If your answer to Question (d)(1) is "Yes," state:

Type of motion or petition:_____

Name and location of the court where the motion or petition was filed:_____

_____

Docket or case number (if you know):_____

Date of the court's decision:_____

Remark (attach a copy of the court's opinion or order, if available):_____
_____

(3) Did you receive a hearing on your motion or petition?
Yes ___ No ___

(4) Did you appeal from the denial of your motion or petition?
Yes ___ No ___

(5) If your answer to Question (d)(4) is "Yes," did you raise this issue in the appeal?
Yes ___ No ___

(6) If your answer to Question (d)(4) is "Yes," state

Name and location of the court where the appeal was filed:_____
_____

Docket or case number (if you know):_____

Date of the court's decision:_____

Results (attach a copy of the court's opinion or order if available)_____
_____

(7) If your answer to Question (d)(4) or Questions (d)(5) is "No," explain why you did not raise
this issue:_____
_____
_____

 (e) **Other Remedies:** Describe any other procedures (such as habeas corpus, administrative remedies, etc)
that you have used to exhaust your state remedies on Ground Three:_____
_____
_____

GROUND FOUR:_____
_____
_____

(a) Supporting facts (Do not argue or cite law. Just state the specific facts that support your claim):

_____
_____
_____
_____
_____
_____

(b) If you did not exhaust your state remedies on Ground Four, explain why:_____
_____
_____
_____

(c) Direct Appeal of Ground Four:

(1) If you appealed from the judgment of conviction, did you raise this issue?

Yes _____   No ___

(2) If you did <u>not</u> raise this issue in your direct appeal, explain why?_____

_____

_____

(d) Post-Conviction Proceedings:

(1) Did you raise this issue through a post-conviction motion or petition for habeas corpus in a state trial court?

Yes ___   No ___

(2) If your answer to Question (d)(1) is "Yes," state:

Type of motion or petition:_____

Name and location of the court where the motion or petition was filed:_____

_____

Docket or case number (if you know):_____

Date of the court's decision:_____

Result (attach of copy of the court's opinion or order, if available):_____

_____

(3) Did you receive a hearing on your motion or petition?

Yes ___   No ___

(4) Did you appeal from the denial of your motion or petition?

Yes ___   No___

(5) If your answer to Question (d)(4) is "Yes," did you raise this issue in the appeal?

Yes ___   No___

(6) If your answer to Question (d)(4) is "Yes," state:

Name and location of the court where the appeal was filed:_____

_____

Docket or case number (if you know):_____

Date of the court's decision:_____

Result (attach a copy of the court's opinion or order if available)_____

_____

(7) If your answer to Question (d)(4) or Questions (d)(5) is "No", explain why you did not raise this issue:_____
_____

(e) **Other Remedies**: Describe any other procedures (such as habeas corpus, administrative remedies, etc) that you have used to exhaust your state remedies on Ground Four:_____
_____
_____

13. Please answer these additional questions about the petition you are filing:

(a) Have all grounds for relief that you have raised in this petition been presented to the highest state court having jurisdiction?   Yes ___   No___

If your answer is "No," state which grounds have not been so presented and give your reason(s) for not presenting them:_____
_____
_____

(b) Is there any ground in this petition that has not been presented in some state or federal court? If so, which ground or grounds have not been presented, and state your reasons for not presenting them:_____
_____
_____
_____

14. Have you previously filed any type of petition, application, or motion in a federal court regarding the conviction that you challenge in this petition? Yes ___   No ___

If "Yes," state the name and location of the court, the docket or case number, the type of proceeding, the issues raised, the date of the court's decision, and the result for each petition, application, or motion filed. Attach of copy of any court opinion or order, if available:_____
_____
_____
_____
_____
_____

15. Do you have any petition or appeal now pending (filed and not decided yet) in any court, either state or federal for the judgment you are challenging? Yes ___   No ___

If "Yes," state the name and location of the court, the docket or case number, the type of proceeding, and the issues raised: _____
_____
_____
_____
_____
_____

16. Give the name and address, if you know, of each attorney who represented you in the following state of the judgment you are challenging:

(a) At preliminary hearing:_____

(b) At arraignment and plea:_____

(c) At trial: _____

(d) At sentencing:_____

(e) On appeal:_____

(f) In any post-conviction proceeding:_____

(g) On appeal from any ruling against you in a post-conviction proceeding:_____
   _____
   _____

17. Do you have any future sentence to serve after you complete the sentence for the judgment you are challenging?   Yes ___   No ___

(a) If so, give name and location of court that imposed the other sentence you will serve in the future:
   _____
   _____

(b) Give the date the other sentence was imposed:_____

(c) Give the length of the other sentence:_____

(d) Have you filed, or do you plan to file, any petition that challenges the judgment or sentence to be served in the future?   Yes ___   No ___

18. TIMELINESS OF PETITION: If your judgment of conviction became final over one year ago, you must explain why the one-year statute of limitations as contained in 28 U.S.C. § 2244(d) does not bar your petition.*(see below)_____
_____
_____
_____
_____
_____
_____
_____
_____
_____

*The Antiterrorism and Effective Death Penalty Act of 1996 ("AEDPA") as contained in 28 U.S.C. § 2244(d) provides in part that:

(1) A one-year period limitations shall apply to an application for writ of habeas corpus by a person in custody pursuant to the judgment of a State court. The limitations period shall run from the latest of:
(A) the date on which the judgment became final by the conclusion of direct review or the

expiration of the time for seeking such review;

(B) the date on which the impediment to filing an application created by State action in violation of the constitution or laws of the United States is removed, if the applicant was prevented from filing by such state action;

(C) the date on which the constitution right asserted was initially recognized by the Supreme Court, if the right has been newly recognized by the Supreme Court and made retroactively applicable to cases on collateral review; or

(D) the date on which the factual predicate of the claim or claims presented could have been discovered through the exercise of true diligence.

(2) The time during which a properly filed application for State post-conviction or other collateral review with respect to the pertinent judgment or claim is pending shall not be counted toward any period of limitations under this subsection.

_____

Therefore, petitioner asks that the Court grant the following relief:_____
_____
_____
or any other relief to which petitioner is entitled.

_____
Signature of Attorney (if any)

I declare (or certify, verify, or state) under penalty of perjury that the foregoing is true and correct and that this Petition for Writ of Habeas Corpus was placed in the prison mailing system on _____ (month, date, year).

Executed (signed) on _____ (Date).

_____
Signature of Petitioner

If the person signing is not petitioner, state relationship to petitioner and explain why petitioner is not signing this petition._____
_____
_____

BLANK AFFIDAVIT IN SUPPORT OF REQUEST TO PROCEED *IN FORMA PAUPERIS*

Note: The blank affidavit will appear on the following 3 single-sided pages without headers or page numbers.

```
_____     )
Plaintiff, Petitioner or Movant )
                                )
          v.                    )     Case No._____
                                )
_____     )
Defendant(s) or Respondent(s)   )
```

AFFIDAVIT IN SUPPORT OF REQUEST TO
PROCEED *IN FORMA PAUPERIS* -- PRISONER CASES

I, _____ declare (1) that I am the _____ in this case; (2) that in support of my motion to proceed without being required to **prepay** fees or costs, I state that because of my poverty, I am unable to pay the costs of this proceeding; and (3) that I believe I am entitled to relief. (Note: Prisoners must pay the full filing fee of $350.00 in civil rights cases and $5.00 in habeas corpus cases in accordance with 28 U.S.C. § 1915.) See instructions provided with this packet.

1. Place of confinement of plaintiff: _____

    _____

2. Crime(s) for which you have been convicted, date and sentence on each:

    _____

    _____

3. Are you presently employed?   Yes ___   No ___

    a.   If the answer is "Yes," state the amount of your salary or wages per month, and give the name and address of your employer.

         _____

         _____

    b.   If the answer is "no", state the date of last employment and the amount of the salary and wages per month which you received.

         _____

         _____

4. Have you received, within the past twelve (12) months, money from any of the following sources?

	Yes	No
Business, profession of form of self-employment?	___	___
Rent payments, interest or dividends?	___	___
Pensions, annuities or life insurance payments?	___	___
Gifts or inheritances?	___	___
Any other sources?	___	___

    If the answer to any of the above is "yes," describe the source and amount of money received from each during the past twelve (12) months.

    _____

    _____

5. Do you own any cash, or do you have money in a checking or savings account? (Include any funds in prison accounts during the last six (6) months.) Yes ___ No ___

    If the answer is "Yes," state the total amount of cash owned, and the average monthly balance in all checking, savings or prison accounts during the last six (6) months.

    _____

    _____

6. Do you own real estate, stocks, bonds, notes, automobiles, jewelry or other valuable property (excluding ordinary household furnishings and clothing)? Yes ___ No ___

    If the answer is "yes," describe the property and state its approximate value.

    _____

    _____

7. List the persons who are dependent upon you for support, state your relationship to those persons, and indicate how much you contribute toward their support.

    _____

    _____

    _____

    _____

    _____

I DECLARE UNDER PENALTY OF PERJURY THAT THE ABOVE INFORMATION IS TRUE AND CORRECT. I UNDERSTAND THAT PROVIDING FALSE INFORMATION MAY RESULT IN DISMISSAL OF THE CASE, SUBJECT ME TO CRIMINAL PROSECUTION, IMPOSITION OF A FINE, OR OTHER SANCTION THAT MAY ADVERSELY AFFECT MY ABILITY TO PURSUE THIS CASE OR OTHER CASES. I HAVE REVIEWED MY ANSWERS TO INSURE THEIR ACCURACY.

Executed (signed) this _____ day of _____, 20___ .

_____
(Signature of Plaintiff, Petitioner or Movant)

==

Authorization for Release of Institutional Account Information and Payment of the Filing Fee

I, _____

(Name of Plaintiff, Petitioner or Movant)   (Register Number)

authorize the Clerk of Court to obtain, from the agency having custody of my person, information about my institutional account, including balances, deposits and withdrawals, to determine my eligibility to proceed *in forma pauperis*. 28 U.S.C. § 1915. The Clerk of Court may obtain my account information from the past six months and in the future until the filing fee is paid. I also authorize the agency having custody of my person to withdraw funds from my account and forward payments to the Clerk of the Court, in accord with 28 U.S.C. § 1915.

Executed (signed) this _____ day of _____, 20___ .

_____
(Signature of Plaintiff, Petitioner or Movant)

EXAMPLE PETITION FOR WRIT OF HABEAS CORPUS

IN THE UNITED STATES DISTRICT COURT
WESTERN DISTRICT OF MISSOURI
PERSONS IN STATE CUSTODY APPLICATION FOR
HABEAS CORPUS UNDER 28 U.S.C. §2254

Name: **ZACHARY SMITH**

Prison Number: **521163**

Place of Confinement: **Crossroads Correctional Center, Cameron, MO**

United States District Court, Western District of Missouri

Case No:

Zachary Smith

v.

Mike Kemna, RESPONDENT

and

THE ATTORNEY GENERAL OF THE STATE OF MISSOURI, ADDITIONAL
RESPONDENT

PETITION

1.   Name and location of court which entered the judgment of conviction under

attack: **Circuit Court of Jackson County, Missouri, Kansas City, Missouri**

2.   Date of judgment of conviction: **June 16, 2000**

3.   Length of sentence: **Life imprisonment, without possibility of parole; ninety-**

nine years' imprisonment.

4.   Nature of offense involved (all counts): **murder first degree, armed criminal**

action.

1

EXAMPLE PETITION FOR WRIT OF HABEAS CORPUS (Continued)

5.   What was your plea? (Check one)

(a) Not guilty   __X__

(b) Guilty   _____

(c) Nolo contendere   _____

If you entered a guilty plea to one count or indictment, and a not guilty plea to another count or indictment, give details:

6.   Kind of trial: (Check one) (a) Jury _X_ (b) Judge only ___

7.   Did you testify at the trial? Yes [ ] No [X]

8.   Did you appeal from the judgment of conviction Yes [X] No [ ]

9.   If you did appeal, answer the following:

(a) Name of court: **Missouri Court of Appeals, Western District**

(b) Result: **Conviction affirmed**

(c) Date of result: **September 24, 2004**

10. Other than a direct appeal from the judgment of conviction and sentence, have you previously filed any petitions, applications or motions with respect to this judgment in any court, state or federal?

Yes [X]   No [ ]

11.   If your answer to 10 was "yes," give the following information:

(a)   (1)   Name of court: **Missouri Supreme Court**

(2)   Nature of proceeding: **Application for transfer**

(3)   Grounds raised:

(4)   Did you receive an evidentiary hearing on your petition, application, or motion? Yes [ ] No [X]

(5)   Result: **Transfer denied**

(6)   Date of result: **December 24, 2002**

2

EXAMPLE PETITION FOR WRIT OF HABEAS CORPUS (Continued)

(b) As to any second petition, application, or motion give the same information:

    (1) Name of court: **United States Supreme Court**

    (2) Nature of proceeding: **Petition for certiorari**

    (3) Grounds raised:

    (4) Did you receive an evidentiary hearing on your petition, application, or motion? Yes [ ] No [X]

    (5) Result: **Certiorari denied**

    (6) Date of result:

(c) As to any third petition, application, or motion give the same information:

    (1) Name of court: **Circuit Court of Jackson County**

    (2) Nature of proceeding: **Post-conviction proceeding under Mo. Sup. Ct. R. 29.15**

    (3) Grounds raised:

    (4) Did you receive an evidentiary hearing on your petition, application, or motion? Yes [X] No []

    (5) Result: **Relief denied**

    (6) Date of result: **September 19, 2006, Court of appeals opinion; December 18, 2006 (transfer to Mo. Sup. Ct. denied)**

(d) Did you appeal to the highest state court having jurisdiction the result of the action taken on any petition, application or motion?

    (1) First petition, etc.   Yes [ ] No [X]

    (2) Second petition, etc.   Yes [ ] No [X]

3

EXAMPLE PETITION FOR WRIT OF HABEAS CORPUS (Continued)

---

(3)   Third petition, etc.   Yes [X] No [ ]

(e)   If you did <u>not</u> appeal from the adverse action on any petition, application, or motion, explain why you did not: **No appeal was available from the first and second petitions.**

12.   State <u>concisely</u> every ground on which you claim that you are being held unlawfully. Summarize <u>briefly</u> the facts supporting each ground. If necessary, you may attach pages stating additional grounds and <u>facts</u> supporting same.

A.   Ground one: **Mr. Smith's was denied due process of law under the Fourteenth Amendment to the United States Constitution when the prosecutor was permitted to testify about Mr. Smith's brother's alleged attempt to intimidate prosecution witness Kevin Glavin.**

Supporting **FACTS** (tell your story <u>briefly</u> without citing cases or law):

During Mr. Smith's trial, the state's principal witness was Kevin Glavin, who was allegedly an eyewitness to the events in question. Mr. Glavin informed the court that he was not "mentally capable to go through with this testimony." He said that he could not remember the facts of the case. Mr. Glavin testified before the jury that he could not remember any of the circumstances of Derek Hoskins's (the victim) death. The prosecutor began to impeach Mr. Glavin with his prior statements. Then, the prosecutor asked Mr. Glavin whether he remembered Mr. Smith's brother Tory (Torrid) Smith nodding at him as he sat in the hall before testifying. After an objection from trial counsel the trial court specifically instructed the prosecutor not to ask about what Tory Smith did, but

4

EXAMPLE PETITION FOR WRIT OF HABEAS CORPUS (Continued)

rather about what motion Mr. Glavin himself made to Tory Smith. However,

instead, the prosecutor questioned Mr. Glavin as follows:

> A little bit ago when we were out there in the hallway, 10
> or 15 minutes ago, the brother of the defendant walked
> by, he nodded, he went like this (indicating) and the
> defendant nodded again.

The testimony of Mr. Glavin, the only eyewitness who testified, was critical

to the prosecution in this case. The prosecutor was forced to present his

testimony by impeachment. The suggestion that this was due to actions by Mr.

Smith's brother under Mr. Smith's direction was implicit in the prosecutor's

questioning, and was prejudicial to Mr. Smith.

B.   Ground two: **Mr. Smith was denied due process of law under the Fourteenth**

Amendment to the United States Constitution when the trial court permitted the

jury to view the videotaped prior statement prosecution witness Kevin Glavin

during deliberations.

Supporting **FACTS** (tell your story briefly without citing cases or law):

During their deliberations, the jury requested the right to see the

videotaped unsworn prior statement of state's witness Kevin Glavin. The judge

granted this request. As noted above, Mr. Glavin's previous statement was

critical to the state's case because he testified at trial that he did not remember

what happened the night of the murder. Allowing the jury to hear this unsworn

statement twice was highly prejudicial to Mr. Smith.

5

EXAMPLE PETITION FOR WRIT OF HABEAS CORPUS (Continued)

C.   Ground Three: **Mr. Smith was denied his right to effective assistance of counsel under the Sixth Amendment to the United States Constitution when trial counsel failed to call Alvino Carrillo as a witness.**

Supporting **FACTS** (tell your story briefly without citing cases or law):

At trial, the state presented evidence that shells from the gun that Mr. Smith allegedly fired outside 411 Indiana St. two weeks before the death of Mr. Hoskins matched the shells from the gun that killed Mr. Hoskins. Alvino Carrillo testified at the post-conviction hearing that he was present for the shooting incident outside 411 Indiana, and that no shots were fired by Zachary Smith. He would have been available and willing to testify at Mr. Smith's trial, but was never contacted by trial counsel. Mr. Smith informed trial counsel in writing of Mr. Carrillo's identity, the knowledge he had about the case, and how he could be contacted.

Had Mr. Carrillo been called as a witness at trial, Mr. Smith would also have exercised his right to testify. He would have testified not only that he did not fire the shots outside 411 Indiana, but that Kevin Glavin, and not he, had killed Derek Hoskins. He would also have explained that the shell casings found in his yard were there because Mr. Sosa fired two shots in his yard the same night of the 411 Indiana incident. He would further have testified that when he entered the vehicle the first time, he sat in the back seat. This would have explained how Mr. Smith's fingerprint came to be on the back window of the vehicle.

6

EXAMPLE PETITION FOR WRIT OF HABEAS CORPUS (Continued)

Had Mr. Carrillo been called as a witness, there is a reasonable probability of a different outcome.[1]

D.   Ground Four: **Mr. Smith was denied his right to effective assistance of counsel under the Sixth Amendment to the United States Constitution when trial counsel failed to object to the prosecutor's testimony about the alleged attempt to intimidate Kevin Glavin.**

Supporting **FACTS** (tell your story <u>briefly</u> without citing cases or law):

As described in Ground One above, the prosecutor asked Mr. Glavin about a supposed incident that occurred in the hall before his testimony in terms that amounted to testimony by the prosecutor about the incident. Trial counsel did not object to this "question." Moreover, although the court told trial counsel that he could request a limiting instruction after the prosecutor questioned the witness, trial counsel never requested such an instruction. Because the prosecutor had to convince the jury to believe Mr. Glavin's prior statement rather than his sworn trial testimony that he did not remember what happened the night of the murder, this prosecutorial testimony was prejudicial to Mr. Smith. Had trial counsel objected, there is a reasonable probability of a different outcome.

---

[1] In this and all other grounds asserting ineffective assistance of counsel, Mr. Smith contends that even if this instance of ineffectiveness is not itself sufficiently prejudicial to required reversal, the cumulative instances of ineffective assistance of counsel clearly create the reasonable probability of a different outcome.

7

EXAMPLE PETITION FOR WRIT OF HABEAS CORPUS (Continued)

E.   Ground Five: **Mr. Smith was denied effective assistance of counsel under the Sixth Amendment to the United States Constitution when trial counsel failed to object to the jury's viewing the videotaped prior statement of Kevin Glavin during deliberations.**

Supporting **FACTS** (tell your story briefly without citing cases or law):

As described under Ground Two above, the jury requested to see the videotaped statement of Kevin Glavin. This effectively allowed them to hear the testimony twice, in violation of both Missouri and federal constitutional law. Trial counsel made no objection. Had he objected, it is likely that the objection would have been sustained. There is a reasonable probability of a different outcome absent this error of counsel.

F.   Ground Six: **Mr. Smith was denied due process of law under the Fourteenth Amendment to the United States Constitution when the prosecutor made baseless allegations tending to suggest that Mr. Smith's brother had influenced the trial testimony of prosecution witnesses Catherine and Lori Stone, and threatened Lori Stone with prosecution if she did not testify as the prosecutor wished.**

Supporting **FACTS** (tell your story briefly without citing cases or law):

The prior testimony of Lori and Cathy Stone was read into evidence at Mr. Smith's trial.[2] They testified that they were present at the Indiana Street location

---

[2] Mr. Smith was tried twice. After the first trial, his conviction was reversed for a Fourth Amendment violation. See Ground Eight, below.

EXAMPLE PETITION FOR WRIT OF HABEAS CORPUS (Continued)

when shots were fired by Mr. Smith. At the post-conviction hearing, Lori Stone testified that the prosecutor threatened her with prosecution if she did not testify as he wished, but she did not actually see what occurred on Indiana Street. Because this testimony was critical to tying the murder weapon to Mr. Smith, there is a reasonable probability of a different outcome absent this prosecutorial misconduct.

G.   Ground Seven: **Mr. Smith was denied effective assistance of counsel under the Sixth Amendment to the United States Constitution when trial counsel failed to impeach prosecution witness Kevin Glavin with the fact that he had previously been convicted of theft, and had lied to officers investigating that offense.**

Supporting **FACTS** (tell your story <u>briefly</u> without citing cases or law):

Trial counsel had available to him, had he conducted a reasonable investigation, a report of the Randolph, Missouri, Police Department regarding the arrest of state's witness Kevin Glavin for theft. The report indicated that although Glavin had been captured on videotape stealing cigarettes, he denied doing so when confronted by police officers. Movant's Ex. 10. Trial counsel failed to impeach Mr. Glavin with this document. Such impeachment with prior false allegations is proper under Missouri law.

9

EXAMPLE PETITION FOR WRIT OF HABEAS CORPUS (Continued)

H.   Ground Eight: **Mr. Smith was denied effective assistance of counsel under the Sixth Amendment to the United States Constitution when trial counsel failed to present evidence in support of his motion to suppress the evidence seized in the search of a safe in Mr. Smith's apartment.**

Supporting **FACTS** (tell your story briefly without citing cases or law):

After Mr. Smith's first trial, his conviction was reversed because the Missouri Court of Appeals found prejudicial error when the state failed to establish that Cynthia Frost, Mr. Smith's sometimes paramour, had authority to consent to the opening of a locked shape in his home. *State v. Smith,* **966 S.W.2d 1 (Mo. App. 1997). On retrial, Mr. Smith renewed his motion to suppress, and the state presented additional evidence on the consent issue.**

Trial counsel failed to support properly his motion to suppress evidence in the face of this new evidence. He failed to present evidence that, at the time Ms. Frost "consented" to the search, an order of protection was in effect directing that she not associate with Mr. Smith. Because such orders were furnished to the Kansas City Police Department, the officers were charged with knowledge that Ms. Frost could not consent to a search of Mr. Smith's belongings. Nor did counsel present to the court the fact that, under the Kansas City, Missouri Police Department procedure manual, searches were not to be conducted without *written* **consent, and none was obtained here. Finally trial counsel failed to impeach the testimony of the police officers with the fact that Mr. Smith had a pending civil rights complain against them alleging that the search was improper. Had trial counsel presented this evidence, there is a reasonable probability that**

10

EXAMPLE PETITION FOR WRIT OF HABEAS CORPUS (Continued)

the motion to suppress would have been granted, and that the outcome of the

proceeding would have been different.

13.   If any grounds listed in 12A-H were not previously presented, state <u>briefly</u> what

        grounds were not so presented, and give your reasons for not presenting them:

        N/A

14.   Do you have any petition or appeal now pending in any court, either state or

        federal, as to the judgment under attack?   Yes [ ] No [X]

15.   Give the name and address, if known, of each attorney who represented you in
        the following stages of the judgment attacked herein:

        (a)   At preliminary hearing: **None**

        (b)   At arraignment and plea **Daniel Franco, address unknown**

        (c)   At trial: **Daniel Franco**

        (d)   At sentencing **Daniel Franco**

        (e)   On appeal **Andrew Schroeder, 2842 W. Hwy 116, Plattsburg, MO**

             64477

        (f)   In any post-conviction proceeding: **Elizabeth Unger Carlyle, P.O. Box**

    962, Columbus, MS 39703

        (g)   On appeal from any adverse ruling in a post-conviction proceeding:

    Elizabeth Unger Carlyle

16.   Were you sentenced on more than one count of an indictment, or on more than
        one indictment, in the same court and at approximately the same time?

        Yes [X] No [ ]

EXAMPLE PETITION FOR WRIT OF HABEAS CORPUS (Concluded)

17.   Do you have any future sentence to serve after you complete the sentence imposed by the judgment under attack?

Yes [ ] No [X]

(a)   If so, give name and location of court which imposed sentence to be served in the future:

(b)   And give date and length of sentence to be served in the future:

(c)   Have you filed, or do you contemplate filing any petition attacking the judgment which imposed the sentence to be served in the future?
Yes [ ] No [ ]

Wherefore, petitioner prays that this court grant and issue a writ of habeas corpus, conduct such hearings as may be required, and, upon hearing, grant petitioner relief from his unlawful convictions and sentences.

/s/ Elizabeth Unger Carlyle
_____
ELIZABETH UNGER CARLYLE
P.O. Box 962
Columbus, MS 39703
Missouri Bar Number 41930

ATTORNEY FOR PETITIONER

I declare under penalty of perjury that the foregoing is true and correct.
Executed on June 18, 2007.

/s/ Elizabeth Unger Carlyle
_____
ELIZABETH UNGER CARLYLE

12

3. STATE'S RESPONSE TO ORDER TO SHOW CAUSE

STATE'S RESPONSE

Shortly after your petition for a writ of habeas corpus is filed, the district court will order the respondent to show cause why a writ of habeas corpus should not be granted. Once they receive notice of the court's order, the attorney general's office will assign an assistant attorney general to represent the respondent.

It is common practice for assistant attorneys general to file motions for extensions of time to file their response. In my experience with these motions, the assistant attorney usually asks for sixty additional days at a time. Sometimes they will file additional motions for extensions of time, which the court almost always grants.

When the state's response is filed, it will include: copies of trial transcripts; your direct appeal legal file; all direct appeal briefs, from both you and the state; opinion of the court of appeals; post-conviction hearing transcripts, if an evidentiary hearing was held; post-conviction review legal file; post-conviction appellate briefs; reply briefs, if any, from you and the state; and the opinion of the court of appeals. They never provide you with these copies; only the court receives them. All the documents will be cited by the state as, for example, "Resp. Exh. 1 at 1." When you prepare your traverse, you may also refer to these exhibits in support of your arguments without having to file duplicate exhibits.

AFFIRMATIVE DEFENSES

The number one defense the state will assert is the one-year statute of limitations period of 28 U.S.C. §2244(d). There are a lot of prisoners who wait until the last minute to file their petitions without considering the tolling provisions stated in chapter one. In doing so, their petitions are untimely, providing the state with a valid defense that results in the dismissal of the petition without review of the prisoners' constitutional claims. As you will see in the example copy of a state's response at the end of this chapter, the state was thorough in their calculations to determine the timeliness of my petition for a writ of habeas corpus in federal court.

Next, the state lists all the claims you presented in state court that are preserved for federal review. If the claims were never presented, or not properly presented (in a properly filed application, or presented to the state's highest appellate court), they will assert a procedural default defense.

The state will then address the properly preserved claims and basically reassert the same position the state courts took in denying your claims. They merely point out the findings of fact and law made by the state courts that supported the decision to deny you relief.

REQUESTING AN EXTENSION OF TIME TO FILE YOUR TRAVERSE

Once the state's response is filed with the court, you'll want to immediately file a motion for an extension of time to file a traverse. I've provided an example copy for you to use as a template at the end of this chapter. I always ask for ninety days; sometimes the court only grants sixty. But you can always later request another thirty or sixty days if you have good cause. Examples of good cause include your placement in administration segregation, a lack of access to the law library, or the death of a family member.

EXAMPLE OF STATE'S RESPONSE

IN THE UNITED STATES DISTRICT COURT
WESTERN DISTRICT OF MISSOURI
ST. JOSEPH DIVISION

ZACHARY SMITH,	)	
Petitioner,	)	
	)	
v.	)	07-06068-CV-SJ-005
	)	
MIKE KEMNA,	)	
Respondent.	)	

RESPONSE TO ORDER TO SHOW CAUSE WHY THE WRIT OF HABEAS CORPUS SHOULD NOT BE GRANTED

Statement of Custody and Parties

Zachary Smith is confined in Crossroads Correctional Center in Cameron, Missouri.

He was convicted by a jury in Jackson County, Missouri of first degree murder and armed

criminal action. The Circuit Court of Jackson County, Missouri sentenced Smith to

concurrent terms of imprisonment of life without the possibility of parole and ninety-nine

years. Mike Kemna the Superintendent of the Crossroads Correctional Center is the proper

party respondent 28 U.S.C. §2254 Rule 2(a).

Statement of Exhibits

1a Volume 1 of the trial transcript

1b Volume 2 of the trial transcript

2   The direct appeal legal file

3   Smith's direct appeal brief

4   The State of Missouri's direct appeal brief

Case 5:07-cv-06068-ODS   Document 6   Filed 10/09/2007   Page 1 of 12

EXAMPLE OF STATE'S RESPONSE (continued)

5 The opinion of the Missouri Court of Appeals affirming the judgment of conviction and sentence

6 The post-conviction review hearing transcript

7 The post-conviction review legal file

8 Smith's post-conviction review appellate brief

9 The State's post-conviction review appellate brief

10 Smith's post-conviction review appellate reply brief

11 The decision of the Missouri Court of Appeals affirming the denial of post-conviction relief

12 The docket sheets from the direct and post-conviction appeals.

Timeliness

The petition for certiorari in the direct appeal was denied on March 21, 2003. *Smith v. Missouri*, 538 U.S. 948 (2003). The motion for post-conviction relief under Missouri Supreme Court Rule 29.15 was filed on February 3, 2003 tolling the one year statute of limitations before it began to run (Resp. Exh. 7 at 1).

The mandate in the post-conviction appeal was issued on December 22, 2006 (Resp. Exh. 11 Docket Entry December 22, 2006). That started the one year limitations period of 28 U.S.C. §2244(d). The habeas petition in this case was filed on June 18, 2007 within the one year time limit (Document 4).

Smith's Claims

Smith alleges the following grounds for relief

Case 5:07-cv-06068-ODS   Document 6   Filed 10/09/2007   Page 2 of 12

EXAMPLE OF STATE'S RESPONSE (continued)

1)   The prosecutor allegedly implied in his questioning that Smith's brother had threatened witness Glavin, violating the Due Process Clause.

2)   The trial court allegedly violated the Due Process Clause by allowing the jury to view the videotape of witness Glavin's statement, during deliberations.

3)   Trial counsel was allegedly ineffective for not calling Alvin Carrillo as a defense witness.

4)   Trial counsel was allegedly ineffective for not objecting when the prosecutor questioned witness Glavin about an interaction with Smith's brother in the hall before Glavin's testimony.

5)   Trial counsel was ineffective for not objecting when the trial court permitted the jury to view the videotaped statement of Glavin during deliberations.

6)   The prosecutor allegedly committed misconduct by allegedly implying that Smith's brother had influenced the testimony of witnesses Catherine Stone, and Lori Stone by allegedly threatening Lori Stone to procure her testimony.

7)   Trial counsel was allegedly ineffective for failing to impeach Glavin with his prior conviction for stealing cigarettes and his denial of committing the offense that resulted in the conviction.

8)   Trial counsel was ineffective for not presenting additional evidence to support the motion to suppress evidence found in a safe in Smith's apartment. Specifically, counsel allegedly should have pointed out that Smith had filed a civil rights complaint alleging the search was illegal.

Procedural Default

Case 5:07-cv-06068-ODS   Document 6   Filed 10/09/2007   Page 3 of 12

EXAMPLE OF STATE'S RESPONSE (continued)

Smith's grounds 1, 2 and 6 are direct appeal claims. Grounds 1 and 2 correspond to points I and III in the direct appeal brief (Resp. Exh. 4 at 21-25). But the Missouri Court of Appeals rejected the claim that is now Smith's Ground 1 by finding that it was not preserved for appellate review and did not rise to the level of plain error. *State v. Smith*, 90 S.W.3d 132, 137-139 (Mo. App. W.D. 2002). There is an intra-circuit split on whether plain error review of a defaulted claim should be treated as complete procedural bar to federal habeas corpus review or should be interpreted to permit a federal habeas court to also conduct review for plain error. *Hornbuckle v. Groose*, 106 F.3d 253, 257 (8th Cir. 1997); *Mitchell v. Kemna*, 109 F.3d 494, 496 (8th Cir. 1997). Respondent asserts a defense of complete procedural bar. But, if this Court chooses to follow the line of cases permitting federal plain error review, such review should be highly deferential. *See James v. Bowersox*, 187 F.3d 866, 869 (8th Cir. 1999) (noting that plain error review of a claim defaulted in state court should not be *de novo* plain error review, but rather should be based on the standard that relief will be denied unless any reasonable judge would have *sua sponte* declared a mistrial.)

Smith's ground two is subject to the same procedural default analysis as his ground one. The Missouri Court of Appeals rejected the claim based on plain error review because it was not properly preserved. *State v. Smith*, 90 S.W.3d at 142. The claim is either completely barred from review or subject to the heightened standard of plain error review set out in *James v. Bowersox*.

Smith's ground six, the claim that the prosecutor acted improperly concerning the testimony of Catherine Stone and Lori Stone is not contained in the direct appeal brief (Resp. Exh. 3 at 21-25). Because this direct appeal claim was not raised on direct appeal it is

EXAMPLE OF STATE'S RESPONSE (continued)

procedurally defaulted. See *Reese v. Delo*, 94 F.3d 1177, 1185 (8th Cir. 1996). But the post-conviction court reviewed the claim on the merits to the extent it alleged that the prosecutor threatened Lori Stone, even though the claim was defaulted when it was not raised on direct appeal (Resp. Exh. 11 at 16-17). Therefore, Ground six is barred only to the extent it exceeds the claim that the prosecutor threatened Lori Stone.

In his ground three Smith alleges that trial counsel was ineffective for not calling Alvin Carrillo. This claim was rejected on the merits by the Missouri Court of Appeals and is preserved for review (Resp. Exh. 11 at 14-16).

In ground four Smith alleges that trial counsel was ineffective for not properly objecting when the prosecutor questioned Glavin about alleged intimidation by Smith's brother and that counsel was ineffective for not requesting a limiting instruction. The claim was rejected on the merits by Missouri Court of Appeals (Resp. Exh. 11 at 6-10). The claim is therefore preserved for habeas review.

In ground five Smith alleges that counsel was ineffective for not objecting to the jury being allowed to hear the videotaped statement of Glavin during deliberations. The Missouri Court of Appeals rejected this claim on the merits and it is preserved for appellate review (Resp. Exh. 11 at 10-11).

Ground seven is a claim that trial counsel was ineffective for failing to impeach witness Glavin with his prior conviction for stealing cigarettes. The Missouri Court of Appeals rejected this claim on the merits (Resp. Exh. 11 at 12-13). The claim is preserved for habeas review.

Case 5:07-cv-06068-ODS   Document 6   Filed 10/09/2007   Page 5 of 12

EXAMPLE OF STATE'S RESPONSE (continued)

In ground eight Smith alleges that trial counsel was ineffective for not presenting additional evidence in support of the motion to suppress. The Missouri Court of Appeals rejected the claim on the merits (Resp. Exh. 11 at 19-21). The claim is preserved for appellate review.

Merits Analysis

Ground 1: Smith alleges that the prosecutor violated the Due Process Clause by implying that Glavin had been threatened by Smith's brother, when Glavin alleged he not had no recollection of the events concerning the crime, about which he testified at am earlier trial of Smith.

The Missouri Court of Appeals rejected the claims Smith raised on appeal. The Missouri Court of Appeals rejected the claim made by Smith that the prosecutor did not lay a proper foundation for questioning of Glavin on this point, holding that defense counsel objected to the answer to the question on the ground that it was non-responsive and that defense counsel did not ask that the answer be struck. *State v. Smith*, 90 S.W.3d at 138-139. The Missouri Court of Appeals held that the trial court did not err in not giving a limiting instruction, as the trial court offered to give such an instruction after the prosecutor finished the line of questioning, but defense counsel did not take up the offer. *Id.* at 139.

In Order for a Due Process violation to have occurred from an evidentiary ruling improprieties so egregious that they fatally infected the proceedings and made the entire trial fundamentally unfair must have occurred *Anderson v. Goeke*, 44F3d 675, 679 (8th Cir. 1995). In a case of plain error analysis the standard of review is even higher. *See James v.*

EXAMPLE OF STATE'S RESPONSE (continued)

Bowersox, 187 F3d at 869 (equating plain error in a habeas case with a trial judge failing to act *sua sponte* when any reasonable judge would have done so.)

In this case the conduct complained of would not rise to the level of a Due Process Clause violation, on *de novo* review. It certainly does not rise to the level on plain error set out in *James.*

Ground 2: Smith alleges the trial court violated the Due Process Clause by allowing a videotape of Glavin's statement to be played to the jury. The Missouri Court of Appeals rejected this claim finding that whether to send an exhibit to the jury during deliberations is a matter of discretion with the trial court and that an objecting party has the burden of showing the trial court that prejudice will result. *State v. Smith*, 90 S.W.3d at 142. The Court of Appeals pointed out that defense counsel did not object to the jury reviewing the videotaped statement *Id.* at 142. The analysis of this claim is similar to that of Ground I. No Due Process Clause violation resulted as the entire trial was not made fundamentally unfair by allowing the jury to review properly admitted evidence during its deliberations when it asked to do so. See *Anderson v. Goeke*, 44 F3d at 679. Further, it cannot be said that all reasonable judges would have *sua sponte* denied jury access to the videotape, when both parties apparently had no objection to their reviewing it *See James v. Bowersox*, 187 F.3d at 869.

Ground 3: Smith alleges trial counsel was ineffective for not calling Alvin Carillo as a witness. Carrillo allegedly would have testified about an incident two weeks before the murder for which Smith was on trial, in which he was with Smith and Sosa at 411 Indiana.

EXAMPLE OF STATE'S RESPONSE (continued)

(Resp. Exh. 11 at 14-16). Carrillo allegedly would have testified that Sosa as opposed to Smith exchanged gun fire with a passing car on that occasion (*Id.*)

The Missouri Court of Appeals that not only did Carrillo's testimony not relate to the night of the murder it is not clear that it even related to an incident testified to by witnesses in which Smith had fired a gun into the air (*Id.* at 15). The Missouri Court of Appeals found that Smith failed to demonstrate that the decision not to call Carrillo was not based on reasonable trial strategy (Resp. Exh. 11 at 15). The Missouri Court of Appeals also found that no prejudice resulted because it cannot be said that Carrillo's testimony would have had any effect on the outcome of the trial. (Resp. Exh. 11 at 15). The decision of the Missouri Court of Appeals is consistent with a reasonable application of *Strickland v. Washington*, 446 U.S. 668 (1984) and should be left undisturbed under 28 U.S.C. §2254(d).

Ground 4: Smith alleges trial counsel was ineffective for not objecting to questioning of Glavin, allegedly implying that Glavin had been threatened by Smith's brother and for not requesting a limiting instruction. The Missouri Court of Appeals rejected this claim finding that Smith had failed to show prejudice (Resp. Exh. 11 at 9-10). The decision of the Missouri Court of Appeals is consistent with a reasonable application of *Strickland v. Washington* 466 U.S. 668 (1984), and should be left undisturbed under 28 U.S.C. §2254(d).

Ground 5: Smith alleges that trial counsel was ineffective for not objecting to the jury reviewing Glavin's videotaped statement during deliberations. The Missouri Court of Appeals found that under Missouri law it was proper for the jury to be allowed to view this statement and that counsel cannot have been ineffective for not making an objection that was without legal merit (Resp. Exh. 11 at 10-11). This decision is consistent with a reasonable

Case 5:07-cv-06068-ODS   Document 6   Filed 10/09/2007   Page 8 of 12

EXAMPLE OF STATE'S RESPONSE (continued)

application of *Strickland v. Washington*, and must be left undisturbed under 28 U.S.C. §2254(d).

Ground 6:   Smith alleges that the prosecutor committed misconduct in implying that Smith's brother influenced Catherine Stone and Lori Stone, and he alleges the prosecutor threatened Lori Stone. The part of this claim presented to the Missouri Courts was that the prosecutor threatened Lori Stone in order to obtain favorable testimony (Resp. Exh. 11 at 16). The Missouri Court of Appeals rejected this claim (Resp. Exh. 11 at 15-16). The thrust of Lori Stone's testimony was that she lived next door to 411 Indiana and that two weeks prior to the murder she saw Smith fire a .45 caliber pistol into the air twice (Resp. Exh. 4 at 10 citing, Tr. 772, 775-776). The police later found two shell casings near the curb in front of Smith's house. (Resp. Exh 4 at 10 citing tr. 783-784, 791) Stone's recollection of the incident was supported by the testimony of her sister (Resp. Exh. 4 at 10 citing trial transcript).

Although Smith's allegations concerning the prosecutor implying that Smith had threatened the Stone sisters was not fairly presented to the Missouri Courts and is barred, the record supports the inference that such a threat by Smith occurred. See (Resp. Exh. 4 at 10 citing Tr. At 637 quoting Smith as saying "you guys could get hurt if you snitch or anything.")

In so far as the claim was presented to the Missouri Courts it was rejected consistent with a reasonable application of United States Supreme Court precedent and should be left and the decision should be left undisturbed under 28 U.S.C. §2254(d). In so far as Smith

EXAMPLE OF STATE'S RESPONSE (continued)

exceeds the claim presented in state court, which was that the prosecutor threatened Lori

Stone, the claim is procedurally barred. But the expanded claim is also with legal merit.

Ground 7:   Smith alleges trial counsel was ineffective for failing to impeach Glavin with a

prior conviction for stealing cigarettes. Smith's theory is that Glavin denied stealing the

cigarettes, in a statement to police, but was later convicted and this went to his credibility

(Resp. Exh. 11 at 10). The Missouri Court of Appeals rejected this pointing out that two of

Glavin's prior convictions were before the jury, Glavin's credibility was impaired by being a

co-participant in the murder and under these circumstances evidence that he had lied to the

police about stealing cigarettes would have been of extremely limited value (Resp. Exh. 11 at

12).

The Court also found that Smith presented insufficient evidence at the evidentiary

hearing to overcome the presumption that the decision not to pursue the matter was

reasonable trial strategy (Resp. Exh. 11 at 13). The decision of the Missouri Court of

Appeals is consistent with a reasonable application of *Strickland v. Washington*, 466 U.S.

668 (1984) and should be left undisturbed under 28 U.S.C. §2254(d).

Ground 8:   Smith alleges that the trial counsel was ineffective for not presenting additional

evidence at the hearing on the motion to suppress, specifically evidence Kansas City Police

Department policy requires written consent to searches and that Smith had filed a civil rights

complaint challenging the search. The Missouri Court of Appeals rejected the claim based

on *Illinois v. Rodriquez*, 497 U.S. 177, 186 (1990) (Resp. Exh. 11 at 20-21). The Court

noted that Ms. Frost, Smith's girlfriend, signed a consent form for the search of the house,

informed to police that she was the co-owner of the safe and gave police verbal authorization

EXAMPLE OF STATE'S RESPONSE (continued)

to open it and that under these facts a person of reasonable caution would believe Frost had authority over the safe. (Resp. Exh 11 at 20). The Court of Appeals also found that the probative value of the evidence in the safe, seven live .45 caliber rounds that may not even have been the type of ammunition used in the killing was minimal (*Id.* at 20-21).

The decision of the Missouri Court of Appeals to reject this claim is consistent with a reasonable application of Strickland v. Washington, and should be left undisturbed under 28 U.S.C. §2254(d).

Respectfully submitted,

JEREMIAH W. (JAY) NIXON
Attorney General
/s/Michael J. Spillane

_____
MICHAEL J. SPILLANE
Assistant Attorney General
Missouri Bar No. 40704

Post Office Box 899
Jefferson City, MO 65102-0899
Telephone: (573) 751-3321
Facsimile: (573) 751-2096
Attorneys for Respondent

Case 5:07-cv-06068-ODS   Document 6   Filed 10/09/2007   Page 11 of 12

EXAMPLE OF STATE'S RESPONSE (concluded)

<u>CERTIFICATE OF SERVICE</u>

       I hereby certify that a true and correct copy of the foregoing was should be sent by this Court's electronic filing system to

Elizabeth Unger Carlyle
P.O. Box 962
Columbus, Mississippi, 39703

/s/Michael J. Spillane

_____
Assistant Attorney General

Case 5:07-cv-06068-ODS   Document 6   Filed 10/09/2007   Page 12 of 12

EXAMPLE MOTION REQUESTING AN EXTENSION OF TIME TO FILE TRAVERSE

UNITED STATES DISTRICT COURT
WESTERN DISTRICT OF MISSOURI
WESTERN DIVISION

JOHN DOE,   )
)
                    Petitioner,   )
)
        v.   ) Case No. 0000000000000
)
)
THE WARDEN, et al.,   )
)
                    Respondent.   )

PETITIONER'S MOTION FOR EXTENSION OF TIME TO FILE REPLY TO

RESPONDENT'S RESPONSE TO ORDER TO SHOW CAUSE

COMES NOW Petitioner, John Doe, and respectfully requests this Court to grant him a ninety-day extension of time to file a reply to the Respondent's response to this Court's order to show cause why a writ of habeas corpus should not be granted. In support of request, Petitioner states as follows.

1. Respondent's response to this Court's order was filed on or about June 5, 2010.

2. Petitioner respectfully requests a ninety-day extension of time to thoroughly research the arguments advanced by respondent and prepare a reply for this Court's review.

For the foregoing, Petitioner prays this Court grant the requested relief. He further prays for any other and further relief which the Court may deem just and proper under the circumstances.

Respectfully submitted,

John Doe, #1111111111
Correctional Center
somewhere in Missouri

Petitioner

EXAMPLE MOTION REQUESTING AN EXTENSION OF TIME TO FILE TRAVERSE (concluded)

CERTIFICATE OF SERVICE

The undersigned hereby certifies that a copy of the foregoing was mailed, postage prepaid, this___day of June, 2010, to; Joe Blow, Assistant Attorney General, somewhere in Missouri.

                                       _____
                                       Petitioner

---

4. PETITIONER'S TRAVERSE TO THE STATE'S RESPONSE

STANDARD FOR GRANTING RELIEF

When preparing your traverse, you should start with a standard of review, as set forth in the example copy provided at the end of this chapter. You may want to read over the standard of review in the example a number of times so you'll have a clear understanding of what you must show. You may write your own standard of review, or use the one contained in the example traverse.

You will notice in the example there is no statement of facts; all the facts that support the grounds for relief were already stated in the example petition. If you pleaded all the facts in your petition, there is no need for a statement of facts in the traverse. At this stage of the proceedings, you are required to show that the state court's decision: "(1) resulted in a decision that was contrary to, or involved an unreasonable application of, clearly established Federal law, as determined by the Supreme Court of the United States; or (2) resulted in a decision that was based on an unreasonable determination of the facts in light of the evidence presented in the state court proceedings" to be entitled to relief. *28 U.S.C. §2254(d).*

There are some good cases cited in the example traverse, which explain how the courts interpret §2254(d) when determining whether a habeas corpus petitioner is entitled to relief.

Look for cases that are factually and legally similar to the issue you're arguing. For example, if your argument is that your attorney was ineffective for failing to call a witness, try to find cases that were overturned in your federal circuit on those grounds. If a case is similar to yours, but it's from the Sixth Circuit and you're in the Eighth Circuit, the court isn't bound by that decision. But "to the extent that 'inferior' federal courts have decided factually similar cases, reference to those decisions is appropriate in assessing the reasonableness ... of the state court's treatment of the contested issue." *Copeland v. Washington, 232 F.3d 969, 974 (8th Cir. 2000).*

ARGUING GROUNDS FOR RELIEF

Once you've completed your legal research and are nearly ready to argue the grounds for relief, you'll have to decide which is the best way to present each ground. As you can see from the example traverse, the first two grounds are procedural default arguments. Ground three is an ineffective assistance argument.

First, reference is made to the state court's findings of fact. Next, a restatement of the necessary facts is made to show that the finding by the state court is unreasonable. References to exhibits, which support the facts being relied on, are also made; the exhibits are attached to the back of the traverse. Then argument is made. The facts refuting the state court's findings, the legal arguments, and the legal authority are cited in support.

Depending on the filer's preference, sometimes it may be easier to state the law, the legal authority, the relevant facts, and *then* the legal argument showing the state court's findings are unreasonable and that you're entitled to relief under §2254(d). Once you write out a first draft, read it out loud. If it doesn't sound right to you, it won't sound right to the court, either. Rewrite until it does. If your ground for relief doesn't seem to flow, try different structural variations until it does. You may also reference appellate briefs filed by your attorney in state court, to see how they were structured. If you're not used to making legal arguments, practicing these suggestions will make a big difference in your writing. Sometimes it's not what you argue, but how you argue it.

REQUEST FOR AN EVIDENTIARY HEARING

If you weren't provided an evidentiary hearing in state court, you'll want to prepare a motion requesting one in federal court, and file it in conjunction with your traverse. Evidentiary hearings will be discussed in the next chapter.

EXAMPLE OF PETITIONER'S TRAVERSE

IN THE UNITED STATES DISTRICT COURT
FOR THE WESTERN DISTRICT OF MISSOURI

ZACHARY SMITH   §
                                  §
            Petitioner   §
                                  §
                                  §
      v.   §   No. 07-06068-CV-SJ-ODS
                                  §
MIKE KEMNA   §
                                  §
                                  §
            Respondent   §

PETITIONER'S TRAVERSE TO RESPONSE TO ORDER TO SHOW CAUSE

Elizabeth Unger Carlyle
P.O. Box 962
Columbus, MS 39703
(816)525-6540
FAX (866) 764-1249
Mo. Bar No. 41930

ATTORNEY FOR PETITIONER

EXAMPLE OF PETITIONER'S TRAVERSE (continued)

TABLE OF CONTENTS

EXAMPLE OF PETITIONER'S TRAVERSE (continued)

EXAMPLE OF PETITIONER'S TRAVERSE (continued)

EXAMPLE OF PETITIONER'S TRAVERSE (continued)

Statutes

EXAMPLE OF PETITIONER'S TRAVERSE (continued)

IN THE UNITED STATES DISTRICT COURT
FOR THE WESTERN DISTRICT OF MISSOURI

ZACHARY SMITH	§	
	§	
Petitioner	§	
	§	
v.	§	No. 07-06068-CV-SJ-ODS
	§	
MIKE KEMNA	§	
	§	
Respondent	§	

PETITIONER'S TRAVERSE TO RESPONSE TO ORDER TO SHOW CAUSE

Petitioner Zachary Smith makes his traverse to the response of respondent in this matter.

Standard for granting relief.

As noted by the respondent, 28 U.S.C. §2254(d) provides a standard for when relief can be granted for claims adjudicated on the merits in state court: Relief should be granted when the state court adjudication "resulted in a decision that was contrary to, or involved an unreasonable application of, clearly established Federal law, as determined by the Supreme Court of the United States." The United States Supreme Court interpreted that language in *Williams (Terry) v. Taylor*, 529 U.S. 362 (2000).

The Court held that §2254(d)(1)'s "contrary to" clause required the rejection of state court decisions which were "substantially different from the relevant precedent of this Court." The court gave an example of a misinterpretation of *Strickland v. Washington*, 466 U.S. 668, 694 (1984):

> If a state court were to reject a prisoner's claim of ineffective assistance of counsel on the grounds that the prisoner had not established by a preponderance of the evidence that the result of his criminal proceeding would have been different, that decision would be "diametrically different, "opposite in

1

EXAMPLE OF PETITIONER'S TRAVERSE (continued)

character or nature," and "mutually opposed" to our clearly established precedent because we held in *Strickland* that the prisoner need only demonstrate a "reasonable probability that . . . the result of the proceeding would have been different."

Williams (Terry) v. Taylor, 529 U.S. 362, 405-406 (2000).

The Court then considered the situation in which a state court correctly identifies the applicable Supreme Court precedent and the standards contained in that precedent, but applies them unreasonably to the facts of the case. The Court held that this situation requires relief under §2254(d)(1): "A state-court decision that correctly identifies the governing legal rule but applies it unreasonably to the facts of a particular prisoner's case certainly would qualify as a decision 'involving an unreasonable application of . . . clearly established Federal law.'" *Williams (Terry) v. Taylor*, 529 U.S. 362, 407-408 (2000). The court declined to decide how the "unreasonable application" clause applies when a state court decision either extends a legal principle from Supreme Court precedent to a new context or declines to do so.

The Court held in *Williams (Terry)* that an *incorrect* application of law is not the same as an *unreasonable* application of law. But the reasonableness of the state court decision is evaluated objectively by the reviewing court, not by any sort of "majority rule" analysis. The Court specifically rejected the standard of the Fourth Circuit, which had focused on whether "reasonable jurists" would find the state court determination to be reasonable.)*Williams (Terry) v. Taylor*, 529 U.S. 362, 409-410 (2000).

While *Williams (Terry)* did not enunciate standards for the reasonableness determination, it did provide an illustration of the proper analysis when it applied the standard to the decision of the Virginia Supreme Court in Mr. Williams' case, and found that court's decision to be an unreasonable application of clearly established federal

2

EXAMPLE OF PETITIONER'S TRAVERSE (continued)

law. In reaching this conclusion, the Court examined the reasoning of the Virginia Supreme Court both as to the legal standard which it applied and as to the application of that standard to the facts of the case. The court found two aspects of the Virginia Court decision to be unreasonable: First, the Virginia Supreme Court applied the wrong legal standard when it held that the prejudice standard of *Strickland v. Washington*, 466 U.S. 668, 688 (1984) had been modified by *Lockhart v. Fretwell*, 506 U.S. 364 (1993). Second, it failed to evaluate the evidence in the case properly in accordance with the correct standard when it found that the failure of Mr. Williams' counsel to present penalty phase evidence did not prejudice him. *Williams (Terry) v. Taylor,* 529 U.S. 362, 413-414 (2000). Accordingly, the United States Supreme Court reversed Mr. Williams' sentence of death.

The United States Supreme Court recently expanded on its analysis of 28 U.S.C. §2254(d):

> AEDPA does not "require state and federal courts to wait for some nearly identical factual pattern before a legal rule must be applied." *Carey v. Musladin,* . . .127 S.Ct. 649, 656. . . (2006) (KENNEDY, J., concurring in judgment). Nor does AEDPA prohibit a federal court from finding an application of a principle unreasonable when it involves a set of facts "different from those of the case in which the principle was announced." *Lockyer v. Andrade,* 538 U.S. 63, 76. . .(2003). The statute recognizes, to the contrary, that even a general standard may be applied in an unreasonable manner. See, e.g., *Williams v. Taylor,* 529 U.S. 362, . . . (finding a state-court decision both contrary to and involving an unreasonable application of the standard set forth in *Strickland v. Washington,* 466 U.S. 668. . . (1984)).

Panetti v. Quarterman, 127 S.Ct. 2842, 2858 (2007).

In addition to the situation where a state court decision is "contrary to" or "an unreasonable application of clearly established federal constitutional law, 28 U.S.C.

3

EXAMPLE OF PETITIONER'S TRAVERSE (continued)

§2254(d)(2) provides that a state court decision must be reversed, and relief must be

granted if the state court proceeding "resulted in a decision that was based on an

unreasonable determination of the facts in light of the evidence presented in the state

court proceeding." The application of this standard was discussed in *Miller-El v.*

Cockrell, 537 U.S. 322 (2003) (*Miller-El I*):

> Factual determinations by state courts are presumed correct
> absent clear and convincing evidence to the contrary,
> §2254(e)(1), and a decision adjudicated on the merits in a
> state court and based on a factual determination will not be
> overturned on factual grounds unless objectively
> unreasonable in light of the evidence presented in the state-
> court proceeding [citations omitted.] Even in the context of
> federal habeas, deference does not imply abandonment or
> abdication of judicial review. Deference does not by
> definition preclude relief. A federal court can disagree with a
> state court's credibility determination and, when guided by
> AEDPA, conclude the decision was unreasonable or that the
> factual premise was incorrect by clear and convincing
> evidence.

Citing *Miller-El I*, the court in *Collins v. Rice*, 365 F.3d 667, 685 (9th Cir. 2004),

found the appellate court's determination that the trial judge properly accepted proffered

"neutral" bases for peremptory challenges was not supported by the record,

commenting,

> Contrary to the assertion in the dissent, we have not
> substituted our own judgment for that of the state court.
> "Even in the context of federal habeas, deference does not
> imply abandonment or abdication of judicial review.
> Deference does not by definition preclude relief. A federal
> court can disagree with a state court's credibility
> determination and, when guided by AEDPA, conclude the
> decision was unreasonable or that the factual premise was
> incorrect by clear and convincing evidence." *Mille-El*, 123
> S.Ct. at 1041; see also *Hall v. Dir. of Corrs*, 343 F.3d 976,
> 984 n. 8 (9th Cir.2003) ("AEDPA, although emphasizing
> proper and due deference to the state court's findings, did
> not eliminate federal habeas review. Where there are real,
> credible doubts about the veracity of essential evidence and

4

EXAMPLE OF PETITIONER'S TRAVERSE (continued)

the person who created it, AEDPA does not require us to turn a blind eye.").

Also applying *Miller-El I*, the court in *Parsad v. Greiner*, 337 F.3d 175, 180-181 (2nd Cir. 2003), found that the state court's determination that a petitioner was not "in custody" for Miranda purposes was an unreasonable determination of the facts presented to the state court.

Explaining its ruling that the state court decision that the petitioner's plea agreement had not been breached was an unreasonable determination of the facts, the court in *Gunn v. Ignacio*, 263 F.3d 965, 970 (9th Cir. 2001), stated the standard as follows: "We read the 'unreasonable determination of the facts' criterion to require 'more than mere incorrectness,' such that the state court's fact finding is so 'clearly erroneous' as to leave us with a 'firm conviction' that its determination was mistaken on the evidence before it." (Citing *Torres v. Prunty*, 223 F.3d 1103, 1107-1108 (9th Cir.2000). See also *McClain v. Prunty*, 217 F.3d 1209, 1223 (9th Cir. 2000) (Finding state court decision that prosecutor's "race-neutral" reasons justified peremptory strike was unreasonable determination of the facts).

When it revisited Mr. Miller-El's case, the Supreme Court found that the Texas court's determination of the facts was unreasonable under 28 U.S.C. §2254(d)(2): "The state court's conclusion that the prosecutors' strikes of Fields and Warren were not racially determined is shown up as wrong to a clear and convincing degree; the state court's conclusion was unreasonable as well as erroneous." *Miller-El v. Dretke*, 525 U.S. 231, 266 (2005) (*Miller-El II*).

Finally, if a legal issue has not been considered by the state court, this court must review it de novo. *Wiggins v. Smith*, 539 U.S. 510, 531 (2003).

5

EXAMPLE OF PETITIONER'S TRAVERSE (continued)

Merits of Grounds for Relief.

The State has presented its views on the preservation of the issues in a separate

section. Believing that this issue is intertwined with the merits, Mr. Smith will consider

the state's contentions regarding preservation in connection with each separate issue.

**Ground One: Denial of due process of law when prosecutor was permitted
to testify**

The state first contends that this Court's review of this ground is limited because

the Missouri Court of Appeals reviewed it only for plain error. However, ineffective

assistance of counsel provides legal cause for a failure to preserve error, provided that

the instance of ineffective assistance of counsel is raised before the state court.

Coleman v. Thompson, 501 U.S. 722, 754 (1991); *Murray v. Carrier*, 477 U.S. 478, 488

(1986); *Edwards v. Carpenter*, 529 U.S. 446, 450-454 (2000). Mr. Smith raised

counsel's ineffectiveness for failing to preserve this error fully in his state post-conviction

motion, as conceded by the state in its response to Ground Four, which concerns this

instance of ineffective assistance of counsel. Thus, this Court may conduct plenary

review of this ground.

Moreover, while there is contrary Eighth Circuit authority, the majority of circuits

hold that there is no procedural bar where plain error review is conducted by the state

court. See, e.g., *Sanders v. Cotton*, 398 F.3d 572, 579-580 (7th Cir. 2005) (State court's

reliance on procedural bar was not sufficiently explicit to bar review because reference

to the procedural issue was immediately followed by consideration of the merits of the

ground for relief); *Harding v. Sternes*, 380 F.3d 1034, 1043-1044 (7th Cir. 2004), *cert.*

denied, 543 U.S. 1174 (2005). *Clinkscale v. Carter*, 375 F.3d 430, 442 (6th Cir. 2004);

Riley v. Taylor, 277 F.3d 261, 273-275 (3rd Cir. 2001).

6

EXAMPLE OF PETITIONER'S TRAVERSE (continued)

The post-conviction motion court, and the post-conviction appellate opinion, reviewed the merits of this matter without indicating that the ground was procedurally barred. Resp. Ex. 11, p. 17. Because the last state court decision in Mr. Smith's case conducted plenary, albeit cursory, review, there is no procedural bar. *Coleman v. Thompson*, 501 U.S. 722, 754 (1991).

Turning to the merits, the state seems to equate this ground to a complaint about an evidentiary ruling. That is NOT the assertion of this ground. Rather, Mr. Smith asserts that, as an officer of the court sworn to uphold the Missouri and United States Constitution, the prosecutor committed misconduct by testifying in the case, and that his testimonial questions to state's witness Kevin Glavin injected false evidence into the case. Specifically, after Mr. Glavin testified that he did not remember what happened the night of the killing, the prosecutor suggested, falsely, that he had observed Mr. Smith's brother make some sort of threatening contact with Mr. Glavin in the hall of the courthouse before Mr. Glavin testified. Mr. Glavin denied that this had occurred.

In further support of his assertion that the prosecutor' statement was false, Mr. Smith presented, in his post-conviction hearing, the testimony of his brother Torrid (Tory) Smith. Torrid Smith testified that the contact never happened and that he did not even recognize Mr. Glavin as a witness. Resp. Ex. 6, pp. 51, 53. He further testified that the prosecutor had represented him (Torrid) when the prosecutor was a public defender, and that during the prosecutor's representation, he had a confrontation with the prosecutor and thereafter their relationship was hostile. Resp. Ex. 6, p. 52. This evidence, which was not available to the trial court, established that the prosecutor's

7

EXAMPLE OF PETITIONER'S TRAVERSE (continued)

statement at trial that Torrid (or Zachary) Smith had tampered with the witness was false.

The issue of prosecutorial misconduct is controlled by *Miller v. Pate*, 386 U.S. 1 (1967). There, the U.S. Supreme Court reversed a conviction because the prosecutor had argued that a pair of the defendant's shorts, which he knew were stained with paint, were actually stained with blood. The Court held, "More than 30 years ago this Court held that the Fourteenth Amendment cannot tolerate a state criminal conviction obtained by the knowing use of false evidence. . . [Citation omitted]. There has been no deviation from that established principle." *Miller v. Pate*, 386 U.S. 1, 7 (1967). The Missouri Court of Appeals did not discuss *Miller* (or any other case concerning prosecutorial misconduct), but instead relied on *Stewart v. State*, 578 S.W.2d 57, 59 (Mo. App. 1978). That case deals with the standard of relief for trial errors not raised in the trial court, and has nothing to do with prosecutorial misconduct.

The limitation on the prosecutor's injecting his actions and opinions into the case was emphasized in *Hodge v. Hurley*, 426 F.3d 368, 378 (6th Cir. 2005). Quoting *United States v. Young*, 470 U.S. 1, 18-19 (1985), the court observed, "'[T]he prosecutor's opinion carries with it the imprimatur of the Government and may induce the jury to trust the Government's judgment rather than its own view of the evidence.'" In *Hodge*, the court reversed for prosecutorial misconduct in part because the conviction rested almost entirely on the credibility of the witness the prosecutor bolstered. The situation here is analogous. Without the statement of Glavin, the prosecutor had little chance of a conviction. By suggesting to the jury that Mr. Smith, through his brother, had intimidated Mr. Glavin, the prosecutor likely changed the outcome of the case. See also

8

EXAMPLE OF PETITIONER'S TRAVERSE (continued)

United States v. Geston, 299 F.3d 1130 (9ᵗʰ Cir. 2002) (Reversed for improper questioning by prosecutor.)

Because Mr. Smith was denied his right to due process of law by prosecutorial misconduct, the writ must issue and he is entitled to a new trial.

Ground Two: Denial of due process when the jury was permitted to view the videotaped statement of Kevin Glavin.

The state again asserts procedural default. This issue was reviewed for plain error by the Missouri Court of Appeals because there was no trial objection. Mr. Smith raised the issue of ineffectiveness of his trial counsel for failing to object to this error in state court, (Resp. Ex. 7, p. 70; Resp. Ex. 8, p. 45-49) and it is Ground Five of this petition. Ineffectiveness of trial counsel is legal "cause" for failing to raise an issue in state court. Thus, as discussed in connection with Ground One, this Court should grant plenary review.

Turning to the merits, the Eighth Circuit has held that it is error to send exhibits to the jury room when they contain hearsay and summarize the prosecution's evidence. *Sanchez v. United States*, 293 F.2d 260, 269 (8ᵗʰ Cir. 1961); *United States v. Parker*, 491 F.2d 517 (8ᵗʰ Cir. 1973), cited in *United States v. Kirk*, 496 F.2d 947, 951 (8ᵗʰ Cir. 1974). Because Mr. Glavin essentially refused to testify at Mr. Smith's trial, Mr. Smith was effectively unable to cross-examine him concerning the content of his statement. Mr. Glavin was an eyewitness to the murder if he was not the perpetrator. Permitting the jury to hear his "testimony" twice was highly prejudicial to Mr. Smith. The writ must issue and a new trial is required.

9

EXAMPLE OF PETITIONER'S TRAVERSE (continued)

Ground Three: Ineffective assistance of counsel for failing to interview and call as a witness Alvino Carrillo.

As the state noted, the post-conviction court and court of appeals rejected this ground for relief for two reasons. First, the court held that there was an insufficient showing that the failure to call Mr. Carrillo was not reasonable trial strategy.

At trial, the state presented evidence that shells collected at 411 Indiana Street in Kansas City, matched the shells that killed the victim, Mr. Hoskins. (The weapon itself was not found.) Resp. Ex. 1b, pp. 791, 804, 884-885. The state also presented out-of-court statements of witnesses Cathy and Lori Stone that Mr. Smith had fired a weapon at 411 Indiana on the day the shells were recovered there. Resp. Ex. 1b, pp. 625, 675, 782. The testimony of the Stones from Mr. Smith's prior trial and was read to the jury by the state over defense objection; the witnesses could not be located for this trial. Resp. Ex. 1b, pp. 615-618. In their testimony, the Stones repudiated their prior statements. Moreover, physical evidence presented at the trial contradicted the Stones' account. Detective Beard testified that the shells found at 411 Indiana were not located where they would have been had Mr. Smith fired from the location specified by the Stones. Resp. Ex. 1b, pp. 782-784, 787-797. Nonetheless, the state relied on the match between the Indiana Street shells and the shells which killed Mr. Hoskins to connect Mr. Smith to the murder.

Alvino Carrillo testified at the post-conviction hearing that he had been present at the Indiana Street incident referred to by the Stones. He said that Mr. Smith did not fire a weapon that night. Instead, Mr. Carrillo testified that the shots were fired *at* Mr. Smith, among others. Resp. Ex. 1b, p. 43. Thus, had Mr. Carrillo testified, Mr. Smith would

10

EXAMPLE OF PETITIONER'S TRAVERSE (continued)

have had eyewitness evidence refuting the state's bullet match evidence. The uncontradicted evidence from the post-conviction hearing was that Mr. Smith informed trial counsel of Mr. Carrillo and what he would say, and trial counsel never contacted Mr. Carrillo. See Resp. Ex. 6, pp. 44, 49; Movant's Exhibit 13, attached to this traverse as Exhibit A.

The primary reason the motion court gave for finding that Mr. Smith had not overcome the *Strickland* presumption that decisions by trial counsel are strategic was that Mr. Smith did not present the testimony of his trial counsel at the post-conviction hearing. Mr. Smith presented substantial evidence at the post-conviction hearing that he had attempted to present such testimony, but was unable to do so. First, Mr. Smith presented evidence that trial counsel had been disbarred. Movant's Ex. 6, 7, 8, attached to this traverse as Exhibits B, C and D. Post-conviction counsel retained an investigator, Jim Miller, who located Mr. Franco in Sierra Madre, California. Counsel then obtained Letters Rogatory from the circuit court and retained California counsel who caused a deposition subpoena to be issued in California. California counsel diligently attempted to serve the subpoena at the location where Mr. Franco was believed to reside, but were unable to do so. Movant's Ex. 1, 2, 3, 4 (attached to this traverse as Exhibits E, F, G and H). Steven Pietroforte, one of Mr. Smith's California attorneys, stated that on one of his attempts to serve the subpoena, a woman who identified herself as Mr. Franco's sister answered the door. She told Mr. Pietroforte that Mr. Franco had formerly resided there, but no longer did. She would not provide Mr. Pietroforte with a current address. Exhibit H.

11

EXAMPLE OF PETITIONER'S TRAVERSE (continued)

The Missouri Court of Appeals relied on Missouri law construing *Strickland v. Washington*, 466 U.S. 668, 687-88 (1984), but holding that the presumption of trial strategy could *only* be overcome if the post-conviction movant presents the testimony of trial counsel. This authority includes *State v. Tokar*, 918 S.W.2d 753, 768 (Mo. banc 1996); *Taylor v. State*, 126 S.W.3d 755, 758 (Mo. banc 2004); and *State v. Booker*, 945 S.W.2d 457, 459 (Mo. App. 1997). This was a clearly unreasonable interpretation of *Strickland*.

Although *Strickland v. Washington*, 466 U.S. 668, 687-88 (1984), cautions against judging counsel's decisions in hindsight and suggests that a presumption in favor of reasonableness is therefore appropriate, it does not dictate that this presumption can only be overcome by trial counsel's testimony. In *Strickland*, the court held,

> A convicted defendant making a claim of ineffective assistance must identify the acts or omissions of counsel that are alleged not to have been the result of reasonable professional judgment. *The court must then determine whether, in light of all the circumstances, the identified acts or omissions were outside the wide range of professionally competent assistance.* In making that determination, the court should keep in mind that counsel's function, as elaborated in prevailing professional norms, is to make the adversarial testing process work in the particular case. At the same time, the court should recognize that counsel is strongly presumed to have rendered adequate assistance and made all significant decisions in the exercise of reasonable professional judgment.

Strickland v. Washington, 466 U.S. 668, 690 (1984), emphasis added. Nowhere in this formulation did the Court state that the presumption that counsel rendered adequate assistance can only be overcome if the petitioner presents the testimony of trial counsel. That *Strickland* does not require the testimony of trial counsel to

12

EXAMPLE OF PETITIONER'S TRAVERSE (continued)

overcome the presumption of effectiveness is supported by the recent ruling of the

Eighth Circuit Court of Appeals in *White v. Roper*, 416 F.3d 728, (8th Cir. 2005), *cert.*

denied, 546 U.S. 1157 (2006). There, the court found that trial counsel's decision not to

interview and call witnesses was ineffective assistance of counsel. The court noted,

"White's trial counsel, Robert Duncan, died in 1996, before the district court's

evidentiary hearing." *White v. Roper*, 416 F.3d 728, 733 (8th Cir. 2005), cert. denied,

546 U.S. 1157 (2006).

This interpretation of *Strickland* unreasonably places the movant who cannot call

trial counsel as a witness in a different position than that of a movant who does call trial

counsel but trial counsel is unable to recall whether he or she had a reasonable

strategic basis for the challenged decision. In both cases, the court must make its

decision based on an evaluation of the trial transcript and other evidence in the case.

Yet, under the expansive reading of *Tokar* endorsed by the court of appeals, when

unavailable trial counsel is not called he or she is presumed more effective than counsel

who cannot recall the basis for his or her decision. This makes no sense and places, in

a case such as this one, an unfair burden on the movant.

In an analogous case, *Marshall v. Hendricks*, 307 F.3d 36, 110 (3rd Cir. 2002),

the court cautioned against diluting the *Strickland* rule:

> The problem with the [New Jersey] Court's reasoning is that,
> while referencing specific factors on which counsel's
> decision regarding a closing argument can depend, the
> Court actually knew nothing regarding whether those factors
> played any role at all in [counsel's] decision, but assumed
> that a strategic choice was made and was reasonable,
> merely because the choice would have been "difficult.". . .
> [T]he New Jersey Supreme Court has in essence created a
> new standard that would hold any strategy reasonable if the
> choices presented to counsel were "difficult."

13

EXAMPLE OF PETITIONER'S TRAVERSE (continued)

Under *Strickland*, the court should analyze choices made by trial counsel with a bias towards the reasonableness of those choices. But there is no requirement that the claimant present direct evidence of an unreasonable choice. Indeed, even when trial counsel testifies, courts regularly find that their expressed "strategic" choices were unreasonable, particularly where those choices (like that at issue here) were based on inadequate investigation or legal knowledge. *Williams (Terry) v. Taylor*, 120 S. Ct. 1495 (2000); *Wiggins v. Smith*, 539 U.S. 510, 525-526 (2003); and *Rompilla v. Beard*, 525 U.S. 374, 385-386 (2005); the most recent cases in which the U.S. Supreme Court has granted relief for ineffective assistance of counsel, all contain rulings that trial counsel's strategy was NOT reasonable.

The evidence presented at Mr. Smith's post-conviction hearing established that he had informed his counsel of Mr. Carrillo, and that trial counsel had failed even to interview him. Thus, under the *Strickland* standard, the presumption of reasonableness largely evaporates. *White v. Roper*, 416 F.3d 728, 732 (8th Cir. 2005). The evidence also established that no inference favorable to the state could be drawn from Mr. Smith's failure to elicit testimony about this decision from his trial counsel because trial counsel was unavailable to Mr. Smith. Finally, the fact that trial counsel had been disbarred because he committed acts constituting ineffective assistance of counsel also weighs against a finding that his decision not to interview or call Mr. Carrillo was reasonable trial strategy.

The state suggests that because Mr. Smith informed trial counsel that Mr. Carrillo had a criminal record, trial counsel could make a reasonable strategic decision not to interview him. The case law holds otherwise. Counsel simply could not conclude that

14

EXAMPLE OF PETITIONER'S TRAVERSE (continued)

Mr. Carrillo would not make a good witness without interviewing him. As in *Anderson v. Johnson*, 338 F.3d 382, 393 (5th Cir. 2003); "[T]here is no evidence that counsel's decision to forego investigation was reasoned at all, and it is, in our opinion, far from reasonable. Counsel's failure to investigate was not 'part of a calculated trial strategy' but is likely the result of either indolence or incompetence." As the court put it in *Bryant v. Scott*, 28 F.3d 1411, 1415 (5th Cir. 1994), "[A]n attorney must engage in a reasonable amount of pretrial investigation and 'at a minimum, . . . interview potential witnesses and . . . make an independent investigation of the facts and circumstances in the case.'" (quoting *Nealy v. Cabana*, 764 F.2d 1173, 1177 (5th Cir. 1985). Under the circumstances here, the state had the burden to show a strategy supporting the failure to interview Mr. Carrillo. Because it failed to do so, Mr. Smith has met the "performance prong" of the *Strickland v. Washington*, 466 U.S. 668, 687-88 (1984) test. *Riley v. Payne*, 352 F.3d 1313, 1319 (9th Cir. 2003). See also *White v. Roper*, 416 F.3d 728, 732 (8th Cir. 2005).

Alternatively, the state court held that Mr. Smith had not demonstrated prejudice from the failure to call Mr. Carrillo. The court suggested that the evidence against Mr. Smith was "overwhelming," and therefore Mr. Carrillo would have made no difference. This conclusion is likewise an unreasonable interpretation of *Strickland* and its progeny. *Williams (Terry) v. Taylor*, 529 U.S. 362 (2000), emphasizes that in determining *Strickland* prejudice, the court must examine both the trial testimony and the post-conviction evidence to determine whether, had the omitted evidence been presented, there is a reasonable probability of a different outcome.

15

EXAMPLE OF PETITIONER'S TRAVERSE (continued)

A "reasonable probability" of a different outcome does not mean a certainty that the verdict would have been different, but means that the confidence of the court in the outcome is undermined. This does not require that the omitted witness, by himself, would have established a defense. For example, in *White v. Roper*, 416 F.3d 728, (8th Cir. 2005), *cert. denied*, 546 U.S. 1157 (2006), the court found ineffective assistance for failure to interview and present witnesses who would have testified that the defendant did not commit the crime. This finding was made despite the presentation of other evidence supporting this defense. Similarly, in *Smith v. Dretke*, 417 F.3d 438 (5th Cir. 2005), the court found ineffective assistance of counsel for failing to present evidence of self-defense which would have corroborated the defendant's testimony to that defense.

In the closely analogous case of *Stanley v. Bartley*, 465 F.3d 810 (7th Cir. 2006), the court confronted a situation where the state's "eyewitness", like Mr. Glavin in Mr. Smith's case, could easily have been the murderer himself. At least the witness in Mr. Stanley's case was willing to testify in court; Mr. Glavin refused even to do that. And, in *Stanley*, the state presented evidence that Mr. Stanley had made admissions to his sister. No evidence of any admission by Mr. Smith was presented. Nonetheless, under the *Strickland* standard, the federal appeals court in *Stanley* found that the failure of trial counsel to interview and call witnesses was prejudicial, and that the state court's contrary conclusion was not reasonable. The conviction was reversed. See also *Smith v. Dretke*, 417 F.3d 438 (5th Cir. 2005), where the court found ineffective assistance of counsel for failing to present evidence of self-defense which would have corroborated the defendant's testimony to that defense.

16

EXAMPLE OF PETITIONER'S TRAVERSE (continued)

The same result is required here. The state's witnesses in this case were highly suspect, not overwhelmingly compelling. Mr. Glavin, a cocaine addict and convicted felon, could have been the murderer. Cathy and Lori Stone were under the influence of crack at the time the events they testified about occurred, and their testimony was contradicted by the physical evidence. Nonetheless, the state relied on the match between the casings found at 411 Indiana and the bullet which killed Hoskins to convict Mr. Smith. The testimony of Mr. Carrillo would have contradicted their testimony. Moreover, had Mr. Carrillo testified, Mr. Smith would also have done so. In his testimony, he would have set out the facts contained in his amended post-conviction motion, Resp. Ex. 7, pp. 91-97. Resp. Ex. 6, pp. 65-66.[1]

Specifically, Mr. Smith would have explained that on the evening of Mr. Hoskins's murder, he, Kevin Glavin, and Ricky Sosa were driving around in Mr. Hampton's car looking for cocaine and saw Derek Hoskins. Mr. Hoskins and Mr. Glavin (who was intoxicated) began arguing about Mr. Glavin's alleged theft of cocaine from a friend of Mr. Hoskins. Mr. Smith intervened and cooled the parties down. Eventually, Mr. Hoskins got in the car with them, and Mr. Glavin apologized and shook hands with him.

After a fruitless search for drugs, Mr. Glavin and Mr. Hoskins dropped Mr. Smith off at the home of Flo Brown. Later, Mr. Glavin returned alone and told Mr. Smith, his friend Rose Sanchez, and Ricky Sosa that he had an argument with Mr. Hoskins and killed him. Mr. Glavin brought Mr. Hoskins's bike back in the car. Mr. Smith took the bike out of the car and returned the car to the owner; he gave the bike to Sandra Cordray in exchange for a power drill she was trying to sell.

---

[1] In his evidentiary hearing testimony, Mr. Smith referred to pages 16(i) through 16(o) of his post-conviction motion. Those pages are found in the post-conviction legal file, Resp. Ex, 7, pp. 91-97.

17

EXAMPLE OF PETITIONER'S TRAVERSE (continued)

Mr. Smith would also have explained that he did not fire any shots during the incident at 411 Indiana described by the Stones.

Mr. Smith never made any admissions to the police. The closest thing to direct evidence connecting him to the crime was the testimony of Kevin Glavin. Had the jury heard the testimony of Mr. Carrillo and the testimony of Mr. Smith, there is a reasonable probability of a different outcome.

The writ must issue, and the state must be ordered to release or retry Mr. Smith.

Ground Four: Ineffective assistance of counsel for failing to object to the prosecutor's improper testimony.

The facts relevant to the prosecutor's misconduct are set out in Ground One above. Trial counsel attempted an objection to the prosecutor's misconduct, but failed to follow up. After a bench conference in which the court instructed the prosecutor not to ask questions about the conduct of Mr. Smith's brother, the prosecutor blatantly disregarded this instruction and suggested that *Mr. Smith* had intimidated the witness. There was no further objection. Moreover, the trial court invited trial counsel to request an instruction that the supposed conduct of Mr. Smith's brother could not be imputed to Mr. Smith, but trial counsel failed to make any such request.

The Missouri Court of Appeals's memorandum opinion disposed of the issue this way:

> At the evidentiary hearing the prosecutor denied impropriety. The prosecutor acknowledged that he misspoke when he said "*the defendant* nodded again." It was an obvious misstatement in which the prosecutor intended to say *the defendant's brother* nodded again. Torrid Smith testified that the alleged interaction in the hallway with Glavin never

18

EXAMPLE OF PETITIONER'S TRAVERSE (continued)

> happened and that he did not know Glavin. Glavin also
> testified that there was no such incident.

Resp. Ex, 11, p. 9. This reading of the facts reveals several problems. First, the court's conclusion that the prosecutor's misstatement was unintentional is completely speculative. It is clear from the context of the trial transcript that the prosecutor was attempting to suggest that Mr. Smith, through his brother, was intimidating the witness. Second, it is not clear from this summary that Torrid Smith did not testify at trial. He testified only at the evidentiary hearing. Thus, the jury did not have the benefit of his testimony. At trial, only Mr. Glavin denied the incident. The Missouri Court of Appeals memorandum constitutes an unreasonable determination of the facts.

28 U.S.C. §2254(d)(2) provides that a state court decision must be reversed, and relief must be granted, if the state court proceeding "resulted in a decision that was based on an unreasonable determination of the facts in light of the evidence presented in the state court proceeding." *Miller-El v. Cockrell*, 537 U.S. 322, 340 (2003) (*Miller-El I*). The court made clear that the district court may not simply defer to the fact findings of the state court:

> Even in the context of federal habeas, deference does not
> imply abandonment or abdication of judicial review.
> Deference does not by definition preclude relief. A federal
> court can disagree with a state court's credibility
> determination and, when guided by AEDPA, conclude the
> decision was unreasonable or that the factual premise was
> incorrect by clear and convincing evidence.

Citing *Miller-El I*, the court in *Collins v. Rice*, 365 F.3d 667, 685 (9th Cir. 2004), found the appellate court's determination that the trial judge properly accepted proffered "neutral" bases for peremptory challenges was not supported by the record. The court also relied on *Hall v. Dir. of Corrs*, 343 F.3d 976, 984 n. 8 (9th Cir. 2003):

19

EXAMPLE OF PETITIONER'S TRAVERSE (continued)

> AEDPA, although emphasizing proper and due deference to the state court's findings, did not eliminate federal habeas review. Where there are real, credible doubts about the veracity of essential evidence and the person who created it, AEDPA does not require us to turn a blind eye.

In *Miller-El v. Dretke*, 545 U.S. 231, 266 (2005) (*Miller-El II*), the Supreme Court found that the Texas court's determination of the facts was unreasonable under 28 U.S.C. §2254(d)(2): "The state court's conclusion that the prosecutors' strikes of Fields and Warren were not racially determined is shown up as wrong to a clear and convincing degree; the state court's conclusion was unreasonable as well as erroneous."

Applying these principles, the Eighth Circuit Court of Appeals granted relief in *Simmons v. Luebbers*, 299 F.3d 929, 937 (8th Cir. 2002). There, the court held that the Missouri Supreme Court's finding that certain evidence was introduced during trial was an "unreasonable determination of the facts in light of the evidence presented in the State court proceeding." 28 U.S.C. § 2254(d): "Our independent review of the record leads us to conclude that the Missouri Supreme Court's conclusions regarding the evidence that was presented during the penalty phase of that trial are completely inaccurate."

As the Fifth Circuit put it,

> Federal courts in habeas corpus proceedings are required to accord a presumption of correctness to state court findings of fact, unless they lack fair support in the record.FN19 This deference is not absolute, however, and section 2554(d)(2) allows "issuance of the writ if the state court decision was based on an unreasonable determination of the facts in light of the evidence presented."

Finding the state court's determination of the basis of the petitioner's parole revocation to be erroneous, the court granted relief. *Alexander v. Cockrell*, 294 F.3d

20

EXAMPLE OF PETITIONER'S TRAVERSE (continued)

626, 630 (5th Cir. 2002). See also *Norton v. Spencer*, 351 F.3d 1, 6-7 (1st Cir. 2003) (State court determination that affidavits of newly discovered evidence were incredible was unreasonable); *Bui v. Haley*, 321 F.3d 1304, 1315-1316 (11th Cir. 2003) (State court determination that prosecutor's reasons for jury strike were race-neutral was unreasonable where there was no evidence in the state record to support it).

The conclusion of the state court of appeals here that Torrid Smith testified at Mr. Smith's trial, and that the prosecutor did not disobey the court's instructions, are likewise inaccurate, and insofar as they are the basis for the state court's prejudice finding, must be rejected by this court.

Turning to the applicable law, the court of appeals misapplied *Strickland v. Washington*, 466 U.S. 668, 687-88 (1984), holding,

> The failure to object to objectionable evidence or argument constitutes ineffective assistance of counsel only where the comment was of such a character that it resulted in a substantial deprivation of the accused's right to a fair trial. . .. find the prosecutor's questions in this case so egregious as to have denied Smith a fair trial.

Resp. Ex. 11, p. 9. The court went on to say, "Failure to request a limiting instruction is not necessarily ineffective assistance of counsel; it must be so prejudicial that the movant was denied a fair trial." Resp. Ex. 11, p. 10.

The *Strickland v. Washington*, 466 U.S. 668, 687-88 (1984) prejudice standard is NOT whether trial counsel's actions "substantially deprived" or "denied" the defendant a fair trial. That standard was specifically rejected in *Williams (Terry) v. Taylor*, 529 U.S. 362 (2000). There, the court reiterated that under *Strickland*, the defendant must only show a reasonable probability of a different outcome. The court of appeals applied the wrong standard.

21

EXAMPLE OF PETITIONER'S TRAVERSE (continued)

Had the *Strickland* standard been properly applied, Mr. Smith would have been granted relief. The Eighth Circuit has found counsel ineffective for failing to object to a verdict-directing jury instruction that omitted an element of the offense. *Reagan v. Norris*, 365 F.3d 616 (8th Cir. 2004). Also quite similar to this case is *Chatom v. White*, 858 F.2d 1479, 1486 (11th Cir. 1988). There, the court found trial counsel ineffective for failing to object to questionable test results: "[C]ounsel's failure to object under the circumstances present in this case fell below standards of reasonable performance causing the adversarial testing contemplated by the Sixth Amendment to falter concerning this critical issue." See also *Joshua v. DeWitt*, 341 F.3d 430 (6th Cir. 2003) (Counsel failed to move to suppress evidence based on unlawful detention); *United States v. Horey*, 333 F.3d 1185 (10th Cir. 2003) (Counsel failed to object to impermissible sentence enhancement which increased the defendant's sentence).

The prejudice from the prosecutor's improper actions is discussed in connection with Ground One, and the court is respectfully referred thereto.

The writ must issue, and Mr. Smith is entitled to a new trial.

Ground Five: Ineffective assistance of counsel for failure to object to the jury's viewing the videotaped statement of Glavin during deliberations.

Had Mr. Glavin testified at Mr. Smith's trial, the jury would have heard, once, his account of how Mr. Smith allegedly killed Mr. Hoskins. But Mr. Glavin refused to so testify. As a result, the state was permitted, under Missouri law, to use the prior videotaped statement in its case in chief. The state received a windfall, though, because not only did the jury view the videotape once, it requested and received

22

EXAMPLE OF PETITIONER'S TRAVERSE (continued)

permission to see it **again** during deliberations. Contrary to the state's contention and the holding of the Missouri Court of Appeals, this is a violation of Missouri law, and had trial counsel objected, it is likely that such an objection would have been sustained. Under *State v. Evans*, 639 S.W.2d 792, 795 (Mo. 1982), testimonial exhibits other than confessions should not be given to the jury during deliberations: "The general rule is that exhibits that are testimonial in nature cannot be given to the jury during its deliberation." See also *O'Neal v, Pipes Entertainment, Inc.*, 930 S.W.2d 416, 421 (Mo. App. 1995). Recorded statements by witnesses qualify as testimonial exhibits under this rule. *State v. Jennings*, 815 S.W.2d 424 (Mo. App. 1991).

Thus, the holding of the Missouri Court of Appeals was BOTH an unreasonable determination of the facts and an unreasonable application of the *Strickland v. Washington*, 466 U.S. 668, 687-88 (1984), standard. The authorities relevant to failure to make proper objections, and to the prejudice standard, are discussed above, and the court is respectfully referred thereto.

The writ must issue, and Mr. Smith is entitled to a new trial.

Ground Six: Prosecutorial misconduct: threats to witness and suborning perjury.

At Mr. Smith's trial, the prosecutor presented written statements by Cathy and Lori Stone. In their statements, they alleged that Mr. Smith had fired a weapon at 411 Indiana Street in Kansas City days before Mr. Hoskins was killed. Resp. Ex. 1b, pp. 625, 675, 782. Their testimony from a prior trial and was read to the jury by the state over defense objection; the witnesses could not be located for this trial. Resp. Ex. 1b,

23

EXAMPLE OF PETITIONER'S TRAVERSE (continued)

pp. 615-618. In their testimony, they repudiated their prior statements, and Cathy Stone testified that the prosecutor had threatened her. Resp. Ex. 1b, p. 638.

The state asserts that Cathy Stone testified that *Mr. Smith* had threatened her, citing Resp. Ex. 1b, p. 638. However, as the prosecutor acknowledged in this evidentiary hearing testimony, Ms. Stone testified instead that *the prosecutor* threatened her if she did not testify as he wished. See Resp. Ex. 6, p. 25.

The Missouri Court of Appeals did not specifically address this issue, but it was raised in Mr. Smith's post-conviction motion and appeal brief. It is clearly improper for the prosecutor to threaten witnesses to obtain favorable testimony. *Kyles v. Whitley*, 514 U.S. 419.. 437 (1995); *Miller v. Pate*, 386 U.S. 1 (1967). As discussed in connection with Ground Three above, the state relied on the testimony of the Stones to establish that Mr. Smith fired a gun which was later matched to the weapon that killed Hoskins. In light of the lack of any inculpatory statements by Mr. Smith and the weak "eyewitness" testimony from a co-participant, prejudice is clear. *Stanley v. Bartley*, 465 F.3d 810 (7th Cir. 2006).

The writ must issue and Mr. Smith is entitled to relief.

Ground Seven: Ineffective assistance of counsel for failure to impeach Kevin Glavin.

At the post-conviction hearing, Mr. Smith presented a report of the Randolph Police Department regarding the arrest of state's witness Kevin Glavin for theft. The report indicated that although Glavin had been captured on videotape stealing cigarettes, he denied doing so when confronted by police officers, and implicated

24

EXAMPLE OF PETITIONER'S TRAVERSE (continued)

another person as the perpetrator. Movant's Ex. 10, attached to this traverse as Exhibit I. Mr. Smith testified at the post-conviction hearing that he had discovered this document in trial counsel's file after he received that file from appellate counsel. Resp. Ex. 6, pp. 70-71. Thus, the document was available to trial counsel. But trial counsel failed to impeach Mr. Glavin with it. Resp. Ex. 1a, pp. 473-602.

The court of appeals found that trial counsel's failure to use this document was not prejudicial to Mr. Smith because Mr. Glavin's two prior convictions were before the jury. However, the Randolph report specifically related to Mr. Glavin's propensity to lie to police officers. In the Randolph case, Mr. Glavin lied to the police and attempted to implicate another person as the criminal. Given that the evidence presented here was a similar statement to police officers implicating another person, the Missouri Court of Appeals unreasonably discounted the value of the evidence.

Alternatively, the court found that Mr. Smith had not demonstrated a lack of trial strategy because he did not present the testimony of his trial counsel. As discussed in connection with Ground Three above, this represents an unreasonable application of *Strickland*. Since there was no evidence that there WAS a strategic decision not to use the evidence, no reasonable basis for not using this readily available impeachment material, and Mr. Smith was unable to present the testimony of trial counsel, the court of appeals erred in relying on the *Strickland* presumption of reasonableness here.

Properly impeaching prosecution witnesses is certainly an important element of effective assistance of counsel. Applying the *Strickland* standard, the court in *Steinkuhler v. Meschner*, 176 F.3d 448 (8th Cir. 1999), found prejudicial ineffectiveness when trial counsel failed to impeach the state's witnesses with evidence that their

25

EXAMPLE OF PETITIONER'S TRAVERSE (continued)

employer, the Sheriff, had told them that he "forgets" all the time when faced with the

need to avoid giving exculpatory testimony.

Because Mr. Smith has met both prongs of the *Strickland* standard, the writ must

issue and he is entitled to a new trial.

Ground Eight: Ineffective assistance of counsel for failing to present

evidence in support of motion to suppress.

The post-conviction motion court failed to issue findings of fact and conclusions

of law concerning Mr. Smith's allegation that trial counsel should have presented, in

support of his motion to suppress evidence, the following evidence: 1) Evidence that at

the time of the consent to search Mr. Smith's safe by his former girlfriend, Cynthia Frost,

an order of protection was in effect which forbade her from coming to his house or

having any contact with him; 2) evidence that although the officers relied on Ms. Frost's

oral consent for the search of Mr. Smith's safe, Kansas City Police Department policy

required written consent to search which was not obtained, and 3) evidence that Mr.

Smith had pending a civil lawsuit against the officers who conducted the search.

The court of appeals substituted its own opinion for the missing findings of the

court of appeals, and found that this evidence would not have changed the ruling of the

trial court and court of appeals that the search was proper. In so holding, the court did

not cite the "reasonable probability" standard required by *Strickland*, but simply said,

"Smith fails to persuade us that introduction of these documents would have changed

[the decision]." Resp. Ex. 11, p. 20. Of course, Mr. Smith need only "persuade" the

26

EXAMPLE OF PETITIONER'S TRAVERSE (continued)

court that trial counsel's failure to support the motion *had a reasonable probability* of affecting the outcome.

In holding that it was "unpersuaded," the court of appeals completely disregarded the significance of Mr. Smith's civil suit, finding it "wholly irrelevant to this analysis." Resp. Ex, 11, p. 20. But Mr. Smith's civil suit provided an incentive to the officers to lie, not only to convict Mr. Smith, but to avoid personal liability. When all of this evidence is considered together, there is a reasonable probability of a different outcome. And the exclusion of the bullets found in the safe would have made a difference in this case. A finding of guilt was far from a foregone conclusion, particularly when as required by *Strickland* and *Williams (Terry) v. Taylor,* 529 U.S. 362 (2000), this Court considers the totality of circumstances. That includes not only the evidence actually offered at trial, but the evidence that was presented in post-conviction proceedings. Given the weak "eyewitness" testimony here, and the lack of any inculpatory statements by Mr. Smith, prejudice is evident. See *Stanley v. Bartley,* 465 F.3d 810 (7th Cir. 2006).

The writ must issue, and Mr. Smith is entitled to a new trial.

Cumulative prejudice.

In this traverse, Mr. Smith has addressed why each particular ground for relief was prejudicial to him. Without waiving his contention that each instance, by itself, merits relief, Mr. Smith points out that, in assessing prejudice, this Court must consider all of the instances of prosecutorial misconduct and ineffective assistance of counsel which the court finds to have been established together.

27

EXAMPLE OF PETITIONER'S TRAVERSE (continued)

In *White v. Roper*, 416 F.3d 728, (8th Cir. 2005), *cert. denied*, 546 U.S. 1157 (2006), the court found prejudice from counsel's ineffectiveness in failing to investigate and call two witnesses. In *Cargle v. Mullin*, 317 F.3d 1196 (10th Cir. 2003), the court found prejudice both because of numerous instances of ineffective assistance of trial counsel and because of prosecutorial misconduct (*Brady* violations.) See also *Harris ex rel. Ramseyer v. Wood*, 64 F.3d 1432, 1434 (9th Cir. 1995) ("Because Benjamin Harris was deprived of his Sixth Amendment right to effective assistance of counsel, we hold that the district court properly granted his petition for a writ of habeas corpus. His defense counsel's many deficiencies cumulatively prejudiced the defense."); *Mak v. Blodgett*, 970 F.2d 614, 622, 624-25 (9th Cir. 1992) (cumulative errors requiring reversal included counsel's failure to present mitigating evidence in the penalty phase, the court's refusal to admit exculpatory evidence and its failure to instruct the jury properly in the penalty phase.).

Cumulative prosecutorial misconduct also can merit relief. *Kyles v. Whitley*, 514 U.S. 419.. 437 (1995); *Vincent v. Seabold*, 226 F.3d 681, 690 (6th Cir. 2000) (errors in trial, taken together, were not harmless); *Depew v. Anderson*, 311 F.3d 742, 751 (6th Cir. 2002) ("Cumulatively, it is clear that these [prosecutorial misconduct] errors are not harmless."); *Jenkins v. Artuz*, 294 F.3d 284 (2nd Cir. 2002) (Cumulative effect of prosecutor's presenting false testimony and improper summation required reversal). Thus, even if no one instance of prosecutorial misconduct or ineffective assistance is found to require relief, they must be considered in the aggregate.

28

EXAMPLE OF PETITIONER'S TRAVERSE (continued)

List of Exhibits

A Letter from Mr. Smith to trial counsel identifying Alvino Carrillo as a witness

B Order of disbarment of trial counsel Daniel Franco

C Report and recommendation of state bar disciplinary counsel regarding Daniel Franco, with exhibits attached

D Application of Daniel Franco to surrender law license

E Request for California deposition subpoena for Daniel Franco

F California subpoena

G Affidavit of George Halterman, California counsel, concerning attempts to serve Daniel Franco

H Affidavit of Steven Pietroforte, California counsel, concerning attempts to serve Daniel Franco

I Randolph, Missouri police report concerning lies by Kevin Glavin

29

EXAMPLE OF PETITIONER'S TRAVERSE (concluded)

Conclusion

For the foregoing reasons, Mr. Smith prays the court to issue the writ, and to

vacate his conviction and sentence and order that Mr. Smith be afforded a new trial

within 60 days of the court's order, or be released from custody.

Respectfully submitted,

/S/ ELIZABETH UNGER CARLYLE

Elizabeth Unger Carlyle
P.O. Box 962
Columbus, MS 39703
Missouri Bar No. 41930
(816)525-6540
FAX (866) 764-1240
elizcar@bellsouth.net

ATTORNEY FOR PETITIONER

CERTIFICATE REGARDING SERVICE

I hereby certify that it is my belief and
understanding that counsel for respondent,
Asst. Atty. Gen. Stephen D. Hawke, is a
participant in the Court's CM/ECF program and
that separate service of the foregoing
document is not required beyond the
Notification of Electronic Filing to be forwarded
on January 3, 2008 upon the filing of the
foregoing document.

/S/ ELIZABETH UNGER CARLYLE

30

5. REQUEST FOR EVIDENTIARY HEARING

STANDARD FOR GRANTING EVIDENTIARY HEARING

28 U.S.C. §2254

(e)

(1) In a proceeding instituted by an application for a writ of habeas corpus by a person in custody pursuant to the judgment of a state court, a determination of a factual issue made by a state court shall be presumed to be correct. The applicant shall have the burden of rebutting the presumption of correctness by clear and convincing evidence.

(2) If the applicant has failed to develop the factual basis of a claim in state court proceedings, the court shall not hold an evidentiary hearing on the claim unless the applicant shows that --

> (A) the claim relies on --
>
> > (i) a new rule of constitutional law, made retroactive to cases on collateral review by the Supreme Court, that was previously unavailable; or
> >
> > (ii) a factual predicate that could not have been previously discovered through the exercise of due diligence; and
>
> (B) the facts underlying the claim would be sufficient to establish by clear and convincing evidence that but for the constitutional error, no reasonable fact finder would have found the applicant guilty of the underlying offense.

If an evidentiary hearing is denied in state court, a federal district court must grant an evidentiary hearing to a habeas corpus petitioner under the following circumstances: if (1) the merits of the factual dispute were not resolved in the state hearing; (2) the state's factual determination is not fairly supported by the record as a whole; (3) the fact-finding procedure employed by the state court was not adequate to afford a full and fair hearing; (4) there is a substantial allegation of newly discovered evidence; (5) the material facts were not adequately developed at the state court hearing; or (6) for any reason it appears that the state trier of fact did not afford the habeas petitioner a full and fair fact hearing. *Townsend v. Sain, 83 S.Ct. 745 (U.S. Ill 1963)*

Under *Townsend*, you must first allege facts which, if proved, would entitle you to relief. *Id. at 314, 83 S.Ct. 754*. This mandate requires you to demonstrate that the state court's decision was "contrary to, or involved an unreasonable application of, clearly established federal law," as determined by the Supreme Court of the United States pursuant to *28 U.S.C. §2254(d)(1)*, or that the state court's decision "resulted in a decision that was based on an unreasonable determination of the facts in light of the evidence presented in the state court proceeding" pursuant to *28 U.S.C. §2254(d)(2)*.

Put simply: if the state court denied you an evidentiary hearing on the basis that you were not entitled to relief and that a hearing was unnecessary, you will first need to rebut the state court's factual findings with clear and convincing evidence. Secondly, you must show that you are entitled to relief under *28 U.S.C. §2254(d)(1) or (d)(2)* in a motion requesting an evidentiary hearing. An example motion is provided at the end of this chapter.

However, if you failed to develop the factual basis of a claim in state court proceedings for some other reason, you must meet one of the statutory conditions stated in *28 U.S.C. §2254(e)(2)* for excusing the deficiency. In such an instance, you must show you are entitled to relief under *28 U.S.C. §2254 (d)(1) or (d)(2)*. For a clearer understanding, I recommend reading *Williams v. Taylor, 120 S.Ct. 1479 (U.S. Va. 2000)*.

EXAMPLE REQUEST FOR EVIDENTIARY HEARING

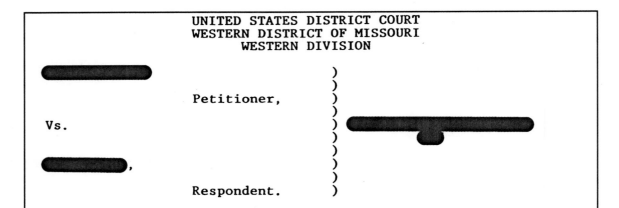

UNITED STATES DISTRICT COURT
WESTERN DISTRICT OF MISSOURI
WESTERN DIVISION

▬▬▬▬▬	)	
	)	
Petitioner,	)	
	)	
Vs.	)	▬▬▬▬▬▬▬
	)	
	)	
▬▬▬▬,	)	
	)	
Respondent.	)	

PETITIONER'S REQUEST FOR AN EVIDENTIARY HEARING

WITH HIS SUGGESTIONS IN SUPPORT

COMES NOW Petitioner, ▬▬▬▬▬, and moves this Court to hold an evidentiary hearing on his two claims of ineffective assistance of counsel. And for his suggestions in support of evidentiary hearing, Petitioner states as follows.

Statement of Facts

Before trial, Mr. ▬▬ filed a motion to suppress to exclude items seized from the apartment where police found Mr. ▬▬ sleeping (L.F. 8-15). Theses items included an assault rifle, a .25 caliber handgun, a .38 special revolver, 21 live rounds of ammunition, 3 empty cartridge boxes, a gun case and other physical evidence and pictures of the items (L.F. 8). The motion also asked that testimony about the illegal search and statements made during the search be excluded (.L.F. 8). The basis for the motion to suppress was simple; the police had no search warrant, did not obtain valid consent and had no other exception to the warrant requirement (L.F. 8-15).

The trial court held a hearing on the motion (Tr. 9-40).

1

EXAMPLE REQUEST FOR EVIDENTIARY HEARING (continued)

Officer Travis Williams was the point man of the tactical response team that responded to the shooting of the officers (Tr. 10-11). Many officers responded behind a library at 31st and Prospect and set up a command post for the operation 100 (Tr. 10-11). Williams arrived at 12:40 am (Tr. 18). They gathered information and were relatively sure they had an apartment targeted, ███████████████ (Tr. 11). However, the officers did not choose to apply for a warrant, rather they decided to do a "knock and talk" of the apartments (Tr. 19). Under this procedure they went from building to building and from door to door to see if residents were okay and whether they had any information about the offense (Tr. 19). If there was no answer, they moved on (Tr. 19). If they were not invited in, they did not go inside the apartment (Tr. 19).

At 3:20 am, the officers, with guns in a "low position," approached apartment 1E at ███████████████ from the east along the front facade, parallel to the apartment (Tr. 12). The guns had flashlights attached to them (Tr. 21). Officers knocked on the door and a young lady, ██████████ answered (Tr. 12, 20, 33).

█████ recalled being awakened by heavy knocking on the metallic door (Tr. 33). She asked who was it and heard a response, "This is the police, open up" (Tr. 33, 37). █████ looked through the peep hole and saw a line of police officers with a battering ram (Tr. 33). They were dressed in black SWAT outfits, covered from head to toe; they had heavy machinery with bright lights (Tr. 33-34, 36). █████ testified that when

2

EXAMPLE REQUEST FOR EVIDENTIARY HEARING (continued)

she opened the door, the police came rushing in and asked if anyone else was in the apartment (Tr. 34, 38, 39). She said, "yes," and two officers held a gun on her, while the other officers cleared the hallway and each room (Tr. 34-36, 39). ▇▇▇ described the encounter as a "raid" (Tr. 36). She never invited the officers inside (Tr. 35).

Officer Williams testified that he explained to ▇▇▇ that they were the police, told her about the incident that occurred in front of the apartment, and asked to speak to her (Tr. 12). ▇▇▇ allowed them in, but said it was not her apartment, that she was staying there with a friend (Tr. 12, 20). The lease-holder was asleep in a back bedroom (Tr. 13, 20). When Williams asked for her consent, ▇▇▇ said she could not grant consent, that he would have to speak with the tenant and she pointed to the back bedroom (Tr. 13, 22, 23). ▇▇▇ told Williams that the lady was asleep with several small children and there was no one else in the apartment (Tr. 13-14).

As the officers moved in the darkness--the only light on was a blue flicker from the television--they saw movement in the back bedroom (Tr. 14, 21, 27). They went into the bedroom and found Mr. ▇▇▇ lying in a fetal position facing away from the door (Tr. 15). ▇▇▇▇▇▇ was crouched down on the floor attempting to hide (Tr. 15, 28). Officer Williams had both men stand up and place their hands on top of their heads (Tr. 15). ▇▇▇ had a handgun (Tr. 16). On the bed, officers saw an assault weapon and several boxes of 7.62 ammunition

EXAMPLE REQUEST FOR EVIDENTIARY HEARING (continued)

(Tr. 16). They took the occupants into custody, secured the scene and continued with knocks and talks in the building (Tr. 17).

Officers then obtained a search warrant and fully searched the apartment (Tr. 18, 29-30). The warrant was signed by the judge at 7:54 am (Tr. 30).

The trial court denied the motion to suppress, finding that the police had probable cause to search the resident's apartment, they were invited to the apartment by a guest and directed to a room where they could obtain permission to search (L.F. 40). Further, the court found police had probable cause to enter the back bedroom when they observed movement there, since they had been told that no one else was in the apartment (L.F. 40).

At trial, Mr. ▇▇▇ renewed his motion to suppress and objected when the State offered evidence seized during the search (Tr. 143, 306-07, 343-45, 349-53, 366-67). The court overruled all these objections. **Id.**

Based on their interviews with the occupants, police developed evidence that Mr. ▇▇▇ had committed the crime. According to his friends, Mr. ▇▇▇ was mad that an officer shone his light on him (Tr. 227-28, 230-31, 257). Mr. ▇▇▇ said if the police rode back by again he was going to shoot them (Tr. 230-31, 232-33, 396). According to ▇▇▇▇▇▇▇, Mr. ▇▇▇ said, "he's got a New Year's resolution to shoot the police" (Tr. 271). When the police car circled the block and came back by, Mr. ▇▇▇ fired at the car (Tr. 272, 274, 397).

4

EXAMPLE REQUEST FOR EVIDENTIARY HEARING (continued)

He said, "I think I hit them" (Tr. 229).

However, the State's eyewitnesses had biases and motives to lie. ███████████ was given immunity for his testimony, having invoked the Fifth Amendment when questioned under oath during a deposition (Tr. 220, 235-36). ███████████ struck a deal with the State for his testimony; he was facing up to seven years for a probation violation on a conviction of possessing cocaine and 15 years on a new charge of trafficking cocaine (Tr. 276-78). As a result of his testimony, he would be placed in a 120 day drug treatment program and receive probation. ███████████ also had a deal to testify (Tr. 203-05), but recanted his earlier statements to police and could not remember any of his statements or any of the events on December 31st (Tr. 205-12). ███████████ had slept with ███████ (Tr. 248).

Additionally, these witnesses' accounts were inconsistent with each other and contrary to accounts by police officers. ███████ said he never left his car on New Year's Eve, but Officer Johnson saw him on the front porch of the apartment building at ███████████, where the shooting occurred (Tr. 204-05, 216, 431-33). Similarly, Officer Colvin saw ███████ ███████ on the front steps of the apartment (Tr. 191-92), yet ███████ denied being there, saying he went inside earlier and was asleep (Tr. 227-28). ███████ also said he went inside before the shooting and witnessed the shooting from inside (Tr. 272-74). However, the crime scene photos call this into question, due to the placement of the windows and furniture

5

EXAMPLE REQUEST FOR EVIDENTIARY HEARING (continued)

(Tr. 354-55, Ex. 64-67). ███████ said 15 minutes passed between the time the officer shone his lights on them and the shooting (Tr. 295), but all three officers remembered a much shorter time, just long enough to drive around the block (Tr. 157, 172-74, 191-92).

Mr. ████ maintained his innocence, saying that he had been at the apartment at 1E at ███████████████████, but that he passed out before the shooting of the officers occurred (Tr. 453). At the close of the evidence, the trial court denied Mr. ████'s motion for judgment of acquittal (Tr. 498). The jury deliberated for nearly 6 hours, before convicting Mr. ████ of all four counts of assaulting law enforcement officers and four counts of armed criminal action (Tr. 545, 553).

The Missouri Court of Appeals, for the Western District, affirmed Mr. ████'s convictions and sentences on direct appeal in State V. ████████████████████████ (Mo.App.WD 2003). The court issued its mandate on October 2, 2003.

On March 11, 2002, Mr. ████ prematurely filed a pro se Rule 29.15 motion for postconviction relief (PCR L.F. 1-6). The postconviction court suspended the proceedings until such time as the mandate issued in the direct appeal case (S.L.F. 3). Thereafter, appointed counsel timely filed an amended motion on December 29, 2003 (S.L.F. 4, PCR L.F. 7, 11, 12-25).

In claim 8(a) and 9(a) of his amended motion, Mr. ████ alleged that trial counsel was ineffective for failing "to request the submission of instructions on the lesser included offenses of assault of a law enforcement officer in the second

6

EXAMPLE REQUEST FOR EVIDENTIARY HEARING (continued)

degree and assault of a law enforcement officer in the third degree" (PCR L.F. 14-15, 16-19).

In claim 8(b) and 9(b), Mr. ⬤ alleged that counsel was ineffective "by failing to call ⬤ as a witness to testify that Mr. ⬤ was an overnight guest at her home the night of the charged incident" in order to establish that Mr. ⬤ had standing to challenge the warrantless search and seizure (PCR L.F. 15, 20).

On November 3, 2004, the motion court entered its judgment, which denied postconviction relief without an evidentiary hearing (PCR L.F. 30-36).

As to the claim that trial counsel was ineffective for failing to request instructions for the lesser included offenses of assault of a law enforcement officer in the second and in the third degree, the court found that "[t]he outcome of the case is in no way undermined by the lack of lesser included instructions. Therefore, the prejudice required by Strickland has not been met in this case..."(PCR L.F. 33). The court wrote further that "movant's motion does not set forth the evidence which provided a conviction only of the lesser charge" (PCR L.F. 33).

As to the claim that trial counsel was ineffective for failing to call ⬤ as a witness, the court held that "movant's amended motion fails to show that the testimony of ⬤ would have provided movant with a viable defense..."(PCR L.F. 35).

Mr. ⬤ timely filed a Notice of Appeal on December 4,

EXAMPLE REQUEST FOR EVIDENTIARY HEARING (continued)

2004, (PCR L.F. 38-39). The Missouri Court of Appeals concluded first, Ms. ██████ was an overnight guest in Ms. ████'s apartment she, therefore, had a reasonable expectation of privacy in the apartment and also had authority to consent to the entry of the police officers into the apartment. Secondly, that exigent circumstances justified the officers warrantless entry into the back bedomm of the apartment. Therefore, Ms. ████'s testimony would not have provided Mr. ████ with a viable defense. ████████████████████████████ (App.WD 2006). As to the lesser included offense instructions issue, the court concluded that Mr. ████ would not have been entitled to the instruction based upon the State's evidence. Id.

Suggestions in Support of Evidentiary Hearing

A federal court must grant an evidentiary hearing to a habeas applicant under the following circumstances: if (1) the merits of the factual dispute were not resolved in the state hearing; (2) the state factual determination is not fairly supported by the record as a whole; (3) the fact-finding procedure employed by the state court was not adequate to afford a full and fair hearing; (4) there is a substantial allegation of newly discovered evidence; (5) the material facts were not adequately developed at the state-court hearing; or (6) for any reason it appears that the state trier of fact did not afford the habeas applicant a full and fair fact hearing. **Townsend V. Sain,** 83 S.Ct. 745 (U.S. Ill 1963).

Under Townsend, Mr. ████ must first "allege facts which, if proved, would entitle him to relief." **Id.,** at 312, 83 S.Ct.

8

EXAMPLE REQUEST FOR EVIDENTIARY HEARING (continued)

745. This mandate requires Mr. ▮▮▮ to demonstrate that the state court's decision was "contrary to, or involved an unreasonable application of, clearly established federal law," as determined by the Supreme Court of the United States pursuant to 28 U.S.C. §2254(d)(1), or the state court's decision "resulted in a decision that was based on an unreasonable determination of the facts in light of the evidence presented in the state court proceeding" pursuant to 28 U.S.C. §2254(d)(2).

Ground Six- ineffective assistance in failing to call ▮▮▮▮▮

The Missouri Court of Appeals' decision concluding that trial counsel was not ineffective in failing to call ▮▮▮ ▮▮▮ to testify at the suppression hearing to establish that Mr. ▮▮▮ was a overnight guest and had a legitimate expectation of privacy in the back bedroom of Ms. ▮▮▮'s apartment because her testimony would not have provided him with a viable defense, is an unreasonable application of clearly established federal and also an unreasonable determination of the facts in light of the evidence presented. First, the Missouri Court of Appeals unreasonably concluded that Ms. ▮▮▮ consented to the entry of the police officers into the apartment in light of the evidence presented in the state court proceeding. Ms. ▮▮▮

9

EXAMPLE REQUEST FOR EVIDENTIARY HEARING (continued)

testified that she was told, "This is the police, open up"
(Tr. 33, 37). ⬛⬛⬛ looked through the peep hole and saw a
line of police officers with a battering ram (Tr. 33). They
were dressed in black SWAT outfits, covered from head to toe,
they had heavy machinery (big guns) with bright lights attached
to them (Tr. 21, 33-34, 36). When she opened the door, the
police rushed in and if anyone else was in the apartment (Tr.
34, 38, 39). She said, "Yes", and two officers held a gun on
her, while the other officers cleared the hallway, and each
room (Tr. 34-36, 39). ⬛⬛⬛ described the encounter as a "raid"
(TR. 36). She never invited the officers inside and never give
a consent to search (Tr. 22-23, 25-26, 33-40).

A federal court can disagree with a state court's
credibility determination and, when guided by AEDPA, conclude
the decision was unreasonable or that the factual premise was
incorrect by clear and convincing evidence. **Miller-El V.
Cockrell,** 123 S.Ct. 1029, 1041 (2003). The state court's factual
determination that ⬛⬛⬛ consented to the police entry is
objectively unreasonable because it is neither logical or
reasonable to conclude that ⬛⬛⬛ believed she could have denied
the police entry into the apartment without the police using
their battering ram upon the front door if she refused to "open
up" in light of the evidence. ⬛⬛⬛ simply succumbed to police
authority. This case is like that in **Johnson V. United States,**
33 U.S. 10, 68 S.Ct. 367 (1948). There, police officers smelled
an unmistakable odor of opium outside a hotel room. They knocked
in the door, identified themselves, and told the occupant that

10

EXAMPLE REQUEST FOR EVIDENTIARY HEARING (continued)

they wanted to talk to her. The occupant stepped back acquiescently and admitted the officers. The United States Supreme Court found that the entry was granted in submission to authority, and did not constitute valid consent.

Secondly, the Missouri Court of Appeals unreasonably concluded that ▇▇▇ give the police consent to search. A third party may provide consent, but only if they possess common authority over or other sufficient relationship to the premises or effects sought to be inspected. **United States V. Matlock,** 94 S.Ct. 988 (1974). Police officers must reasonably believe that the person granting consent has authority to do so. **Id.** See also **U.S. V. Reid,** 226 F.3d 1020 (9th Cir. 2000).

There was no evidence for the state court to conclude that ▇▇▇ consented to any search, or any evidence showing that the police believed that ▇▇▇ had possessed common authority over or any mutual use of any other room in the apartment other then the front room where she was at when the police knocked on the door, and where one might expect their guest to have use of. Even Officer Williams admitted that ▇▇▇ told the officers she was not the owner or a tenant, and she had no authority to provide permission for their entry or search (Tr. 12, 20, 23). Yet, he continued down the hallway in search of a resident who could give him permission (Tr. 20). The police could not have reasonably believed that ▇▇▇ had any authority to consent to them to search for a person to give consent, yet they ignored her and went further into the apartment to allegedly search for someone else who could give them consent

11

EXAMPLE REQUEST FOR EVIDENTIARY HEARING (continued)

to secure the apartment (Tr. 22, 25). Once the officers knew ████ had no authority to let them into the apartment, they should have left and obtained a warrant if they wanted to search it, which would of been consistent with clearly established federal law.

This case is also like **Mincey V. Arizona,** 437 U.S. 385, 391-92 (1978), where the Supreme Court rejected a homicide scene exception to the warrant requirement of the Fourth Amendment. In **Mincey,** an undercover narcotics officer had gone to the defendant's apartment, with other officers, where he was shot and killed by Mincey. **Id.,** at 387. Other narcotic officers searched for the injured and secured the scene. **Id.,** at 388. Homicide detectives arrived at the scene and fully searched the entire apartment, without obtaining a warrant. **Id.,** at 388-89. The court found the search unconstitutional. **Id.,** at 391-94.

The Missouri Court of Appeals' decision is both an unreasonable application of clearly established federal law and an unreasonable determination of the facts in light of the evidence presented in the state court proceeding, because the search of the apartment was unconstitutional since the police did not have a valid warrant and did not obtain valid consent to search the apartment.

████████'s testimony that Mr. ███ was an overnight guest in her home would have provided Mr. ███ with a viable defense because it would have established that Mr. ███ had a legitimate expectation of privacy in Ms. ███'s back bedroom.

12

EXAMPLE REQUEST FOR EVIDENTIARY HEARING (continued)

Thus, the evidence seized from Ms. ⬤'s apartment and statements obtained during the search would have been suppressed. By failing to call Ms. ⬤ as a witness, trial counsel failed to exercise the customary skill and diligence that a reasonably competent attorney would have exercised under the same or similar circumstances.

Mr. ⬤ was prejudiced by the unconstitutional search and seizures. The officers utilized the assault weapon and other evidence to prove the assaults and armed criminal actions. The prosecutor argued, "Our defendant here is curled up around his friend, the assault weapon, in a fetal position" (Tr. 508). He told jurors that Mr. ⬤ was ready "For his revolution" against the police (Tr. 508, 542). He emphasized that "Men like this have assault weapons" (Tr. 544). The weapons and ammunition seized from the apartment where Mr. ⬤ slept were the center-piece of the state's case because several of the eyewitnesses testified inconsistently and had motives to lie (Tr. 157, 172-274, 276-278, 354-355, 431-433).

Mr. ⬤ is entitled to an evidentiary hearing to present evidence that counsel was ineffective for failing to call Ms. ⬤ as a witness and that he was prejudiced thereby under Townsend V. Sain, because the state court's factual determination is not supported by the record as a whole, and Mr. ⬤ was not afforded a full and fair fact hearing to develop the material facts of his ineffective assistance claim in state court. Mr. ⬤ therefore prays this Court grant him an evidentiary hearing, and thereafter, issue a writ of habeas

13

EXAMPLE REQUEST FOR EVIDENTIARY HEARING (concluded)

corpus because he is entitled to relief.

Ground Seven- failing to request lesser instructions

Mr. ⬛ hereby incorporates by reference the arguments advanced in state court and asks this Court to review the briefs filed and grant him an evidentiary hearing on this claim also.

Based upon the foregoing reasons, Mr. ⬛ prays this Court grant him an evidentiary hearing, and thereafter, issue a writ of habeas corpus because he is entitled to relief. He further prays for any other and further relief which this Court may deem just and proper under the circumstances.

Respectfully submitted,

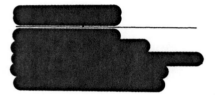

Petitioner

CERTIFICATE OF SERVICE

The undersigned hereby certifies that a copy of the foregoing was mailed, postage prepaid, this 20th day of ___January___, 2007, to; Ryan F. Haigh, Assistant Attorney General, 221 West High Street, 6th Floor, P.O. Box 899, Jefferson City, MO 65101,
Attorney for Respondent.

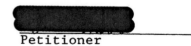

Petitioner

14

6. DECISION OF DISTRICT COURT

ORDER AND OPINION GRANTING OR DENYING PETITION

The district court will issue a written order and opinion stating its reasons granting or denying your petition for a writ of habeas corpus. *Federal Rules of Civil Procedure Rule 58(a).* An example order and opinion denying petition for writ of habeas corpus is provided at the end of this chapter.

The district court may also deny you a certificate of appealability when it issues its order and opinion denying the petition. Sometimes they wait until a formal motion requesting a certificate of appealability is filed. Filing these requests will be discussed in the next chapter.

DECISIONS BY MAGISTRATE JUDGES

Federal Rules of Civil Procedure Rule 72

(b) Dispositive Motions and Prisoner Petitions. A magistrate judge assigned without consent of the parties to hear a pretrial matter dispositive of a claim or defense of a party or a prisoner petition challenging the conditions of confinement shall promptly conduct such proceedings as are required. A record shall be made of all evidentiary proceedings before the magistrate judge, and a record may be made of such other proceedings as the magistrate judge deems necessary. The magistrate judge shall enter into the record a recommendation for disposition of the matter, including proposed findings of fact when appropriate. The clerk shall forthwith mail copies to all parties. A party objecting to the recommended disposition of the matter shall promptly arrange for the transcription of the record, or portions of it as all parties may agree upon or the magistrate judge deems sufficient, unless the district judge otherwise directs. Within 10 days after being served with a copy of the recommended disposition, a party may serve and file specific, written objections to the proposed findings and recommendations. A party may respond to another party's objections within 10 days after being served with a copy thereof. The district judge to whom the case is assigned shall make a de novo determination upon the record, or after additional evidence, of any portion of the magistrate judge's disposition to which specific written objection been has made in accordance with this rule. The district judge may accept, reject, or modify the recommended decision, receive further evidence, or recommit the matter to the magistrate judge with instructions.

Some federal district courts assign magistrate judges to habeas corpus petitions by prisoners. If that occurs, you must file specific, written objections to the proposed findings and recommendations by the magistrate judge. The district court in your district may also ask for your consent before assigning a magistrate judge. In that instance, you may either consent or object to your case being decided by a magistrate judge.

AMENDMENT OF JUDGMENT

Federal Rules of Civil Procedure Rule 59

(e) Motion to Alter or Amend Judgment. Any motion to alter or amend a judgment shall be filed no later than 10 days after entry of the judgment.

You may file a motion to alter or amend judgment. An example motion to alter or amend judgment, suggestions in opposition filed by the state, reply suggestions, and order and opinion denying motion to alter or amend judgment are provided at the end of this chapter.

RELIEF FROM JUDGEMENT OR ORDER

Federal Rules of Civil Procedure Rule 60

(b) Mistakes; Inadvertence; Excusable Neglect; Newly Discovered Evidence; Fraud, etc. On motion and upon such terms as are just, the court may relieve a party or a party's legal representative from a final judgment, order, or proceeding for the following reasons:

(1) mistake, inadvertence, surprise, or excusable neglect;

(2) newly discovered evidence which by due diligence could not have been discovered in time to move for a new trial under Rule 59 (b);

(3) fraud (whether heretofore denominated intrinsic or extrinsic), misrepresentation, or other misconduct of an adverse party;

(4) the judgment is void;

(5) the judgment had been satisfied, released, or discharged, or a prior judgment upon which it is based has been reversed or otherwise vacated, or it is no longer equitable that the judgment should have prospective application; or

(6) any other reason justifying relief from the operation of the judgment.

The motion shall be made within a reasonable time, and for reasons (1), (2), and (3) not more than one year after the judgment, order, or proceeding was entered or taken. A motion under this subdivision (b) does not affect the finality of a judgment or suspend its operation. This rule does not limit the power of a court to entertain an independent action to relieve a party from a judgment, order, or proceeding, or to grant relief to a defendant not actually personally notified as provided in Title 28, U.S.C., §1655, or to set aside a judgment for fraud upon the court. Writs of coram nobis, coram vobis, audita querela, and bills of review, are abolished, and the procedure for obtaining any relief from a judgment shall be by motion as prescribed in these rules or by an independent action.

Motions under Rule 60(b) are rarely filed, and depend upon the specific facts and circumstances of the case such as newly discovered evidence of actual innocence, or something substantial like fraud upon the court.

EXAMPLE ORDER AND OPINION DENYING PETITION

IN THE UNITED STATES DISTRICT COURT FOR THE
WESTERN DISTRICT OF MISSOURI
ST. JOSEPH DIVISION

ZACHARY SMITH,   )
)
                Petitioner,   )
)
vs.   )   Case No. 07-06068-CV-SJ-ODS
)
MIKE KEMNA,   )
Superintendent,   )
Crossroads Correctional Center   )
)
                Respondent.   )

ORDER AND OPINION DENYING PETITION FOR WRIT OF HABEAS CORPUS

Pending is Petitioner's Petition for Writ of Habeas Corpus filed pursuant to 28 U.S.C. § 2254. After reviewing the Record and the parties' arguments, the Court concludes the Petition must be denied.

I. BACKGROUND

Petitioner Zachary Smith is presently incarcerated at the Crossroads Correctional Center in Cameron, Missouri, in the custody of Respondent. He was convicted by a jury in Jackson County, Missouri of first degree murder and armed criminal action and sentenced to concurrent terms of imprisonment of life without the possibility of parole and ninety-nine years. In this action, Petitioner alleges eight grounds for relief involving ineffective assistance of counsel, prosecutorial misconduct, and trial error.

The following recitation of facts comes from the Missouri Court of Appeals' opinion affirming the denial of post-conviction relief in this case:

> On June 23, 1995, at around 10:00 p.m., Smith and two other men, Kevin Glavin and Jose Sosa, were driving around in a maroon-colored vehicle when they stopped to talk to Derek Hoskins. Smith told Hoskins to get into the car, and Sosa put the bicycle Hoskins had been riding into the car's trunk. Smith persuaded Hoskins, who owed Smith money, to burglarize a house to repay him. After the burglary, Smith drove the three others to Cliff Drive, a remote area in

EXAMPLE ORDER AND OPINION DENYING PETITION (continued)

the northeast part of Kansas City. While there, Smith shot Hoskins in the head, then drove off and left him lying in the street.

Two security officers in the area reported that they heard gunshots sometime between 3:00 and 4:00 a.m. on June 24th. After receiving a report of someone lying in the street, the security officers drove to the scene, where they found Hoskins' dead body. Investigating officers found two spent .45-caliber bullets and two .45-caliber shell casings on the ground near Hoskins' body. The police later found two .45-caliber shell casings on the ground at Smith's residence and two more near Smith's father's house at 411 Indiana, where Smith recently had been staying. A criminalist from the Kansas City Regional Crime Laboratory determined that all six shell casings had been fired from the same .45-caliber pistol.

Lori Stone, who lived next door to Smith's father's house, told an officer that two weeks before Hoskins' death, she saw Smith fire a black .45-caliber handgun into the air twice. Her sister-in-law, Catherine, told officers that she also had seen Smith shoot his gun into the air.

Kevin Glavin, one of the occupants of the car, gave a statement to the police, in which he provided the details of the murder and identified Zachary Smith as the murderer. When the police went to arrest Smith, they found him hiding under a bed. In his statement to the police, Smith said that he and several friends had been bowling on the night of the murder and that they then went to his father's house, where they remained until 11:00 a.m. the next morning. Smith denied owning a gun, claimed not to know Glavin, and stated that he had not seen Hoskins for a month. He also told police that he did not have Hoskins' bicycle, he had not been in a maroon car, and he had not been to Cliff Drive in at least three to four months.

Much of what Smith told the police was refuted by others. Sosa's girlfriend told police that Smith, Sosa, and Glavin had arrived at her house the morning after the murder in a burgundy or red car and that Smith had a gun tucked into his waistband. Catherine Stone also reported seeing Smith standing next to a maroon car later that morning. Another witness testified that on the night of the murder, she saw Hoskins talking to Smith and two other men and then get into Smith's car. She also saw one of the men put Hoskins' bicycle into the trunk. Police recovered Hoskins' bicycle from a young boy who testified at trial that Smith had given it to him after the murder.

Cynthia Frost, Smith's girlfriend and co-habitant, signed a form consenting to the search of Smith's house. In one of the bedrooms, police detectives found a locked safe. Frost told the officers that the safe was "her and Zach's" and authorized them to open it. The detectives carried the safe out to the front porch, where they forced it open using a hammer, a crowbar, and a heavy-duty

2

EXAMPLE ORDER AND OPINION DENYING PETITION (continued)

screwdriver. Inside the safe the detectives found a small bag containing several live .45 rounds and an empty box of .45-caliber ammunition. The safe also contained Zachary Smith's Missouri identification card and a Missouri inmate card for Jose Sosa.

Smith v. State, No. WD 65643, slip op. at 1-3 (Mo. Ct. App. Sept. 19, 2006).

The Missouri Court of Appeals affirmed Petitioner's conviction on September 24, 2002. See State v. Smith, 90 S.W.3d 132 (Mo. Ct. App. 2002). The court later affirmed the denial of Petitioner's motion for post-conviction relief. See Smith v. State, No. WD 65643, slip op. (Mo. Ct. App. Sept. 19, 2006). Petitioner's Petition for Writ of Habeas Corpus now raises eight grounds for relief involving ineffective assistance of counsel, prosecutorial misconduct, and trial error.

II. DISCUSSION

An application for a writ of habeas corpus cannot be granted unless the state court adjudication

(1) resulted in a decision that was contrary to, or involved an unreasonable application of, clearly established Federal law, as determined by the Supreme Court of the United States; or

(2) resulted in a decision that was based on an unreasonable determination of the facts in light of the evidence presented in the State court proceedings.

28 U.S.C. § 2254(d).

The "contrary to" clause is satisfied if a state court has arrived "at a conclusion opposite to that reached by [the Supreme Court] on a question of law" or "confronts facts that are materially indistinguishable from a relevant Supreme Court precedent" but arrives at the opposite result. A state court "unreasonably applies" clearly established federal law when it "identifies the correct governing legal principle from [the Supreme] Court's decisions but unreasonably applies that principle to the facts of the prisoner's case." *A case cannot be overturned merely because it incorrectly applies federal law, for the application must also be "unreasonable."*

3

EXAMPLE ORDER AND OPINION DENYING PETITION (continued)

Shafer v. Bowersox, 329 F.3d 637, 646-47 (8th Cir. 2003) (emphasis added) (quoting Williams v. Taylor, 529 U.S. 362, 405, 411, 413 (2000)). In addition, the Court must defer to the state courts' findings of fact, presuming them to be correct unless they are not fairly supported by the record. Simmons v. Luebbers, 299 F.3d 929, 942 (8th Cir. 2002), cert. denied, 538 U.S. 923 (2003).

A. Ineffective Assistance of Counsel

A claim of ineffective assistance of counsel is governed by the standard set forth in Strickland v. Washington, 466 U.S. 668 (1984). "This standard requires [Petitioner] to show that his 'trial counsel's performance was so deficient as to fall below an objective standard of reasonable competence, and that the deficient performance prejudiced his defense.'" Nave v. Delo, 62 F.3d 1024, 1035 (8th Cir. 1995), cert. denied, 517 U.S. 1214 (1996) (quoting Lawrence v. Armontrout, 961 F.2d 113, 115 (8th Cir. 1992)). This analysis contains two components: a performance prong and a prejudice prong.

> Under the performance prong, the court must apply an objective standard and "determine whether, in light of all the circumstances, the identified acts or omissions were outside the wide range of professionally competent assistance," Strickland, 466 U.S. at 690, while at the same time refraining from engaging in hindsight or second-guessing of trial counsel's strategic decisions. Id. at 689. Assuming the performance was deficient, the prejudice prong "requires proof 'that there is a reasonable probability that, but for a counsel's unprofessional errors, the result of the proceeding would have been different.'" Lawrence, 961 F.2d at 115 (quoting Strickland, 466 U.S. at 694).

Id. Failure to satisfy both prongs is fatal to the claim. Pryor v. Norris, 103 F.3d 710, 713 (8th Cir. 1997) (stating there is no need to "reach the performance prong if we determine that the defendant suffered no prejudice from the alleged ineffectiveness"). "An ineffective assistance of counsel claim is a mixed question of law and fact." McReynolds v. Kemna, 208 F.3d 721, 723 (8th Cir. 2000). Consequently, the state courts' findings of historical fact are entitled to a presumption of correctness, and their application of Strickland to those facts must stand unless they applied those standards

4

EXAMPLE ORDER AND OPINION DENYING PETITION (continued)

in an unreasonable manner.

Petitioner presents five allegations of ineffective assistance of counsel. Claims of ineffective assistance cannot be considered cumulatively; each claim of ineffective assistance of counsel must rise or fall on its own merits. E.g., Pryor, 103 F.3d at 714 n.6; United States. v. Stewart, 20 F.3d 911, 917-18 (8th Cir. 1994). Consequently, the Court will consider the allegations separately.

i. Failing to interview and call as a witness Alvino Carrillo

At trial, the state presented evidence that shells collected at Petitioner's father's residence at 411 Indiana Street in Kansas City, matched the shells that killed Mr. Hoskins. The State also presented statements of witnesses Catherine and Lori Stone that Petitioner had fired a weapon into the air at 411 Indiana two weeks before Mr. Hoskins' death. Alvino Carillo allegedly would have testified about an incident two weeks before the murder in which he was with Petitioner and Sosa at 411 Indiana. He would have testified that Sosa, not Petitioner, exchanged gun fire with a passing car during that incident. Carillo, who was incarcerated at the time of Petitioner's trial, said he was available and willing to testify at the time of trial but was never contacted. Petitioner presented a letter he wrote to his trial counsel identifying Carrillo as a possible witness. Petitioner also testified that had counsel called Carrillo as a witness to corroborate his story, Petitioner would have testified on his own behalf.

The post-conviction court held, and the court of appeals agreed, that Petitioner had not overcome the Strickland presumption that decisions by trial counsel are strategic because Petitioner did not present his attorney's testimony at the post-conviction hearing.[1] Without his counsel's testimony, the court held, Petitioner could not demonstrate that his counsel's decision was not based on reasonable trial strategy. The court noted that Petitioner's letter to his counsel concluded "Mr. Carillo has a record for selling drugs, so I don't know if you want to use him." Additionally, the court found that Carillo's testimony would not have been very helpful to Petitioner because not only

---

[1] Petitioner's trial counsel had relocated to California. Petitioner was unable to serve him despite substantial efforts to do so.

5

EXAMPLE ORDER AND OPINION DENYING PETITION (continued)

did it "not pertain to the night of the murder, it also is not clear that the shooting incident Carrillo referred to is the same one the State's witnesses described. The State's witnesses described an incident where Smith fired a gun into the air, while Carillo described two groups of individuals shooting at each other." Smith, No. WD 65643, slip op. at 15.

The court also held that Petitioner had not demonstrated any resulting prejudice from not calling Carrillo to testify based on the other overwhelming evidence of Petitioner's guilt and concluded it was "unlikely that [Petitioner's] decision on whether to testify in his own defense would have hinged on such a peripheral matter." Id. at 16. This Court agrees. Even assuming trial counsel's decision not to investigate Mr. Carillo as a possible witness was unreasonable, there is no reasonable probability that the verdict would have been any different if Mr. Carrillo had testified. Accordingly, Petitioner has not satisfied the prejudice prong of Strickland.

ii. Failing to object to line of questioning by prosecutor

Petitioner argues that his trial counsel was ineffective for failing to timely object and to request a limiting instruction regarding allegedly improper questioning by the prosecutor. Glavin, who had testified in an earlier trial that he witnessed the murder, claimed he had lost his memory of the event at this trial. The prosecutor attempted to demonstrate that his memory loss was feigned and was the result of a hallway encounter between Glavin and Petitioner's brother, Torrid (Tory) Smith, before Glavin testified. The prosecutor asked Glavin:

> Q: Okay. Do you remember what just happened out in the hall a little bit ago, maybe 10, 15 minutes ago?
> A: What are you referring to?
> Q: You know what I am referring to. I was out there, went into the hall and you were there walking this way, and the defendant's brother Tory Smith walked by you.
> Remember what happened out there?
> A: No, Sir.
> Q: You don't remember Tory nodding to you? You don't remember –
> A: No.

Trial Tr. at 480-81.

EXAMPLE ORDER AND OPINION DENYING PETITION (continued)

Petitioner's counsel objected. Out of the presence of the jury, the prosecutor explained that the purpose of discussing the hallway incident was to show that Glavin did not really lose his memory. The judge stated that he would allow the questioning. Petitioner's counsel then asked the court to give a limiting instruction so that the jury should not "infer that his brother's actions were in any way known to [Zachary Smith]." The court then stated that it would "allow the question," and suggested that if trial counsel would request such an instruction after the answer was given, then "I'll be happy to."

Resuming the questioning, the prosecutor asked Glavin:

Q: A little bit ago when we were out there in the hallway, 10 to 15 minutes ago, the brother of the defendant walked by, he nodded, he went like this (indicating) and the *defendant*[2] nodded again. Didn't that happen? (Emphasis added).

A: No, sir. I have only heard Zach's brother by name. I don't know Zach's brother.

Trial Tr. at 485.

Petitioner's counsel objected on the basis that Glavin's answer was nonresponsive, and the court sustained the objection. Counsel did not seek a limiting instruction. The prosecutor then moved on to a different line of questioning.

The post-conviction court found that another objection by counsel to the prosecutor's questioning would have been non-meritorious because the prosecutor did nothing outside the court's instructions other than mistakenly indicate that it was Petitioner that nodded instead of his brother. Additionally, the court held that even if counsel's failure to request a limiting instruction was not based on reasonable trial strategy, Petitioner had not demonstrated how the discussion of Petitioner's brother's actions may have influenced the jury's decision. Rather, it is not reasonably likely that

---

[2] At the post-conviction motion hearing the prosecutor acknowledged that he misspoke when he said "the *defendant* nodded again." The court found that it was an obvious misstatement in which the prosecutor intended to say the *defendant's brother* nodded again. The court further stated that the jury would have recognized it as a mere misstatement because there was every indication that the defendant was never present in the hallway.

7

EXAMPLE ORDER AND OPINION DENYING PETITION (continued)

the jury's verdict would have been different if it had been instructed that Petitioner had no knowledge of his brother's conduct in the hallway, conduct that Glavin testified had never occurred. Moreover, because Glavin denied the incident, the need for the limiting instruction as worded disappeared; Petitioner did not need to disassociate himself from a nonevent. Thus, Petitioner's claim of ineffective assistance of counsel on this point must be denied.

iii. Failing to object to jury's viewing of videotaped statement during deliberations

Because Glavin repudiated his statement describing the night of the murder and Petitioner as the shooter, Glavin's pretrial videotaped statement was played for the jury during trial. Petitioner acknowledges that Missouri law allows the use of the prior videotaped statement. During deliberations, the jury requested to see the videotape again. Trial counsel did not object, and the trial court granted the request. The jury was brought into the courtroom, the entire videotape was played for them, and the jury returned to the jury room to continue deliberations.

Petitioner argues that his counsel did not act as a reasonably competent attorney by failing to object to the replaying of the videotape. However, the court of appeals found that any such objection would have been meritless. The court noted that under Missouri law the general rule is that exhibits that are testimonial in nature should not be given to the jury during its deliberations. State v. Evans, 639 S.W.2d 792, 795 (Mo. 1982). However, the court stated that there are exceptions for confessions by the defendant and for a witness' out-of-court statement that contains admissions by the defendant. State v. Jennings, 815 S.W.2d 434, 440 (Mo. Ct. App. 1991).

The court of appeals found that Glavin's videotaped statement fit the second exception because it recounted numerous admissions by Petitioner, including his statement that he was the "mastermind" of Hoskins' murder. Accordingly, counsel's performance cannot be deficient for failing to object to admissible evidence. Furthermore, Petitioner has failed to demonstrate how the replaying of the videotape was prejudicial. Therefore, Petitioner's claim of ineffective assistance of counsel must fail.

8

EXAMPLE ORDER AND OPINION DENYING PETITION (continued)

iv. Failing to impeach State's witness

Petitioner contends that his counsel was ineffective in failing to impeach Glavin's testimony with evidence of a prior false statement Glavin gave to police regarding a separate offense. After getting caught on videotape stealing cigarettes, Glavin denied doing so and implicated another person as the perpetrator. The court of appeals held that Petitioner had not established prejudice; Glavin's credibility had already been attacked, not only by evidence of two prior convictions, but also by the fact that he was present during the murder and therefore had a motive to protect himself. This Court agrees that Glavin's credibility was already significantly undermined. Therefore, additional impeachment evidence that he lied to police about stealing cigarettes would have had no reasonable probability of changing the jury's verdict in this case. Accordingly, Petitioner has failed to satisfy Strickland's two-prong test for establishing ineffective assistance of counsel.

v. Failing to present certain evidence in support of motion to suppress

Petitioner claims his counsel was ineffective in failing to present certain evidence in support of his motion to suppress evidence found during a search of a safe in Petitioner's house. The police obtained consent to search the house and safe from Petitioner's girlfriend and co-habitant, Cynthia Frost. According to Petitioner, counsel should have supported the motion to suppress with evidence of (1) Petitioner's order of protection against Ms. Frost, (2) the Kansas City Police Department's policy requiring consent for searches to be in writing,[3] and (3) Petitioner's civil rights action against the officers who conducted the search.

On direct appeal, the court of appeals rejected Petitioner's claim that the search of the safe was unlawful. The court relied on Illinois v. Rodriguez, 497 U.S. 177, 186 (1990), for the proposition that a warrantless search based on consent is valid if the

_____

[3] The police obtained written consent to search the house but only oral consent to search the safe.

9

EXAMPLE ORDER AND OPINION DENYING PETITION (continued)

police officers involved reasonably believed that the person granting consent had the authority to do so, even if that belief later turns out to be erroneous. The key question is whether the facts available to the officers at the time of the search would warrant a person of reasonable caution to believe that the consenting party had authority over the premises. Id. at 188-89. The evidence at the suppression hearing was that Ms. Frost was a co-habitant of the house, she signed a consent form for the search of the house, she informed the police that the safe belonged to both her and Petitioner, and she gave her verbal consent to open the safe. The court of appeals found that "these facts would warrant a person of reasonable caution to believe that Frost had authority over the safe," and therefore had authority to consent to its search. Smith, 90 S.W.3d at 141-42.

In its post-conviction motion order, the court of appeals held that the additional evidence would not have altered its original holding. Rather, Ms. Frost's assertion that she was a co-owner of the safe is not refuted by the order of protection. Likewise, the Department policy on obtaining written consent does not show that the officers could not reasonably rely on Ms. Frost's claim that she had the authority to consent. Petitioner's civil rights action, which was initiated after the search occurred, also could not impact the officers' reasonable reliance on Ms. Frost's consent.

The court of appeals then went on to state that the outcome of the trial would not likely have been affected even if the evidence in the safe had been suppressed. Rather, as the court of appeals noted in Petitioner's first direct appeal:

> [T]he only evidence found in the safe were seven live .45 caliber rounds of ammunition. . . .The probative value of the live ammunition found in Smith's safe was minimal. The most that evidence could have established for the jury was that Smith owned or had access to the same type of ammunition used in the killing, although, from the testimony at trial, it is questionable whether those rounds were even the same type used to kill Hoskins.

Smith, 966 S.W.2d 1, 9 (Mo. Ct. App. 1997). The court of appeals concluded that "[i]n light of the other evidence of Smith's guilt and the relative insignificance of the evidence found in the safe," counsel's failure to introduce the additional documents in support of the motion to suppress likely did not affect the outcome of the trial. Smith, No. WD 65643, slip op. at 21. This determination was not an unreasonable application of

10

EXAMPLE ORDER AND OPINION DENYING PETITION (continued)

Strickland v. Washington and must therefore be left undisturbed.

B. Prosecutorial Misconduct

i. Improper line of questioning

As discussed in section II.A.ii. above, Petitioner argued that his trial counsel was ineffective for failing to object to an allegedly improper line of questioning by the prosecutor. Petitioner also raises a substantive claim of prosecutorial misconduct, alleging the prosecutor "testif[ied]" through his questions about what he witnessed in the hallway between Petitioner's brother and Glavin. The court of appeals held that the claim was not preserved for appellate review because three questions were asked and answered concerning the hallway incident before counsel objected. The court then stated that the conduct did not rise to the level of plain error.

Because the court of appeals reviewed for plain error, the issue becomes whether the review for plain error excuses the procedural default. There are conflicting panel decisions from the Eighth Circuit on this issue. See Hornbuckle v. Groose, 106 F.3d 253, 257 (8th Cir.), cert. denied, 118 S. Ct. 189 (1997) (noting conflict); Mack v. Caspari, 92 F.3d 637, 641 n.6 (8th Cir. 1996), cert. denied, 117 S. Ct. 1117 (1997) (same). Until the issue is resolved by either the Supreme Court or the Eighth Circuit sitting en banc, federal courts in this circuit must pick one of the two lines of cases to follow. Hornbuckle, 106 F.3d at 257 ("Although we cannot resolve this divergence in our holdings, we may choose which line of cases to follow."). The decision as to which line of cases to follow appears to be discretionary. Sweet, 125 F.3d at 1152. In this case, the Court will also review for plain error, but such review is highly deferential. See James v. Bowersox, 187 F.3d 866, 869 (8th Cir. 1999) (stating that plain error review of a claim defaulted in state court should not be *de novo* plain error review, but rather should be based on the standard that relief will be denied unless any reasonable judge would have *sua sponte* declared a mistrial).

"The test for prosecutorial misconduct has two parts. First, the remarks must have been improper, and second, the remarks must have been so prejudicial as to deprive the defendant of a fair trial." Young v. Bowersox, 161 F.3d 1159, 1162 (8th Cir.

11

EXAMPLE ORDER AND OPINION DENYING PETITION (continued)

1998), cert. denied, 528 U.S. 880 (1999). Needless to say, if the remarks were not improper, there is no unfair prejudice to be gauged and the second component of the analysis is unnecessary. However, in the event an improper comment is revealed, it must be remembered that the standard of prejudice is relatively high. "The petitioner must show that the alleged improprieties were 'so egregious that they fatally infected the proceedings and rendered his entire trial fundamentally unfair.' Under this standard, a petitioner must show that there is a reasonable probability that the error complained of affected the outcome of the trial--i.e., that absent the alleged impropriety, the verdict probably would have been different." Newlon v. Armontrout, 885 F.2d 1328, 1336-37 (8th Cir. 1989), cert. denied, 497 U.S. 1038 (1990) (quoting Moore v. Wyrick, 760 F.2d 884, 886 (8th Cir. 1985) (second quotation omitted); see also Darden v. Wainwright, 477 U.S. 168, 181 (1986).

Petitioner contends that in questioning Glavin about the hallway incident, the prosecutor violated the court's restrictions on the questioning, interjected his own personal opinion into the trial, and improperly asked about "facts" he knew to be false. As discussed in section II.A.ii. above, even assuming the prosecutor's questions were improper, Petitioner has not demonstrated the requisite prejudice. The trial transcript as quoted above shows that the prosecutor only asked a few questions regarding the hallway incident and moved on quickly after Glavin denied knowing Petitioner's brother. Accordingly, Petitioner has failed to show "that absent the alleged impropriety, the verdict probably would have been different."

ii. Alleged threats to witness

Petitioner also alleges that the prosecutor threatened Catherine Stone in order to obtain favorable testimony. Petitioner failed to raise this allegation on direct appeal. The post-conviction court of appeals noted that claims of prosecutorial misconduct are generally not cognizable in a Rule 29.15 proceeding. Tisius v. State, 183 S.W.3d 207, 212 (Mo. banc 2006). Nevertheless, the motion court reviewed the claims and stated that Petitioner had failed to produce any evidence to support his allegation that the prosecutor had suborned perjury from Ms. Stone. Petitioner's claim must fail.

12

EXAMPLE ORDER AND OPINION DENYING PETITION (continued)

C. Trial Error

Petitioner alleges his due process rights were violated when the jury was permitted to view the videotaped statement of Kevin Glavin during its deliberations. As discussed in section II.A.iii., trial counsel did not object to the jury viewing this exhibit. On direct appeal, the court of appeals stated that the claim of error was not preserved and then proceeded to find no plain error. Accordingly, this Court can also review for plain error, but such review is highly deferential to the state court's determination. See James v. Bowersox, 187 F.3d 866, 869 (8th Cir. 1999).

The court of appeals stated that whether to send an exhibit to the jury during deliberations is a matter within the discretion of the trial court, citing State v. Barnett, 980 S.W.2d 297, 308 (Mo. banc 1998). Even if this Court accepts Petitioner's claim that the state evidentiary ruling was in error, "not every trial error amounts to a constitutional deprivation." Anderson v. Goeke, 44 F.3d 675, 679 (8th Cir. 1995). The Eighth Circuit has consistently recognized that in a § 2254 habeas corpus proceeding, "a federal court's review of alleged due process violations stemming from a state court conviction is narrow." Id. (citing Newlon v. Armontrout, 885 F.2d 1328, 1336 (8th Cir. 1989), cert. denied, 497 U.S. 1038 (1990)).

Accordingly, this Court will reverse a state court evidentiary ruling only if the "petitioner . . . show[s] that the alleged improprieties were so egregious that they fatally infected the proceedings and rendered his trial fundamentally unfair. To carry that burden, the petitioner must show that there is a reasonable probability that the error complained of affected the outcome of the trial-i.e., that absent the alleged impropriety the verdict probably would have been different." Id. (quotations omitted). Petitioner merely makes the broad assertion that "[p]ermitting the jury to hear [Glavin's] 'testimony' twice was highly prejudicial to Mr. Smith." Traverse at 9. Petitioner has failed to carry his burden in demonstrating prejudice.

III. CONCLUSION

For the foregoing reasons, Petitioner's application for relief pursuant to 28 U.S.C.

13

EXAMPLE ORDER AND OPINION DENYING PETITION (concluded)

§ 2254 is denied.

IT IS SO ORDERED.

                                    /s/ Ortrie D. Smith
                                    ORTRIE D. SMITH, JUDGE
DATE: January 29, 2008   UNITED STATES DISTRICT COURT

14

EXAMPLE MOTION TO ALTER OR AMEND JUDGMENT

IN THE UNITED STATES DISTRICT COURT
FOR THE WESTERN DISTRICT OF MISSOURI

ZACHARY SMITH §
§
   Petitioner §
§
    v. § No. 07-06068-CV-SJ-ODS
§
MIKE KEMNA §
§
   Respondent §

SUPPLEMENT TO MOTION TO ALTER OR AMEND JUDGMENT

Zachary Smith, petitioner, moves the court pursuant to Fed. R. Civ. P. 59(e) to alter or amend the judgment entered in this case on January 29, 2008, in order to correct manifest errors of law and fact. In this motion, petitioner addresses some, but not all, of the grounds in his original petition. The failure to address a particular ground in this motion is not intended as a waiver of the right to seek appellate review of that ground.

As counsel for Mr. Smith was preparing this motion, she learned that Mr. Smith had filed a motion, pro se. This motion is intended to incorporate by reference and supplement that motion. Page 1 of Mr. Smith's pro se motion contains a similar request.

In support of this motion, Mr. Smith states:

Standard for relief under Rule 59(e).

In *Innovative Home Health Care, Inc. v. P.T.-O.T. Associates of the Black Hills*, 141 F.3d 1284, 1287 (8th Cir. 1998), the court explained the purpose of a motion under Fed. R. Civ. P. 59(e) to correct errors in the judgment:

1

EXAMPLE MOTION TO ALTER OR AMEND JUDGMENT (continued)

Federal Rule of Civil Procedure 59(e) was adopted to clarify a district court's power to correct its own mistakes in the time period immediately following entry of judgment. *Norman [v. Arkansas Dept. of Education]*, 79 F.3d [748,] 750 [(8th Cir. 1996)] (citing *White v. New Hampshire Dep't of Employment Sec.*, 455 U.S. 445. . . (1982)). Rule 59(e) motions serve a limited function of correcting "'manifest errors of law or fact or to present newly discovered evidence.'" *Hagerman [v. Yukon Energy Corp.]*, 839 F.2d [407] 414 [(8th 1998)] (quoting *Rothwell Cotton Co. v. Rosenthal & Co.*, 827 F.2d 246, 251 (7th Cir.), as amended, 835 F.2d 710 (7th Cir.1987)).

The court in *Innovative Home Health Care* affirmed relief granted under Rule 59(e), noting that "the district judge in this case expressly cited 'errors or changes of heart regarding the merits of the legal arguments' related to. . . the merits of its prior decision. . ." *Id.* Similarly, in *Margolies v. McCleary, Inc.*, 447 F.3d 1115, 1125 (8th Cir. 2006), the court affirmed the district court's grant of a Rule 59(e) motion based on a legal error in the original judgment. See also *Perkins v. U.S. West Communications*, 138 F.3d 336, 340 (8th Cir. 1998) (Affirming relief granted under Rule 59(e)); *Twin City Construction Co. of Fargo v. Turtle Mountain Band of Chippewa Indians*, 911 F.3d 137, 138 (8th Cir. 1990) (Reversal for failure to grant Rule 59(e) motion); *Kort v. Western Surety Co.*, 705 F.2d 278, 281 (8th Cir. 1983) (Affirming relief granted under Rule 59(e)).

Errors of fact and law

1. The failure to investigate and present the testimony of Alvino Carrillo was prejudicial to Mr. Smith. This Court endorsed the finding of the Missouri courts

2

EXAMPLE MOTION TO ALTER OR AMEND JUDGMENT (continued)

that the lack of testimony by Mr. Carrillo was not prejudicial to Mr. Smith.[1] That finding

was based on several errors of fact and law.

    A. *Mr. Carrillo was clearly talking about the same incident as Cathy and Lorie*

Stone. The Missouri court reasoned (and this Court adopted that reasoning) that Mr.

Carrillo might have been talking about a different incident because his description of the

incident was so different from the (repudiated) description given by the Stones. But the

context of Mr. Carrillo's testimony made it clear that he was talking about the same

incident. The time period and location matched that to which the Stones referred. Mr.

Carrillo testified, as did the Stones, that Mr. Smith was present. He described the

arrival of a car as the event which precipitated the shooting. His testimony, unlike that

of the Stones, did not contradict the physical evidence seized at the scene. The fact

that his description of the incident was different was precisely what made his testimony

such powerful impeaching evidence. The Stones fabricated their description. Mr.

Carrillo's, on the other hand, was accurate, and the jury would likely have so found.

    B. *There was "other overwhelming evidence" of Mr. Smith's guilt.* The evidence

against Mr. Smith consisted primarily of the repudiated statement of Kevin Glavin, a

convicted felon who was present at the scene of the murder and had every motive to

conceal his own guilt. He was the only "eyewitness" who placed the weapon in the

hand of Mr. Smith. Rose Sanchez testified at trial that she had never told police that Mr.

Smith had a gun that night; she was confronted with her prior statement to police, which

she said was not her statement. The other evidence was extremely circumstantial: the

---

[1] This Court assumed that the failure to investigate Mr. Carrillo's testimony was not reasonably effective. Obviously, Mr. Smith does not contest that assumption. Should this Court be inclined to revisit it, Mr. Smith would reiterate that the state court finding that he had not established the "practice prong" was based primarily on the fact that he did not present trial counsel's testimony, despite evidence that he was unable to secure such testimony.

3

EXAMPLE MOTION TO ALTER OR AMEND JUDGMENT (continued)

fact that Mr. Smith later gave away Mr. Hoskins's bike, and that he gave inconsistent statements about the offense. By itself, this evidence is clearly insufficient to prove guilt.

To support this testimony, the state relied heavily on the ballistics evidence—the match between bullets fired at another time on Indiana Street and the bullet that killed the victim here. That evidence, in turn, was based on the testimony of Cathy and Lorie Stone, whose prior testimony was read into evidence, that Mr. Smith had fired shots. They also repudiated their initial statements to the police. Lorie Stone testified that she had been intimidated and coerced into lying by the prosecutor. Both of the Stones testified that they were under the influence of crack cocaine at the time of the incident. And their testimony was further weakened by the fact that the place where the expended shells were found on Indiana Street was inconsistent with their testimony about Mr. Smith's location at the time he supposedly fired into the air. Resp. Ex. 1b, pp. 782-784.

This was hardly "overwhelming evidence" of Mr. Smith's guilt. The statement by the Missouri Courts to this effect is simply not supported by the record. As noted earlier, the first trial of Mr. Smith's case resulted in a mistrial because of a hung jury. The jury sent out a note reading, "Can we find guilty of being present but not actually shooting the gun?"[2] These jurors clearly did not credit either the weak ballistics evidence or the testimony of Kevin Glavin. And one of the jurors at the most recent trial contacted trial counsel and said that he was confused and wished to change his mind. Resp. Ex. 1b, p. 1061.

---

[2] A copy of the cover and relevant page of the mistrial transcript, which were filed in the Missouri Court of Appeals as a supplemental legal file in Mr. Smith's first appeal, is attached for the court's convenience.

4

EXAMPLE MOTION TO ALTER OR AMEND JUDGMENT (continued)

In addition to erroneous factual findings, the Missouri court, and this Court, unreasonably applied the *Strickland v. Washington,* 466 U.S. 668, 687-88 (1984), standard for prejudice. In determining whether Mr. Smith was prejudiced, the reviewing court must consider all of the evidence that would have been available had Mr. Smith had competent counsel. The fact that there was other evidence of guilt is not dispositive; the court must examine the whole record. *Wiggins v. Smith,* 539 U.S. 510, 534 (2003). Because Mr. Carrillo's testimony would have impeached the state's only physical evidence connecting Mr. Smith with the weapon, Mr. Smith was clearly prejudiced by the failure to present it. Such evidence creates a "reasonable probability" that the outcome would have been different. *Stanley v. Bartley,* 465 F.3d 810 (7th Cir. 2006).

2. Mr. Smith was prejudiced by the failure to instruct the jury regarding prosecutorial testimony. This Court reasoned that since Mr. Glavin denied that Mr. Smith's brother had looked at him in a threatening manner, there was nothing about which to instruct the jury. But the prosecutor's "question," in the form of a statement, clearly presented than incident to the jury as a fact: "A little bit ago when we were out there in the hallway, 10 or 15 minutes ago, the brother of the defendant walked by, he nodded, he went like this (indicating) and the defendant nodded again." Resp. Ex. 1a, p. 485. Particularly since the prosecutor misspoke and said that *Mr. Smith* had nodded at the witness, an instruction was needed, and its lack was prejudicial to Mr. Smith.

5

EXAMPLE MOTION TO ALTER OR AMEND JUDGMENT (continued)

3. Certificate of appealability. Mr. Smith will address the issue of a certificate of appealability in a separate pleading. By not addressing it in this motion, he does not intend to waive the right afforded to him in this Court's order to *de novo* review of that issue.

For the foregoing reasons, Mr. Smith prays the court to vacate its judgment, amend its opinion to find that Mr. Smith was prejudiced by trial counsel's failure to interview and call as a witness Alvino Carrillo, and direct the State of Missouri either to release or retry Mr. Smith within a reasonable time.

Respectfully submitted,

/S/ ELIZABETH UNGER CARLYLE

Elizabeth Unger Carlyle
P.O. Box 962
Columbus, MS 39703
Missouri Bar No. 41930
(816)525-6540
FAX (866) 764-1240
elizcar@bellsouth.net

ATTORNEY FOR DEFENDANT

CERTIFICATE REGARDING SERVICE

I hereby certify that it is my belief and understanding that counsel for respondent, Stephen D. Hawke, Asst. Atty. Gen., is a participant in the Court's CM/ECF program and that separate service of the foregoing document is not required beyond the Notification of Electronic Filing to be forwarded on February 12, 2008 upon the filing of the foregoing document.

/S/ ELIZABETH UNGER CARLYLE

6

EXAMPLE MOTION TO ALTER OR AMEND JUDGMENT (continued)

IN THE MISSOURI COURT OF APPEALS
WESTERN DISTRICT

STATE OF MISSOURI,	)	
Respondent,	)	WD# 52,816
	)	
-vs-	)	CR95-4292
	)	
ZACHARY A. SMITH,	)	
	)	
Appellant.	)	

Appeal from the Circuit Court of Jackson County, Missouri,
Sixteenth Judicial Circuit,
Division 7,
The Honorable William F. Mauer, Judge

SUPPLEMENTAL LEGAL FILE

ROSEMARY E. PERCIVAL, #45292
ASSISTANT APPELLATE DEFENDER
Office of the State Public Defender
Western Appellate Division
505 E. 13th Street, Suite 420
Kansas City, MO 64106-2865
(816) 889-2029

Counsel for Appellant

EXAMPLE MOTION TO ALTER OR AMEND JUDGMENT (continued)

EXAMPLE MOTION TO ALTER OR AMEND JUDGMENT (continued)

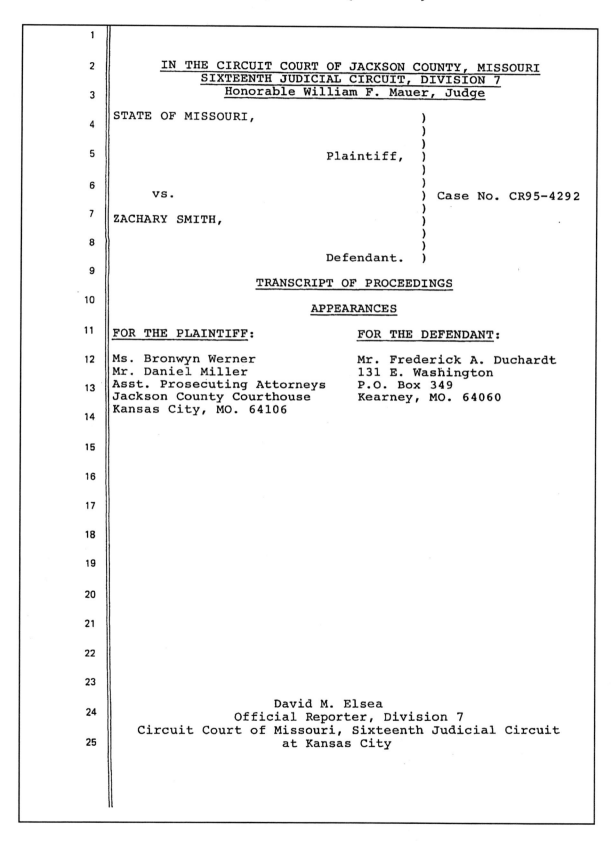

```
 1
 2          IN THE CIRCUIT COURT OF JACKSON COUNTY, MISSOURI
              SIXTEENTH JUDICIAL CIRCUIT, DIVISION 7
 3               Honorable William F. Mauer, Judge

 4    STATE OF MISSOURI,                 )
                                         )
                                         )
 5                      Plaintiff,       )
                                         )
 6        vs.                            ) Case No. CR95-4292
                                         )
 7    ZACHARY SMITH,                     )
                                         )
 8                                       )
                        Defendant.  )
 9
                       TRANSCRIPT OF PROCEEDINGS
10
                            APPEARANCES
11
      FOR THE PLAINTIFF:              FOR THE DEFENDANT:
12
      Ms. Bronwyn Werner              Mr. Frederick A. Duchardt
      Mr. Daniel Miller              131 E. Washington
13    Asst. Prosecuting Attorneys    P.O. Box 349
      Jackson County Courthouse      Kearney, MO. 64060
14    Kansas City, MO. 64106

15

16

17

18

19

20

21

22

23

24                      David M. Elsea
                 Official Reporter, Division 7
25    Circuit Court of Missouri, Sixteenth Judicial Circuit
                       at Kansas City
```

EXAMPLE MOTION TO ALTER OR AMEND JUDGMENT (concluded)

1	which are the clothes of Kevin Glavin. We are
2	sending them, I would note for the record, in the bag
3	they came out of. I would also note for the record
4	that the swatch taken out of the T-shirt and
5	identified as Exhibit 50 is also in the bag and we
6	also have 53 which is the report concerning Rose
7	Sanchez' statement. I believe the parties agree and
8	stipulate that those were the --
9	MS. WERNER: And then there was one more
10	which was the 1901 Lawn Consent to Search which was
11	State's Exhibit No. 3 which didn't come in.
12	MR. DUCHARDT: That's correct. And the
13	parties agree and stipulate that those were the
14	exhibits which were received into evidence.
15	(THE FOLLOWING PROCEEDINGS WERE HAD IN OPEN COURT BUT OUT OF
16	THE PRESENCE AND HEARING OF THE JURY AT 2:40 P.M.:)
17	THE COURT: All right. Let the record show
18	that the Court -- the jury has sent down Court's
19	Exhibit No. 2 which reads, "Can we be a hung jury?
20	We are eight and four after much discussion. Can we
21	find guilty of being present but not actually
22	shooting the gun?" Any suggestions?
23	MS. WERNER: My feeling is it's way to soon
24	in deliberations to even begin to think about a hung
25	jury. So tell them to keep deliberating.

448

EXAMPLE SUGGESTIONS IN OPPOSITION TO MOTION TO AMEND JUDGMENT

IN THE UNITED STATES DISTRICT COURT
WESTERN DISTRICT OF MISSOURI
ST. JOSEPH DIVISION

ZACHARY SMITH,	)	
Petitioner,	)	
	)	
v.	)	07-06068-CV-SJ-ODS
	)	
MIKE KEMNA,	)	
Respondent.	)	

**SUGGESTIONS IN OPPOSITION TO MOTION TO AMEND
JUDGMENT PURSUANT TO RULE 59(E) AND SUPPLEMENT TO MOTION TO
ALTER OR AMEND JUDGMENT**

Comes now Respondent Michael Kemna, by and through Attorney General Jeremiah W. (Jay) Nixon and Assistant Attorney General Michael J. Spillane, and suggests as follows in opposition to the motion to amend judgment.

Standard of Review

A motion to alter or amend must rely on one of three major grounds:

1) An intervening change in controlling law;

2) The availability of new evidence not available previously or;

3) The need to correct a clear error of law or prevent manifest injustice. *Bannister v. Armontrout*, 807 F. Supp. 516, 556 (W.D. Mo. 1991), *aff'd*, 43 F.3d 1434 (8th Cir. 1993), cert. denied 513 U.S. 960 (1994).

Analysis

In his Rule 59(e) motion, Smith does two things. First he argues that this Court misunderstood the facts of the case and re-states them in what he apparently views as a more favorable light. Second, he argues that the state post-conviction

Case 5:07-cv-06068-ODS   Document 20   Filed 02/26/2008   Page 1 of 3

EXAMPLE SUGGESTIONS IN OPPOSITION TO MOTION TO AMEND JUDGMENT (continued)

review court, the state appellate court and this Court erred in their analysis, based on *Strickland v. Washington*, 466 U.S. 668,(1984), that a claim of ineffective assistance of trial counsel for not calling potential witness Carrillo failed both prongs of the *Strickland* test. This Court noted that it was reasonable not to call Carrillo because his testimony was about a peripheral matter and that in any event there was no reasonable probability that if Carrillo would have tested the outcome of the trial would have been changed (Document 15 at 5-6). Smith is not arguing about new previously undiscoverable evidence, or an intervening change in controlling law or that this Court made a clear error of law by using the wrong case law or standard of review. His claim is essentially that he does not like the result of the analysis conducted by the Missouri courts and this Court. That is not a proper Rule 59(e) claim.

The supplement to the Rule 59(e) motion essentially makes two claims. First it alleges that this Court misinterpreted the strength of the state's case and that therefore this Court erred in finding that no *Strickland* prejudice occurred from not calling Carrillo. Second, the supplement argues that the trial court committed a Due Process Clause violation by not *sua sponte* instructing the jury to disregard a question by the prosecutor, even though the defense did not ask for such an instruction. Of course the claim is arguably procedurally barred, and had the trial court *sua sponte* called attention to the questioning by offering an un-requested instruction, Smith would presumably now be arguing that giving the instruction was itself a due process violation, calling unwanted attention to the question, and that double jeopardy concerns prevent retrial allowing Smith to get away with first degree murder. This Court intelligently analyzed the claim

Case 5:07-cv-06068-ODS   Document 20   Filed 02/26/2008   Page 2 of 3

EXAMPLE SUGGESTIONS IN OPPOSITION TO MOTION TO AMEND JUDGMENT (concluded)

and applying the proper precedents rejected the claim. Nothing in the supplement is the proper subject of a Rule 59(e) motion.

Wherefore Respondent prays that the Rule 59(e) motion be denied.

Respectfully submitted,

JEREMIAH W. (JAY) NIXON
Attorney General
/s/Michael J. Spillane

MICHAEL J. SPILLANE
Assistant Attorney General
Missouri Bar No. 40704

Post Office Box 899
Jefferson City, MO 65102-0899
Telephone: (573) 751-3321
Facsimile: (573) 751-2096
Attorneys for Respondent

CERTIFICATE OF SERVICE

I hereby certify that a true and correct copy of the foregoing should be sent by this court's electronic filing system to, this 26thday of February,2008, to:

Elizabeth Unger Carlyle
P.O. Box 962
Columbus, Mississippi, 39703

/s/Michael J.Spillane

Assistant Attorney General

EXAMPLE REPLY SUGGESTIONS IN SUPPORT OF MOTION TO ALTER OR AMEND JUDGEMENT

IN THE UNITED STATES DISTRICT COURT
FOR THE WESTERN DISTRICT OF MISSOURI

ZACHARY SMITH	§	
	§	
Petitioner	§	
	§	
v.	§	No. 07-06068-CV-SJ-ODS
	§	
MIKE KEMNA	§	
	§	
Respondent	§	

REPLY SUGGESTIONS IN SUPPORT OF MOTION TO ALTER OR AMEND JUDGMENT

The state suggests that this Court can alter its judgment only if there is new evidence or if it applied the wrong standard of review. That analysis is incorrect. If this Court, upon reconsideration, perceives that its prior judgment was in error, or if the Court experiences a change of heart about the merits of any issue, relief under Rule 59(e) is proper. *Innovative Home Health Care, Inc. v. P.T.-O.T. Associates of the Black Hills*, 141 F.3d 1284, 1287 (8th Cir. 1998). The rule is interpreted broadly to allow the court to correct its own errors. In considering the merits of the motion to alter or amend judgment, this Court need not attempt to pigeonhole its decision into any particular category. Instead, this Court should exercise its broad discretion, and grant relief.

Respectfully submitted,

/S/ ELIZABETH UNGER CARLYLE

Elizabeth Unger Carlyle
P.O. Box 962
Columbus, MS 39703
Missouri Bar No. 41930
(816)525-6540
FAX (866) 764-1240
elizcar@bellsouth.net
ATTORNEY FOR PETITIONER

1

EXAMPLE REPLY SUGGESTIONS IN SUPPORT OF MOTION TO ALTER OR AMEND JUDGEMENT (concluded)

CERTIFICATE REGARDING SERVICE

I hereby certify that it is my belief and understanding that counsel for respondent, Asst. Atty. Gen. Michael Spillane, is a participant in the Court's CM/ECF program and that separate service of the foregoing document is not required beyond the Notification of Electronic Filing to be forwarded on March 12, 2008, upon the filing of the foregoing document.

/S/ ELIZABETH UNGER CARLYLE

2

EXAMPLE ORDER AND OPINION DENYING MOTION TO ALTER OR AMEND JUDGMENT

IN THE UNITED STATES DISTRICT COURT FOR THE
WESTERN DISTRICT OF MISSOURI
ST. JOSEPH DIVISION

ZACHARY SMITH,	)	
	)	
Petitioner,	)	
	)	
vs.	)	Case No.07-6068-CV-SJ-ODS
	)	
MIKE KEMNA,	)	
Superintendent,	)	
Crossroads Correctional Center	)	
	)	
Respondent.	)	

ORDER AND OPINION DENYING MOTION TO ALTER OR AMEND JUDGMENT

On January 29, 2008, the Court denied Petitioner's Request for a Writ of Habeas Corpus. On February 11th and 12th, 2008, Petitioner timely filed Motions to Alter or Amend the Judgment (Docs. # 18 and 19). For the following reasons, Petitioner's Motions are DENIED.

I. STANDARD

"A motion to alter or amend under Rule 59(e) must rely on one of three major grounds: 1) an intervening change in controlling law; 2) the availability of new evidence not available previously; or 3) the need to correct a clear error of law or prevent manifest injustice." Bannister v. Armontrout, 807 F. Supp. 516, 556 (W.D. Mo. 1991), aff'd, 4 F.3d 1434 (8th Cir. 1993), cert. denied, 115 S. Ct. 418 (1994). On the other hand, the Court need not consider a motion to alter or amend to the extent it merely re-argues issues that were already presented and considered without identifying a change in controlling law or newly discovered facts that were not presented to the Court. E.g., Forsythe v. Saudi Arabian Airlines Corp., 885 F.2d 285, 289 (5th Cir. 1989); see also Lewis v. United States, 555 F.2d 1360, 1362 (8th Cir. 1977) (affirming denial of rule 59(e) motion because, among other reasons, it "stated no basis for relief not already

EXAMPLE ORDER AND OPINION DENYING MOTION TO ALTER OR AMEND JUDGMENT (continued)

rejected by the district court . . . .").

II. DISCUSSION

Principally, Petitioner's Motion simply reasserts arguments that have already been presented and rejected. To that extent, the Motion to Alter or Amend Judgement will be denied. The Motion does contain, however, some arguments that justify further discussion.

Petitioner argues that this Court incorrectly adopted the factual finding of the Missouri court that Mr. Carrillo's testimony would not have contradicted the testimony of Cathy and Lori Stone because his testimony would have described a different incident than the Stones'. The factual findings made by the state courts are entitled to deference. Nave v. Delo, 62 F.3d 1024, 1037 (8th Cir. 1995), cert. denied, 116 S. Ct. 1837 (1996). Specifically, this finding was not "an unreasonable determination of the facts in light of the evidence presented" during Petitioner's trial and post-trial motion hearing. See 28 U.S.C. § 2254(d). The Court has accorded the deference due by law to the state court's factual determinations. Thereafter, the Court independently applied those facts to the law and reached its own legal conclusion that Mr. Carrillo's testimony would not have been helpful to Petitioner's defense, and therefore, Petitioner was not prejudiced by his counsel's failure to investigate or present this testimony.

This Court also held that the failure to present the testimony of Alvino Carrillo was not prejudicial because of the other overwhelming evidence of Petitioner's guilt presented at trial. Petitioner's motion to alter or amend suggests that there was actually very little reliable evidence of Petitioner's guilt. However, Petitioner's motion does not include all of the evidence presented at Petitioner's trial that supported the jury's verdict.[1] The Court still holds that there is no reasonable probability that Alvino Carrillo's testimony would have changed the outcome of the proceeding. See Strickland

---

[1] For the complete version of the evidence supporting the jury's guilty verdict see the Missouri Court of Appeals decision affirming Petitioner's conviction at State v. Smith, 90 S.W.3d 132, 135-37 (Mo. Ct. App. 2002).

EXAMPLE ORDER AND OPINION DENYING MOTION TO ALTER OR AMEND JUDGMENT (concluded)

v. Washington, 466 U.S. 668, 694 (1984).

III. CONCLUSION

For the foregoing reasons, Petitioner's Motions to Alter or Amend (Docs. # 18 and 19) are denied.

IT IS SO ORDERED.

/s/ Ortrie D. Smith
ORTRIE D. SMITH, JUDGE
UNITED STATES DISTRICT COURT

DATE: March 18, 2008

7. NOTICE OF APPEAL

REQUESTING CERTIFICATE OF APPEALABILITY

As mandated by federal statute, a state prisoner seeking a writ of habeas corpus has no absolute entitlement to appeal a district court's denial of his petition. *28 U.S.C. §2253*. Before an appeal may be entertained, a prisoner who was denied habeas relief in the district court must first seek and obtain a COA from a circuit justice or judge. This is a jurisdictional prerequisite because the COA statute mandates that "[u]nless a circuit justice or judge issues a certificate of appealability, an appeal may not be taken to the court of appeals ..." *28 U.S.C. §2253(c)(1)*. As a result, until a COA has been issued, federal courts of appeals lack jurisdiction to rule on the merits of appeals from habeas petitioners.

A petitioner seeking a COA need only demonstrate "a substantial showing of the denial of a constitutional right." *28 U.S.C. §2253(c)(2)*. A petitioner satisfies this standard by demonstrating that jurists of reason could disagree with the district court's resolution of his or her constitutional claims, or that jurists could conclude the issues presented are adequate to deserve encouragement to proceed further. *Slack v. McDaniel, 529 U.S. 473, at 484 (2000)*.

Examples of an application for certificate of appealability, a supplemental application for certificate of appealability, and an order granting in part and denying in part petitioner's motion for certificate of appealability are provided at the end of this chapter. I recommend reading *Miller-El v. Cockrell, 537 U.S. 322, 338 (2003)* for a clearer understanding of what you must show to obtain a COA.

The standard for obtaining a COA does not require you to show that you're entitled to relief:

> We do not require petitioner to prove ... that some jurists would grant the petition for habeas corpus. Indeed, a claim can be debatable even though every jurist of reason might agree, after the COA has been granted and the case has received full consideration, that petitioner will not prevail.

Miller-El v. Cockrell, 537 U.S. 322, 338 (2003). Therefore, doubts whether to issue a certificate of appealability should be resolved in favor of the petitioner. *Fuller v. Johnson, 114 F.3d 491, 495 (5th Cir. 1997); and Buxton v. Collins, 925 F.2d 816, 819 (5th Cir. 1991); Buie v. McAdory, 322 F.3d 980 (7th Cir. 2003)*.

If a ground was dismissed by the district court on procedural grounds, a certificate of appealability must be issued if the petitioner meets the *Barefoot v. Estelle, 463 U.S. 880, 893 (1983)* standard as to the procedural question, and shows, at least, that jurists of reason would find it debatable whether the ground of the petition at issue states a valid claim of a constitutional right. *Slack v. McDaniel, 529 U.S. 473, 483-484 (2000).*

NOTICE OF APPEAL

You must file a notice of appeal, in conjunction to filing your request for a certificate of appealability, within 30 days after the district court's order and opinion denying your petition for a writ of habeas corpus. *Federal Rules of Appellate Procedure Rules 3 and 4.* You must send the district court clerk the original and one copy of the notice of appeal. Your notice must also be accompanied with the filing fee of $455. If you are unable to pay the filing fee, you may ask for leave to proceed *in forma pauperis*. Two example notices of appeal and an example motion for leave to proceed *in forma pauperis* are provided at the end of this chapter.

If the district court denies your request for a certificate of appealability and request for leave to proceed *in forma pauperis*, the court clerk will still process your notice of appeal and forward it to the court of appeals. You may then request that the court of appeals grant you a COA and leave to proceed *in forma pauperis*. Just change the caption and case number on your original COA and motion for leave, then file them with the court of appeals.

DISTRICT COURT TIMELINE

Also provided at the end of this chapter is a docket sheet of an actual case which shows each step taken in the district court. This will give you a general ideal of how long the process takes to litigate a habeas corpus petition in the district court.

EXAMPLE APPLICATION FOR CERTIFICATE OF APPEALABILITY

IN THE UNITED STATES DISTRICT COURT
FOR THE WESTERN DISTRICT OF MISSOURI

ZACHARY SMITH	§	
	§	
Petitioner	§	
	§	
v.	§	No. 07-06068-CV-SJ-ODS
	§	
MIKE KEMNA	§	
	§	
Respondent	§	

APPLICATION FOR CERTIFICATE OF APPEALABILITY

Petitioner Zachary Smith moves the court for a certificate of appealability, and in support states:

A. Standards for granting a certificate of appealability

A petitioner is entitled to a certificate of appealability if he makes "a substantial showing of the denial of a constitutional right." 28 U.S.C. §2253(c)(2). The U.S. Supreme Court in *Barefoot v. Estelle*, 463 U.S. 880, 893 (1983), held this means that the appellant need not show that he would prevail on the merits, but must "demonstrate that the issues are debatable among jurists of reason; that a court could resolve the issues [in a different manner]; or that the questions are 'adequate to deserve encouragement to proceed further.' [Citations omitted]." See *Flieger v. Delo*, 16 F.3d 878, 883 (8th Cir. 1994).

This standard does not require the petitioner to show that he is entitled to relief:

> We do not require petitioner to prove. . . that some jurists would grant the petition for habeas corpus. Indeed, a claim can be debatable even though every jurist of reason might agree, after the COA has been granted and the case has received full consideration, that petitioner will not prevail.

1

EXAMPLE APPLICATION FOR CERTIFICATE OF APPEALABILITY (continued)

Miller-El v. Cockrell, 537 U.S. 322, 338 (2003). Therefore, doubts as to whether to issue a certificate of appealability should be resolved in favor of the appellant. *Fuller v. Johnson*, 114 F.3d 491, 495 (5th Cir. 1997); see *Buxton v. Collins*, 925 F.2d 816, 819 (5th Cir. 1991); *Buie v. McAdory*, 322 F.3d 980 (7th Cir. 2003).

If a ground was dismissed by the district court on procedural grounds, a certificate of appealability must be issued if the petitioner meets the *Barefoot* standard as to the procedural question, and shows, at least, that jurists of reason would find it debatable whether the ground of the petition at issue states a valid claim of a constitutional right. *Slack v. McDaniel*, 529 U.S. 473, 483-484 (2000).

C. Issues as to which a certificate of appealability should be granted.

In its order denying relief, this Court also denied a certificate of appealability, but indicated that a later application by Mr. Smith would be reviewed *de novo*. The Court's order denying relief in this matter reorganized the grounds for relief in the petition. The grounds are discussed below in the order of the petition rather than that of the Court's order denying relief.

1. Mr. Smith was prejudiced by improper prosecutorial testimony. This Court noted that there is a conflict in this circuit concerning the standard of habeas corpus review when, as here, an issue is reviewed by the state court for plain error. *Hornbuckle v. Groose*, 106 F.3d 253, 257 (8th Cir.), *cert. denied*, 118 S. Ct. 189 (1997) (noting conflict); *Mack v. Caspari*, 92 F.3d 637, 641 n.6 (8th Cir. 1996), *cert. denied*, 117 S. Ct. 1117 (1997). This Court then selected a "highly deferential" standard of review, that of *James v. Bowersox*, 187 F.3d 866, 869 (8th Cir. 1999).

2

EXAMPLE APPLICATION FOR CERTIFICATE OF APPEALABILITY (continued)

In so holding, the Court overlooked Mr. Smith's contention that he had demonstrated legal "cause" for failing to preserve error by asserting, both in state court and in federal court, that the failure to preserve error was ineffective assistance of counsel. See *Coleman v. Thompson*, 501 U.S. 722, 754 (1991); *Murray v. Carrier*, 477 U.S. 478, 488 (1986); *Edwards v. Carpenter*, 529 U.S. 446, 450-454 (2000).

In addition to the conflict within the Eighth Circuit concerning the standard of review when a state court reviews for plain error, cases from other circuits support the proposition that plenary review is appropriate when the state court reached the merits of the issue, whether or not the plain error standard was used. See, e.g., *Sanders v. Cotton*, 398 F.3d 572, 579-580 (7th Cir. 2005) (State court's reliance on procedural bar was not sufficiently explicit to bar review because reference to the procedural issue was immediately followed by consideration of the merits of the ground for relief); *Harding v. Sternes*, 380 F.3d 1034, 1043-1044 (7th Cir. 2004), *cert. denied*, 543 U.S. 1174 (2005). *Clinkscale v. Carter*, 375 F.3d 430, 442 (6th Cir. 2004); *Riley v. Taylor,* 277 F.3d 261, 273-275 (3rd Cir. 2001).

Because reasonable jurists could differ about the standard of review applied by this Court, a certificate of appealability should issue as to this ground.

2. Mr. Smith was prejudiced by the jury's viewing the videotaped statement of alleged eyewitness Kevin Glavin again during deliberations.

As with the previous ground the Court selected a "highly deferential" standard of review because the state court reviewed for plain error. This Court again overlooked Mr. Smith's showing of legal "cause", namely, ineffective assistance of counsel. As

3

EXAMPLE APPLICATION FOR CERTIFICATE OF APPEALABILITY (continued)

discussed above, reasonable jurists could disagree on the standard of review used by the Court. Therefore, a certificate of appealability as to this ground is required.

3. Mr. Smith was prejudiced by trial counsel's failure to investigate and call Alvino Carrillo to testify. This Court held, "Even assuming trial counsel's decision not to investigate Mr. Carillo as a possible witness was unreasonable, there is no reasonable probability that the verdict would have been any different if Mr. Carrillo had testified." Order denying relief, p. 6. Reasonable jurists could differ about this conclusion.

In order to find *Strickland* prejudice, the Court need not find that it is more likely that not that the defendant would have been acquitted absent the ineffective assistance of counsel. As the U.S. Supreme Court put it in *Williams (Terry) v. Taylor*, 529 U.S. 362, 405-406 (2000).

> If a state court were to reject a prisoner's claim of ineffective assistance of counsel on the grounds that the prisoner had not established by a preponderance of the evidence that the result of his criminal proceeding would have been different, that decision would be "diametrically different," "opposite in character or nature," and "mutually opposed" to our clearly established precedent because we held in *Strickland* that the prisoner need only demonstrate a "reasonable probability that ... the result of the proceeding would have been different."

[Citations omitted]. The prejudice determination must be based on *all of the evidence* available to the Court, not simply the evidence supporting the verdict. Again, *Williams (Terry)* is instructive on this point: "[T]he State Supreme Court's prejudice determination was unreasonable insofar as it failed to evaluate the totality of the available mitigation evidence—both that adduced at trial, and the evidence adduced in

4

EXAMPLE APPLICATION FOR CERTIFICATE OF APPEALABILITY (continued)

the habeas proceeding—in reweighing it against the evidence in aggravation." *Williams (Terry) v. Taylor*, 529 U.S. 362, 397-398 (2000).

This Court's decision and analysis is substantially different from that in *Stanley v. Bartley*, 465 F.3d 810 (7th Cir. 2006). There, as here, the omitted evidence impeached the testimony of an alleged eyewitness who was a convicted felon and a suspect in the crime. In *Stanley,* the eyewitness testified in court unlike Mr. Glavin, and evidence was presented that Mr. Stanley (unlike Mr. Smith) had made admissions concerning the crime. While this Court may not be convinced by the analysis in *Stanley*, that case, along with the other authorities cited in the traverse, is clearly sufficient to show that reasonable jurists could differ on the prejudice issue in Mr. Smith's case. Therefore, a certificate of appealability is required.

4. Trial counsel's failure to object and request a limiting instruction after prosecutorial misconduct was unreasonable and prejudicial.

This Court's analysis of the facts and the prejudice that resulted is debatable among jurists of reason. The trial court instructed the prosecutor NOT to ask what Mr. Smith's brother did, but only to ask what the witness did. The prosecutor totally disregarded this instruction. After the court's admonition, the next words out of the prosecutor's mouth were a description of what "the defendant" did in the hallway. Not only did he not focus on the acts of the witness as instructed by the court, he said that **"the defendant,"** not Mr. Smith's brother, had nodded at the witness in the hall. The findings of the court of appeals and this court that the prosecutor did not disregard the instruction are without support in the record.

5

EXAMPLE APPLICATION FOR CERTIFICATE OF APPEALABILITY (continued)

Moreover, the fact that Mr. Glavin denied that the event described by the prosecutor had occurred did not cure the error of counsel in failing to object or request a limiting instruction. Contrary to the decision of the Missouri Court of Appeals, Mr. Smith's brother did not testify at Mr. Smith's trial. Thus, the only evidence before the jury was the prosecutor's statement, presented as a fact, that Mr. Smith had nodded at Mr. Glavin, and Mr. Glavin's denial. Under these circumstances, there is more than a reasonable probability that the jury credited the prosecutor and thought the witness had been manipulated by the defendant. The jury did not hear any instruction that they could not draw this conclusion. Mr. Glavin's testimony was clearly crucial to Mr. Smith's conviction. Thus, Mr. Smith was prejudiced by the error of trial counsel.

This Court's failure to recognize this factual discrepancy is debatable among jurists of reason, as demonstrated by *Simmons v. Luebbers*, 299 F.3d 929, 937 (8th Cir. 2002). There, the court found that ""Our independent review of the record leads us to conclude that the Missouri Supreme Court's conclusions regarding the evidence that was presented during the penalty phase of that trial are completely inaccurate."

The conclusion that the prosecutor's misstatement was not prejudicial is likewise debatable among jurists of reason. See *Hodge v. Hurley*, 426 F.3d 368, 378 (6th Cir. 2005). Quoting *United States v. Young*, 470 U.S. 1, 18-19 (1985): "'[T]he prosecutor's opinion carries with it the imprimatur of the Government and may induce the jury to trust the Government's judgment rather than its own view of the evidence.'"

A certificate of appealability should issue.

6

EXAMPLE APPLICATION FOR CERTIFICATE OF APPEALABILITY (continued)

5. An objection to replaying Kevin Glavin's videotaped statement to the jury would likely have been successful.

This Court apparently does not disagree that allowing the jury to hear the state's star witness twice was prejudicial to Mr. Smith. Rather, it finds that as a matter of Missouri law, any objection would likely have been overruled. The only case cited by the Court in support of this proposition is *State v. Jennings*, 815 S.W.2d 454 (Mo. App. 1991). Even that case acknowledges that the general rule is that testimonial exhibits should not be shown to the jury. Other than that case, the only exception generally supported by the case law is for recorded confessions of the defendant to law enforcement. *Jennings* held that it was not an abuse of discretion for the trial court to permit the playing of *parts* of the witness's videotaped statement. But in Mr. Smith's case, the entire statement was played.

More important, in order to establish prejudice, Mr. Smith must show only a reasonable probability that the result would have been different, not that the court would definitely have sustained the objection. The fact that the trial court *might* have overruled the objection and that this *might* have been sustained on appeal does not defeat such a showing here. Since, as the *Jennings* court acknowledged, the general rule disapproves the action here, and the trial court had discretion to refuse the jury's request, there is a reasonable probability of a different result. A certificate of appealability should be issued as to this ground.

7

EXAMPLE APPLICATION FOR CERTIFICATE OF APPEALABILITY (concluded)

Conclusion.

For the foregoing reasons, Mr. Smith prays the court to issue a certificate of appealability as to each issue discussed in this application.

Respectfully submitted,

/S/ ELIZABETH UNGER CARLYLE

Elizabeth Unger Carlyle
P.O. Box 866
Columbus, MS 39703
Missouri Bar No. 41930
(816)525-6540
FAX (866) 764-1240
elizcar@lawalumni.neu.eud

ATTORNEY FOR PETITIONER

<u>CERTIFICATE REGARDING SERVICE</u>

I hereby certify that it is my belief and understanding that counsel for respondent, Stephen D. Hawke, is a participant in the Court's CM/ECF program and that separate service of the foregoing document is not required beyond the Notification of Electronic Filing to be forwarded on April 8, 2008, upon the filing of the foregoing document.

/S/ ELIZABETH UNGER CARLYLE

8

EXAMPLE SUPPLEMENTAL APPLICATION FOR CERTIFICATE OF APPEALABILITY

IN THE UNITED STATES DISTRICT COURT
WESTERN DISTRICT OF MISSOURI

ZACHARY SMITH,   )
)
                Petitioner,   )
)   07-06068-CV-SJ-ODS
v.   )
)
)
MIKE KEMNA, et al.,   )
)
                Respondents.   )

<u>SUPPLEMENTAL APPLICATION FOR CERTIFICATE OF APPEALABILITY</u>

<u>WITH SUGGESTIONS IN SUPPORT</u>

COMES NOW Petitioner, Zachary Smith, and prays this Court issue a certificate of appealability. In support of application, Smith states as follows.

1. Mr. Smith hereby incorporates by reference and asks this Court to consider this supplemental application and the application filed by counsel of record in conjunction with each other. And for his suggestions in support of, Smith states as follows:

Scope of Review for COA

Congress mandates that a prisoner seeking postconviction relief under 28 U.S.C. §2254 has no automatic right to appeal a district court's denial or dismissal of the petition. Instead, petitioner must first seek and obtain a COA. **Slack V. McDaniel**, 529 U.S. 473, 481 (2000). A prisoner seeking a COA need only demonstrate "a substantial showing of the denial of a constitutional right." 28 U.S.C. §2253(c)(2). A petitioner satisfies this standard by demonstrating that jurists of reason could disagree with the district court's resolution of his constitutional claims or that jurists could conclude the issues presented are adequate to deserve encouragement

1

EXAMPLE SUPPLEMENTAL APPLICATION FOR CERTIFICATE OF APPEALABILITY (continued)

to proceed further. **Slack,** supra, at 484.

Applying these principles to Smith's application, a COA should be issued for the following grounds;

     A. Ineffective Assistance of Counsel

     i. Failing to interview and call as a witness Alvino Carrillo

Jurists of reason could disagree with this Court's decision that the Missouri Court of Appeals' factual finding (that Mr. Carrillo's testimony would not have contradicted the testimony of Cathy and Lori Stones' because his testimony would have described a different incident than the Stones') was not an unreasonable determination of the facts in light of the evidence presented. It is debatable among jurists as to whether reasonable jurors would be able to disregard Mr. Carrillo's testimony in light of the fact that the shell casing evidence contradicted the Stones' account of the incident. Detective Beard testified that the shells found at 411 Indiana were not located where they would have been located had Smith fired a gun from the location specified by the Stones', making their statements that they witnessed Smith shoot a gun questionable, and Mr. Carrillo's testimony all the more credible that it was Sosa, and not Smith, that fired the gun.(Resp. Ex. 1b, pp. 782-784, 787-797).

Jurists of reason could also disagree with this Court's decision that the Missouri Court of Appeals' finding that the failure to present the testimony of Mr. Carrillo was not prejudicial because of the other overwhelming evidence of Smith's guilt and that there is no reasonable probability that Carrillo's testimony would have changed the outcome of the proceedings. It is debatable among jurists as to whether the state presented overwhelming evidence of Smith's guilt for first degree murder. As was the case in **Stanley V. Bartley,** 465 F.3d 810 (7th Cir. 2006), the

EXAMPLE SUPPLEMENTAL APPLICATION FOR CERTIFICATE OF APPEALABILITY (continued)

issue is not whether Smith is innocent, but whether if he had a competent lawyer he would have had a reasonable chance (it needn't be a 50 percent or greater chance, Miller V. Anderson, 255 F.3d 455, 459 (7th Cir. 2001) of being acquitted; given that guilt must be proved beyond a reasonable doubt, guilty people are often acquitted.

Similarly, given Glavin's rampant use of crack cocaine leading up to the shooting, his criminal background, and his self-interest in shifting blame for the shooting away from himself and onto Smith, the jury easily could have disbelieved his account of Hoskins' death. In fact, the first trial of Smith's resulted in a mistrial after the jury sent down a note reading, "can we be a hung jury? We are eight to four after much discussion. Can we find guilty of being present but not actually shooting the gun?" Furthermore, defense counsel was contacted by a member of the jury after the third trial who advised counsel of serious reservations and reasonable doubt that existed in his mind, as well as in the mind of other jurors. (Resp. Ex. 1b, pp. 112,1060-1061).

There were other witnesses, but their testimony was distinctly secondary and circumstantial. Smith did not make any admissions to police, and the statements he made, proved nothing. Reasonable jurors could have believed that Smith was merely being uncooperative with the police in their investigation. Smith's possession of the victim's bicycle after the murder is circumstantial and is not conclusive evidence that Smith was the shooter of Hoskins. It was the combination of Glavin's and the Stones' testimony that they saw Smith shoot a gun that matched the shells at the crime scene that convicted Smith of first degree murder. Had Mr. Carrillo been called as a witness and testified that Mr. Sosa fired the gun, and not Smith, there is a reasonable probability that the jury would have disregarded

3

EXAMPLE SUPPLEMENTAL APPLICATION FOR CERTIFICATE OF APPEALABILITY (continued)

the Stones' testimony and the shell casing evidence, because there was no other witnesses that put the murder weapon in Smith's hands before or after Hoskins' death.

Rose Sanchez testified that Smith, Sosa, and Glavin had came to her house and Smith was not in possession of a gun. She testified that Smith and Sosa stayed at her house and Glavin left. She further testified that she had sex with Smith and he stayed with her until morning. (Resp. Ex. 1b, pp. 699-718). Inside the safe there was an inmate Id card for Jose Sosa, which jurors could have easily believed Smith was not the only person who had access to the 45-caliber ammunition. And as found by the first trial jurors, they could have easily believed that Smith was never in possession of the gun used to kill Hoskins on the night in question.

Had the jury thought Glavin a liar and possibly the murderer, Smith would have had a decent shot at an acquittal. This Court and the state's contrary conclusion that the evidence against Smith was overwhelming resulted in an unreasonable application of Strickland V. Washington. Smith is entitled to a COA on this ground because he has made a substantial showing of a denial of his right to effective assistance of counsel, or that this ground is adequate to deserve encouragement to proceed further. Therefore, this Court should grant Smith a COA.

ii. Failing to object to line of questioning by prosecutor

Jurists of reason could disagree with this Court's decision that the Missouri Court of Appeals' finding that the prosecutor's questioning was not improper and did not affect the jury's decision. It is debatable among jurists as to whether the prosecutor's questioning was improper and violated Smith's due process rights, in that it is patently improper for a prosecutor either to comment on the credibility of a witness or to express a personal

4

EXAMPLE SUPPLEMENTAL APPLICATION FOR CERTIFICATE OF APPEALABILITY (continued)

belief that a particular witness is lying. **United State V. Young,** 470 U.S. 1, 17-19 (1985); **Berger,** 295 U.S. at 86-88 (citing prosecutor's statements suggesting that he had personal knowledge that a witness was not being truthful as example of egreglous prosecutorial misconduct).

As the Supreme Court explained in **Young,** there are two separate harms that arise from such misconduct. First, "such comments can convey the impression that evidence not presented to the jury, but known to the prosecutor, supports the charges against the defendant and can thus jeopardize the defendant's right to be tried solely on the basis of the evidence presented to the jury." **Young,** 470 U.S. at 18. Secondly, "the prosecutor's opinion carries with it the imprimatur of the government and may induce the jury to trust the government's judgment rather than its own view of the evidence." **Id.** at 18-19. Both concerns are implicated in this case.

In the prosecutor's questions, his evident purpose was to impugn Glavin's credibility that he didn't remember the facts of the case and to improperly convey to the jury that Smith, through his brother, had intimidated Glavin into refusing to testify. As such, the jury was free to believe that Torrid Smith's alleged actions was an attempt to prevent Glavin from giving unfavorable testimony against Smith and was necessary because of his brother's guilt.

Glavin's denial that any exchange occurred between him and Smith's brother did not remove the prejudice. Rather, the negative responses heightened the truth imputed in the asking of the questions by the prosecutor. **Gross V. United States,** 394 F.2d 216, 221 (8th Cir. 1968). The prosecutor, as a representative of the state, used the questions to "waft an unwarranted innuedo into the jury box," and the conduct is even

5

EXAMPLE SUPPLEMENTAL APPLICATION FOR CERTIFICATE OF APPEALABILITY (continued)

more egregious because the prosecutor had been told to avoid any such

references to what actions, if any, Smith's brother did in the hallway.

The prosecutor's purpose was successful as noted by the trial judge

who stated: "From the court's perspective, he was either a world class

liar and evader or he has a serious memory problem. And my observations

would indicate that he is a world class liar and evader and not trying

to cooperate in this case." (Resp. Ex. 1b., pp. 601). It is debatable among

jurists of reason that there is a reasonable probability that absent the

improper questions, the jury could have easily believed that Glavin's

failure to cooperate was evidence of his consciousness of guilt for shooting

Hoskins and then falsely pointing the finger at Smith. Smith is entitled

to a COA on this ground because he has made a substantial showing of a

denial of his right to effective assistance of counsel and due process

rights, or is adequate to deserve encouragement to proceed further.

Therefore, this Court should issue a COA.

iv. Failing to impeach State's witness

Jurists of reason could disagree with this Court's conclusion that

the Missouri Court of Appeals' decision finding that because Glavin's

credibility was already significantly undermined, Smith could not

demonstrate that the outcome of his trial would have been different if

an additional piece of impeachment evidence had been introduced. It is

debatable among jurists whether the fact that Glavin had been accused of

a crime and falsely implicated another person of a crime Glavin himself

had actually committed, would have tilted the scale of justice in favor

of Smith and the jury believed that the state failed to prove Smith's guilt

beyond a reasonable doubt. Smith is entitled to a COA on this ground because

he has made a substantial showing of the denial of his right to effective

6

EXAMPLE SUPPLEMENTAL APPLICATION FOR CERTIFICATE OF APPEALABILITY (concluded)

assistance of counsel or is adequate to deserve encouragement to proceed further. Therefore, this Court should issue a COA.

CONCLUSION

For the reasons stated, Smith prays this Court issue a COA on each of the grounds set forth in counsel of record's application, as well as, this supplemental application. He further prays for any other and further relief which this Court may deem just and proper under the circumstances.

Respectfully submitted,

ZACHARY A. SMITH,
Reg. No 521163
CRCC
1115 E. Pence Rd.,
Cameron, MO 64429

Petitioner

CERTIFICATE OF SERVICE

The undersigned hereby certifies that a copy of the foregoing was mailed, postage prepaid, this 1st day of April, 2008, to; Michael J. Spillane, Assistant Attorney General, P.O. Box 899, Jefferson City, Missouri 65102, and Elizabeth Carlyle, counsel for Petitioner.

ZACHARY SMITH

7

EXAMPLE ORDER GRANTING IN PART AND DENYING IN PART MOTION FOR COA

IN THE UNITED STATES DISTRICT COURT FOR THE
WESTERN DISTRICT OF MISSOURI
ST. JOSEPH DIVISION

ZACHARY SMITH,	)	
	)	
Petitioner,	)	
	)	
vs.	)	Case No. 07-06068-CV-SJ-ODS
	)	
MIKE KEMNA,	)	
Superintendent,	)	
Crossroads Correctional Center	)	
	)	
Respondent.	)	

ORDER GRANTING IN PART AND DENYING IN PART PETITIONER'S MOTION FOR
CERTIFICATE OF APPEALABILITY

On January 29, 2008, the Court denied Petitioner's Application for a Writ of
Habeas Corpus (Doc. # 15). The Court also denied a Certificate of Appealability (Doc.
16). Petitioner has now filed a Motion for Certificate of Appealability specifying the
issues that he believes should be included and the reasons for doing so (Docs. # 23
and 24).

28 U.S.C. § 2253(c)(2) provides that a Certificate of Appealability should be
granted "only if the applicant has made a substantial showing of the denial of a
constitutional right." This requires Petitioner to demonstrate "that reasonable jurists
could debate whether (or, for that matter, agree that) the petition should have been
resolved in a different manner or that the issues presented were adequate to deserve
encouragement to proceed further." Miller-El v. Cockrell, 537 U.S. 322, 336 (2003)
(quotation omitted).

Upon de novo review of the record and Petitioner's motion, the Court grants a
Certificate of Appealability as to the issue of whether Petitioner received ineffective
assistance of counsel due to his counsel's failure to interview and call as a witness
Alvino Carrillo. The Certificate of Appealability is denied as to the other issues
contained in Petitioner's motion for the reasons stated in the Court's previous order
denying a Certificate of Appealability.

Case 5:07-cv-06068-ODS   Document 26   Filed 04/16/2008   Page 1 of 2

EXAMPLE ORDER GRANTING IN PART AND DENYING IN PART MOTION FOR COA (concluded)

IT IS SO ORDERED.

                                                        /s/ Ortrie D. Smith
                                                        ORTRIE D. SMITH, JUDGE
DATE: April 16, 2008   UNITED STATES DISTRICT COURT

2

Case 5:07-cv-06068-ODS   Document 26   Filed 04/16/2008   Page 2 of 2

EXAMPLE ONE NOTICE OF APPEAL

**IN THE UNITED STATES DISTRICT COURT
FOR THE WESTERN DISTRICT OF MISSOURI**

FILE NUMBER (CASE NO.) 07-06068-CV-SJ-ODS

Zachary Smith   )
     Plaintiff/Petitioner   )
)
)
Mike Kemna   )
     Defendant/Respondent   )

**NOTICE OF APPEAL
TO THE US COURT OF APPEALS FOR THE EIGHTH CIRCUIT**

    Notice is hereby given that Zachary Smith, the petitioner, hereby appeals to the United States Court of Appeals for the Eighth Circuit from the final judgment entered in this action on January 28, 2008.. (This court denied relief under Rule 59(e) on March 18, 2008.)

Respectfully submitted,

/S/ ELIZABETH UNGER CARLYLE

Elizabeth Unger Carlyle
P.O. Box 866
Columbus, MS 39703
Missouri Bar No. 41930
 (816)525-6540
FAX (866) 764-1240
elizcar@lawalumni.neu.edu

ATTORNEY FOR PETITIONER

<u>CERTIFICATE REGARDING SERVICE</u>

I hereby certify that it is my belief and understanding that counsel for respondent, Asst. Atty. Gen. Stephen D. Hawke, is a participant in the Court's CM/ECF program and that separate service of the foregoing document is not required beyond the Notification of Electronic Filing to be forwarded on April 14, 2008 upon the filing of the foregoing document.

/S/ ELIZABETH UNGER CARLYLE

EXAMPLE TWO NOTICE OF APPEAL

UNITED STATES DISTRICT COURT
WESTERN DISTRICT OF MISSOURI
WESTERN DIVISION

JOHN D. COUTS,   )
)
                    Petitioner,   )
)
          v.   ) No. 4:09-CV-00234-DW
)
)
LARRY DENNEY, et al.,   )
)
)
                    Respondent.   )

NOTICE OF APPEAL

Notice is hereby given that John D. Couts hereby appeals to the United States Court of Appeals for the 8th Circuit from the District Court's denial of a writ of habeas corpus in this action on the____day of _____, 200__, and the denial of a certificate of appealability on_____, 200__.

                              Respectfully submitted,

                              _____
                              JOHN D. COUTS
                              Reg. No 524257
                              CRCC
                              1115 E. Pence Rd.,
                              Cameron, MO 64429

                              Petitioner

CERTIFICATE OF SERVICE

The undersigned hereby certifies that a copy of the foregoing was mailed, postage prepaid, this____day of _____, 200__, to; Stephen D. Hawke, Assistant Attorney General, P.O. Box 899, Jefferson City, Missouri 65102.

                              _____
                              Petitioner

EXAMPLE MOTION TO PROCEED *IN FORMA PAUPERIS*

UNITED STATES DISTRICT COURT
WESTERN DISTRICT OF MISSOURI
WESTERN DIVISION

JOHN DOE,   )
)
             Petitioner,   )
)
     v.   ) Case No. 000000000000
)
THE WARDEN, et al.,   )
)
             Respondent.   )

MOTION FOR LEAVE TO PROCEED IN FORMA PAUPERIS

COMES NOW Petitioner, John Doe, and for his motion for leave to proceed in forma pauperis states as follows.

1. Petitioner is proceeding pro se in the above cause and will be proceeding pro se on the appeal as well.

2. Petitioner is incarcerated, unemployed, and without any funds to pay the filing fee in this matter to prefect the appeal. Petitioner only receives $8.50 a month from the Department of Corrections. Other than occasional gifts sent by friends or family, he does not have any other funds. (See attached certified statement of prison account).

3. Petitioner respectfully requests this Court to grant him leave to proceed in forma pauperis and waive the $455 filing fee.

Respectfully submitted,

_____
JOHN DOE, #111111111
Correctional Center
somewhere in Missouri

Petitioner

EXAMPLE MOTION TO PROCEED *IN FORMA PAUPERIS* (concluded)

<u>**CERTIFICATE OF SERVICE**</u>

The undersigned hereby certifies that a copy of the foregoing was mailed, postage prepaid, this___day of June, 2010, to; Joe Blow, Assistant Attorney General, somewhere in Missouri.

_____
Petitioner

EXAMPLE CIVIL DOCKET SHEET OF HABEAS CORPUS CASE

CM/ECF Western District of Missouri   Page 1 of 4

APPEAL, CLOSED, HABEAS

U.S. District Court
United States District Court for the Western District of Missouri (St. Joseph)
CIVIL DOCKET FOR CASE #: 5:07-cv-06068-ODS

Smith v. Kemna   Date Filed: 06/18/2007
Assigned to: District Judge Ortrie D. Smith   Date Terminated: 01/29/2008
Case in other court: 8th Circuit Court of Appeals, 08-01901   Jury Demand: None
Cause: 28:2254 Petition for Writ of Habeas Corpus (State)   Nature of Suit: 530 Habeas Corpus
                                                  (General)
                                                  Jurisdiction: Federal Question

Date Filed	#	Docket Text
06/18/2007	1	PETITION for Writ of Habeas Corpus (Filing fee $ 5 receipt number 1548271.) filed by Elizabeth Unger Carlyle on behalf of Zachary Smith. (Attachments: # 1 Civil Cover Sheet)(Carlyle, Elizabeth) (Entered: 06/18/2007)
07/24/2007	2	ORDER TO SHOW CAUSEShow Cause Response due by 8/13/2007. Signed by Judge Ortrie D. Smith on 07/24/2007. (Will-Fees, Eva) (Entered: 07/25/2007)
08/22/2007	3	SECOND ORDER TO SHOW CAUSEShow Cause Response due by 9/6/2007. Signed by Judge Ortrie D. Smith on 08/22/2007. (Will-Fees, Eva) (Entered: 08/22/2007)
09/07/2007	4	THIRD ORDER TO SHOW CAUSEShow Cause Response due by 10/8/2007. Signed by Judge Ortrie D. Smith on 09/07/2007. (Will-Fees, Eva) (Entered: 09/07/2007)
10/09/2007	5	NOTICE of appearance by Michael Joseph Spillane on behalf of Mike Kemna (Spillane, Michael) (Entered: 10/09/2007)
10/09/2007	6	RESPONSE TO ORDER TO SHOW CAUSEbyMike Kemna. (Attachments: # 1)(Spillane, Michael) (Entered: 10/09/2007)
10/11/2007		***Remark: Notice of filing of Exhibits, Doc. #6-2 received in paper by the Court (Kee, Georgia) (Entered: 10/11/2007)
10/29/2007	7	Consent MOTION for extension of time to file response/reply as to 6 Response to Order to Show Cause filed by Elizabeth Unger Carlyle on behalf of Zachary Smith. Suggestions in opposition/response due by 11/16/2007 unless otherwise directed by the court. (Related document(s) 6) (Carlyle, Elizabeth) (Entered: 10/29/2007)
10/29/2007	8	NOTICE of filing by Zachary Smith *Respondent's Ex. 1b* (Carlyle, Elizabeth) Modified on 11/5/2007 to reflect one copy of Respondent's Exhibit 1b, Vol. 2

EXAMPLE CIVIL DOCKET SHEET OF HABEAS CORPUS CASE (continued)

CM/ECF Western District of Missouri		Page 2 of 4
		of trial transcript received in Clerk's Office on 11/1/2007. (Baldwin, Joella). (Entered: 10/29/2007)
10/31/2007	9	ORDER granting 7 motion for extension of time to file traverse. Traverse due by 12/7/2007 unless otherwise directed by the court. Signed by Judge Ortrie D. Smith on 10/31/2007. (Will-Fees, Eva) (Entered: 10/31/2007)
11/29/2007	10	Consent MOTION for extension of time to file response/reply as to 6 Response to Order to Show Cause filed by Elizabeth Unger Carlyle on behalf of Zachary Smith. Suggestions in opposition/response due by 12/14/2007 unless otherwise directed by the court. (Related document(s) 6) (Carlyle, Elizabeth) (Entered: 11/29/2007)
11/29/2007	11	ORDER granting 10 motion for extension of time to file traverse on or before 12/21/2007. Signed by Judge Ortrie D. Smith on 11/29/2007. (Will-Fees, Eva) (Entered: 11/29/2007)
12/20/2007	12	Consent MOTION for extension of time to file response/reply as to 6 Response to Order to Show Cause filed by Elizabeth Unger Carlyle on behalf of Zachary Smith. Suggestions in opposition/response due by 1/7/2008 unless otherwise directed by the court. (Related document(s) 6) (Carlyle, Elizabeth) (Entered: 12/20/2007)
12/20/2007	13	ORDER granting 12 motion for extension of time to file traverse on or before 01/04/2008. Signed by Judge Ortrie D. Smith on 12/20/2007. (Will-Fees, Eva) Modified on 12/21/2007 to correct traverse due date (Jones, Robin). (Entered: 12/20/2007)
12/21/2007		NOTICE OF DOCKET MODIFICATION. A modification has been made to the document filed on December 20, 2007 as Document No. 13, ORDER. The traverse due date was incorrect in the docket entry. The correct due date is 1/4/2008. The docket text has been corrected. (Related Document 13) This is a text entry only - no document is attached. (Jones, Robin) (Entered: 12/21/2007)
01/03/2008	14	TRAVERSE by Zachary Smith *to response to order to show cause*. (Attachments: # 1 Exhibit A - Letter from Smith to trial counsel# 2 Exhibit B Order of Disbarment of Trial Counsel# 3 Exhibit C Report and recommendations of bar disciplinary counsel# 4 Exhibit D Application of trial counsel to surrender law license# 5 Exhibit D Application for deposition subpoena for trial counsel# 6 Exhibit F Deposition subpoena# 7 Exhibit G Affidavit of California Counsel# 8 Exhibit H Affidavit of California Counsel# 9 Exhibit J Police Report Regarding Kevin Glavin)(Carlyle, Elizabeth) (Entered: 01/03/2008)
01/29/2008	15	ORDER and OPINION denying Petition for Writ of Habeas Corpus. Signed by District Judge Ortrie D. Smith on 01/29/2008. (Will-Fees, Eva) (Entered: 01/29/2008)
01/29/2008	16	ORDER denying Certificate of Appealability. Signed by District Judge Ortrie D. Smith on 01/29/2008. (Will-Fees, Eva) (Entered: 01/29/2008)
01/29/2008	17	CLERK'S JUDGMENT (Will-Fees, Eva) (Entered: 01/29/2008)
02/11/2008	18	MOTION to amend/correct 15 Order filed by Zachary Smith. Suggestions in

EXAMPLE CIVIL DOCKET SHEET OF HABEAS CORPUS CASE (continued)

CM/ECF Western District of Missouri		Page 3 of 4
		opposition/response due by 2/26/2008 unless otherwise directed by the court. (Related document(s) 15) (Kee, Georgia) (Entered: 02/11/2008)
02/12/2008	19	MOTION to alter judgment filed by Elizabeth Unger Carlyle on behalf of Zachary Smith. Suggestions in opposition/response due by 2/27/2008 unless otherwise directed by the court. (Attachments: # 1 Exhibit Transcript excerpt) (Carlyle, Elizabeth) (Entered: 02/12/2008)
02/26/2008	20	SUGGESTIONS in opposition re 19 MOTION to alter judgment, 18 MOTION to amend/correct 15 Order filed by Michael Joseph Spillane on behalf of Respondent Mike Kemna. Reply suggestions due by 3/12/2008 unless otherwise directed by the court (Related document(s) 19 , 18) (Spillane, Michael) (Entered: 02/26/2008)
03/12/2008	21	REPLY SUGGESTIONS to motion re 19 MOTION to alter judgment, 18 MOTION to amend/correct 15 Order filed by Elizabeth Unger Carlyle on behalf of Petitioner Zachary Smith. (Related document(s) 19 , 18) (Carlyle, Elizabeth) (Entered: 03/12/2008)
03/18/2008	22	ORDER denying 18 motion to amend/correct; denying 19 motion to alter judgment. Signed by District Judge Ortrie D. Smith on 03/18/2008. (Will-Fees, Eva) (Entered: 03/18/2008)
04/01/2008	23	PRO SE SUPPLEMENTAL MOTION for certificate of appealability filed by Zachary Smith. Suggestions in opposition/response due by 4/16/2008 unless otherwise directed by the court. (Kee, Georgia) (Entered: 04/01/2008)
04/08/2008	24	MOTION for certificate of appealability filed by Elizabeth Unger Carlyle on behalf of Zachary Smith. Suggestions in opposition/response due by 4/23/2008 unless otherwise directed by the court. (Carlyle, Elizabeth) (Entered: 04/08/2008)
04/14/2008	25	NOTICE OF APPEAL as to 17 Clerk's Judgment, 22 Order on Motion to Amend/Correct, Order on Motion to Alter Judgment, 15 Order by Zachary Smith. Filing fee $ 455, receipt number 08660000000001767851. (Carlyle, Elizabeth) (Entered: 04/14/2008)
04/16/2008	26	ORDER granting in part and denying in part 23 motion for certificate of appealability; granting in part and denying in part 24 motion for certificate of appealability. Signed by District Judge Ortrie D. Smith on 04/16/2008. (Will-Fees, Eva) (Entered: 04/16/2008)
04/16/2008	27	TRANSMISSION of Notice of Appeal Supplement to US Court of Appeals, 8th Circuit via electronic mail. Related document 24 MOTION for certificate of appealability, 23 MOTION for certificate of appealability, 25 Notice of Appeal. (Crespo, Wil) (Entered: 04/16/2008)
04/21/2008	28	USCA Case Number from 8th Circuit Court of Appeals is 08-1901 for 24 MOTION for certificate of appealability filed by Zachary Smith, 23 MOTION for certificate of appealability filed by Zachary Smith, 25 Notice of Appeal filed by Zachary Smith. Briefing schedule entered by the Court of Appeals is attached. (Attachments: # 1 Schedule)(Crespo, Wil) (Entered: 04/21/2008)
05/01/2008	29	MOTION for leave to Appeal in forma pauperis filed by Zachary Smith.

EXAMPLE CIVIL DOCKET SHEET OF HABEAS CORPUS CASE (concluded)

CM/ECF Western District of Missouri		Page 4 of 4
		Suggestions in opposition/response due by 5/16/2008 unless otherwise directed by the court. (Attachments: # 1 Letter from US Court of Appeals)(Kee, Georgia) (Entered: 05/01/2008)
05/01/2008	30	ORDER granting 29 motion for leave to appeal in forma pauperis Signed by District Judge Ortrie D. Smith on 05/01/2008. (Todd, Lindsay) (Entered: 05/01/2008)

PACER Service Center			
Transaction Receipt			
08/04/2008 10:26:26			
PACER Login:	ec0092	Client Code:	smith, z
Description:	Docket Report	Search Criteria:	5:07-cv-06068-ODS
Billable Pages:	3	Cost:	0.24

8. UNITED STATES COURT OF APPEALS

APPOINTMENT OF COUNSEL

If you are granted a certificate of appealability, and granted leave to proceed *in forma pauperis*, the court of appeals will appoint an attorney to represent you on the appeal. The attorney appointed will also be required to file a petition for a writ of certiorari if you're denied relief in the court of appeals and the attorney believes there are grounds to merit review by the United States Supreme Court. However, if you want to proceed pro se, you'll find the necessary steps to take in this chapter and the following chapters.

THE RECORD ON APPEAL

When you've been granted leave to proceed *in forma pauperis* on the appeal, you may file a motion and request leave to use the original record made in the district court. "A party allowed to proceed on appeal *in forma pauperis* may request that the appeal be heard on the original record without reproducing any part. *Federal Rules of Appellate Procedure Rule 24(c)*.

PREPARING APPELLANT BRIEF

Federal Rules of Appellate Procedure Rule 28

(a) Appellant's Brief. The appellant's brief must contain, under appropriate headings and in the order indicated:

> (1) a corporate disclosure statement if required by Rule 26. 1;
>
> (2) a table of contents, with page references;
>
> (3) a table of authorities -- cases (alphabetically arranged), statutes, and other authorities -- with references to the pages of the brief where they are cited;

(4) a jurisdictional statement, including:

(A) the basis for the district court's or agency's subject-matter jurisdiction, with citations to applicable statutory provisions and stating relevant facts establishing jurisdiction;

(B) the basis for the court of appeals' jurisdiction, with citations to applicable statutory provisions and stating relevant facts establishing jurisdiction;

(C) the filing dates establishing the timeliness of the appeal or petition for review; and

(D) an assertion that the appeal is from a final order or judgment that disposes of all parties' claims, or information establishing the court of appeals' jurisdiction on some other basis;

(5) a statement of the issues presented for review;

(6) a statement of the case briefly indicating the nature of the case, the course of proceedings, and the disposition below;

(7) a statement of facts relevant to the issues submitted for review with appropriate references to the record (see Rule 28(e));

(8) a summary of the argument, which must contain a succinct, clear, and accurate statement of the arguments made in the body of the brief, and which must not merely repeat the argument headings;

(9) the argument, which must contain:

(A) appellant's contentions and the reasons for them, with citations to the authorities and parts of the record on which the appellant relies; and

(B) for each issue, a concise statement of the applicable standard of review (which may appear in the discussion of the issue or under a separate heading placed before the discussion of the issue);

(10) a short conclusion stating the precise relief sought; and

(11) the certificate of compliance, if required by Rule 32(a)(7).

(b) Appellee's Brief. The appellee's brief must conform to the requirements of Rule 28(a)(1) through (9) and (11), except that none of the following need appear unless the appellee is dissatisfied with the appellant's statement:

(1) the jurisdictional statement;

(2) the statement of the issues;

(3) the statement of the case;

(4) the statement of the facts; and

(5) the statement of the standard of review.

(e) Reply Brief. The appellant may file a brief in reply to the appellee's brief. An appellee who has cross-appealed may file a brief in reply to the appellant's response to the issues presented by the cross-appeal. Unless the court permits, no further briefs may be filed. A reply brief must contain a table of contents, with page references, and a table of authorities -- cases (alphabetically arranged), statutes, and other authorities -- with references to the pages of the reply brief where they are cited.

(d) References to Parties. In briefs and at oral argument, counsel should minimize use of the terms "appellant" and "appellee." To make briefs clear, counsel should use the parties' actual names or the designations used in the lower court or agency proceeding, or such descriptive terms as "the employee," "the injured person," "the taxpayer," "the ship," "the stevedore."

(e) References to the Record. References to the parts of the record contained in the appendix filed with the appellant's brief must be to the pages of the appendix. If the appendix is prepared after the briefs are filed, a party referring to the record must follow one of the methods detailed in Rule 30(c). If the original record is used under Rule 30(f) and is not consecutively paginated, or if the brief refers to an unreproduced part of the record, any reference must be to the page of the original document. For example:

Answer p. 7;

Motion for Judgment p. 2;

Transcript p. 231.

Only clear abbreviations may be used. A party referring to evidence whose admissibility is in controversy must cite the pages of the appendix or of the transcript at which the evidence was identified, offered, and received or rejected.

(f) Reproduction of statutes, Rules, Regulations, etc. If the court's determination of the issues presented requires the study of statutes, rules, regulations, etc., the relevant parts must be attached at the end, or may be supplied to the court in pamphlet form.

Examples of an appellant's brief, appellee's brief, and appellant's reply brief are provided at the end of this chapter to aid you in preparing your own appellant brief and reply brief, if you choose to proceed pro se on appeal.

APPENDIX TO THE BRIEFS

Federal Rules of Appellate Procedure Rule 30

(a) Appellant's Responsibility.

(1) <u>Contents of the Appendix.</u> The appellant must prepare and file an appendix to the briefs containing:

(A) the relevant docket entries in the proceeding below;

(B) the relevant portions of the pleadings, charge, findings, or opinion;

(C) the judgment, order, or decision in question; and

(D) other parts of the record to which the parties wish to direct the court's attention.

(2) <u>Excluded Material.</u> Memoranda of law in the district court should not be included in the appendix unless they have independent relevance. Parts of the record may be relied on by the court or the parties even though not included in the appendix.

(3) <u>Time to File; Number of Copies.</u> Unless filing is deferred under Rule 30(c), the appellant must file 10 copies of the appendix with the brief and must serve one copy on counsel for each party separately represented. An unrepresented party proceeding *in forma pauperis* must file 4 legible copies with the clerk, and one copy must be served on counsel for each separately represented party. The court may by local rule or by order in a particular case require the filing or service of a different number.

(b) All Parties' Responsibilities.

(1) <u>Determining the Contents of the Appendix</u>. The parties are encouraged to agree on the contents of the appendix. In the absence of an agreement, the appellant must, within 10 days after the record is filed, serve on the appellee a designation of the parts of the record the appellant intends to include in the appendix and a statement of the issues the appellant intends to present for review. The appellee may, within 10 days after receiving the designation, serve on the appellant a designation of additional parts to which it wishes to direct the court's attention. The appellant must include the designated parts in the appendix. The parties must not engage in unnecessary designation of parts of the record, because the entire record is available to the court. This paragraph applies also to a cross-appellant and a cross-appellee.

(2) <u>Costs of Appendix</u>. Unless the parties agree otherwise, the appellant must pay the cost of the appendix. If the appellant considers parts of the record designated by the appellee to be unnecessary, the appellant may advise the appellee, who must then advance the cost of including those parts. The cost of the appendix is a taxable cost. If any party causes unnecessary parts of the record to be included in the appendix, the court may impose the cost of those parts on that party. Each circuit must, by local rule, provide for sanctions against attorneys who unreasonably and vexatiously increase litigation costs by including unnecessary material in the appendix.

(c) Deferred Appendix.

(1) <u>Deferral Until After Briefs Are Filed</u>. The court may provide by rule for classes of cases or by order in a particular case that preparation of the appendix may be deferred until after the briefs have been filed and that the appendix may be filed 21 days after the appellee's brief is served. Even though the filing of the appendix may be deferred, Rule 30(b) applies; except that a party must designate the parts of the record it wants included in the appendix when it serves its brief, and need not include a statement of the issues presented.

(2) <u>References to the Record</u>.

(A) If the deferred appendix is used, the parties may cite in their briefs the pertinent pages of the record. When the appendix is prepared, the record pages cited in the briefs must be indicated by inserting record page numbers, in brackets, at places in the appendix where those pages of the record appear.

(B) A party who wants to refer directly to pages of the appendix may serve and file copies of the brief within the time required by Rule 31(a), containing appropriate references to pertinent pages of the record. In that event, within 14 days after the appendix is filed, the party must serve and file copies of the brief, containing references to the pages of the appendix in place of or in addition to the references to the pertinent pages of the record. Except for the correction of typographical errors, no other changes may be made to the brief.

(d) Format of the Appendix. The appendix must begin with a table of contents identifying the page at which each part begins. The relevant docket entries must follow the table of contents. Other parts of the record must follow chronologically. When pages from the transcript of proceedings are placed in the appendix, the transcript page numbers must be shown in brackets immediately before the included pages. Omissions in the text of papers or of the transcript must be indicated by asterisks. Immaterial formal matters (captions, subscriptions, acknowledgments, etc.) should be omitted.

(e) Reproduction of Exhibits. Exhibits designated for inclusion in the appendix may be reproduced in a separate volume, or volumes, suitably indexed. Four copies must be filed with the appendix, and one copy must be served on counsel for each separately represented party. If a transcript of a proceeding before an administrative agency, board, commission, or officer was used in a district court action and has been designated for inclusion in the appendix, the transcript must be placed in the appendix as an exhibit.

(f) Appeal on the Original Record Without an Appendix. The court may, either by rule for all cases or classes of cases or by order in a particular case, dispense with the appendix and permit an appeal to proceed on the original record with any copies of the record, or relevant parts, that the court may order the parties to file.

When preparing an appendix in a habeas corpus case, your appendix should consist of a docket sheet from the district court, a copy of all pleadings filed by you and the respondent, and all orders and decisions by the court.

FORM OF BRIEFS, APPENDICES, AND OTHER PAPERS

Federal Rules of Appellate Procedure Rule 32

(a) Form of a Brief.

(1) Reproduction.

(A) A brief may be reproduced by any process that yields a clear black image on light paper. The paper must be opaque and unglazed. Only one side of the paper may be used.

(B) Text must be reproduced with a clarity that equals or exceeds the output of a laser printer.

(C) Photographs, illustrations, and tables may be reproduced by any method that results in a good copy of the original; a glossy finish is acceptable if the original is glossy.

(2) Cover. Except for filings by unrepresented parties, the cover of the appellant's brief must be blue; the appellee's, red; an intervenor's or amicus curiae's, green; any reply brief, gray; and any supplemental brief, tan. The front cover of a brief must contain:

(A) the number of the case centered at the top;

(B) the name of the court;

(C) the title of the case (see Rule 12(a));

(D) the nature of the proceeding (e.g., Appeal, Petition for Review) and the name of the court, agency, or board below;

(E) the title of the brief, identifying the party or parties for whom the brief is filed; and

(F) the name, office address, and telephone number of counsel representing the party for whom the brief is filed.

(3) <u>Binding</u>. The briefing must be bound in any manner that is secure, does not obscure the text, and permits the brief to lie reasonably flat when open.

(4) <u>Paper Size, Line Spacing, and Margins</u>. The brief must be on 8.5 by 11 inch paper. The text must be double-spaced, but quotations more than two lines long may be indented and single-spaced. Headings and footnotes may be single-spaced. Margins must be at least one inch on all four sides. Page numbers may be placed in the margins, but no text may appear there.

(5) <u>Typeface</u>. Either a proportionally-spaced or a mono-spaced face may be used.

(A) A proportionally spaced face must include serifs, but sans-serif type may be used in headings and captions. A proportionally spaced face must be 14-point or larger.

(B) A mono-spaced face may not contain more than 10.5 characters per inch.

(6) <u>Type Styles</u>. A brief must be set in a plain, roman style, although italics or boldface may be used for emphasis. Case names must be italicized or underlined.

(7) <u>Length</u>.

(A) Page limitation. A principal brief may not exceed 30 pages, or a reply brief 15 pages, unless it complies with Rule 32(a)(7)(B) and (C).

(B) Type-volume limitation.

(i) A principal brief is acceptable if:

* it contains no more than 14,000 words; or

* it uses a mono-spaced face and contains no more than 1,300 lines of text.

(ii) A reply brief is acceptable if it contains no more than half of the type volume specified in Rule 32(a)(7)(B)(i).

(iii) Headings, footnotes, and quotations count toward the word and line limitations. The corporate disclosure statement, table of contents, table of citations, statement with respect to oral argument, any addendum containing statutes, rules or regulations, and any certificates of counsel do not count toward the limitation.

(C) Certificate of Compliance.

(i) A brief submitted under Rule 32(a)(7)(B) must include a certificate by the attorney, or an unrepresented party, that the brief complies with the type-volume limitation. The person preparing the certificate may rely on the word or line count of the word-processing system used to prepare the brief. The certificate must state either:

* the number of words in the brief; or

* the number of lines of mono-spaced type in the brief.

(ii) Form 6 in the Appendix of Forms is a suggested form of a certificate of compliance. Use of Form 6 must be regarded as sufficient to meet the requirements of Rule 32(a)(7)(C)(i).

(b) Form of an Appendix. An appendix must comply with Rule 32(a)(1), (2), (3), and (4), with the following exceptions:

(1) The cover of a separately bound appendix must be white.

(2) An appendix may include a legible photocopy of any document found in the record or of a printed judicial or agency decision.

(3) When necessary to facilitate inclusion of odd-sized documents such as technical drawings, an appendix may be a size other than 8.5 by 11 inches, and need not lie reasonably flat when opened.

(c) Form of other Papers.

(1) <u>Motion.</u> The form of a motion is governed by Rule 27(d).

(2) <u>Other Papers.</u> Any other paper, including a petition for panel rehearing and a petition for hearing or rehearing en banc, and any response to such as a petition, must be reproduced in the manner prescribed by Rule 32(a), with the following exceptions:

(A) A cover is not necessary if the caption and signature page of the paper together contain the information required by Rule 32(a)(2). If a cover is used, it must be white.

(B) Rule 32(a)(7) does not apply.

(d) Signature. Every brief, motion, or other paper filed with the court must be signed by the party filing the paper or, if the party is represented, by one of the party's attorneys.

(e) Local Variation. Every court of appeals must accept documents that comply with the form requirements of this rule. By local rule or order in a particular case a court of appeals may accept documents that do not meet all of the form requirements of this rule.

SERVING AND FILING BRIEFS

Federal Rules of Appellate procedure Rule 31

(a) Time to Serve and File Brief.

(1) The appellant must serve and file a brief within 40 days after the record is filed. The appellee must serve and file a brief within 30 days after the appellant's brief is served. The appellant may serve and file a reply brief within 14 days after service of the appellee's brief but a reply brief must be filed at least 3 days before argument, unless the court, for good cause, allows a later filing.

(2) A court of appeals that routinely considers cases on the merits promptly after the briefs are filed may shorten the time to serve and file briefs, either by local rule or by order in a particular case.

(b) Number of Copies. Twenty-five copies of each brief must be filed with the clerk and 2 copies must be served on each unrepresented party and on counsel for each separately represented party. An unrepresented party proceeding *in forma pauperis* must file 4 legible copies with the clerk, and one copy must be served on each unrepresented party and on counsel for each separately represented party. The court may by local rule or by order in a particular case require the filing or service of a different number.

(e) Consequence of Failure to File. If an appellant fails to file a brief within the time provided by this rule, or within an extended time, an appellee may move to dismiss the appeal. An appellee who fails to file a brief will not be heard at oral argument unless the court grants permission.

ORAL ARGUMENT

Federal Rules of Appellate Procedure Rule 34

(a) In General.

(1) <u>Party's Statement</u>. Any party may file, or a court may require by local rule, a statement explaining why oral argument should, or need not, be permitted.

(2) <u>Standards.</u> Oral argument must be allowed in every case unless a panel of three judges who have examined the briefs and record unanimously agrees that oral argument is unnecessary for any of the following reasons:

(A) the appeal is frivolous;

(B) the dispositive issue or issues have been authoritatively decided; or

(C) the facts and legal arguments are adequately presented in the briefs and record, and the decisional process would not be significantly aided by oral argument.

(b) Notice of Argument; Postponement. The clerk must advise all parties whether oral argument will be scheduled, and, if so, the date, time, and place for it, and the time allowed for each side. A motion to postpone the argument or to allow longer argument must be filed reasonably in advance of the hearing date.

(c) Order and Contents of Argument. The appellant opens and concludes the argument. Counsel must not read at length from briefs, records, or authorities.

(d) Cross-Appeals and Separate Appeals. If there is a cross-appeal, Rule 28(h) determines which party is the appellant and which is the appellee for purposes of oral argument. Unless the court directs otherwise, a cross-appeal or separate appeal must be argued when the initial appeal is argued. Separate parties should avoid duplicative argument.

(e) Non-appearance of a Party. If the appellee fails to appear for argument, the court must hear appellant's argument. If the appellant fails to appear for argument, the court may hear the appellee's argument. If neither party appears, the case will be decided on the briefs, unless the court orders otherwise.

(f) Submission on Briefs. The parties may agree to submit a case for decision on the briefs, but the court may direct that the case be argued.

(g) Use of Physical Exhibits at Argument; Removal. Counsel intending to use physical exhibits other than documents at the argument must arrange to place them in the courtroom on the day of the argument before the court convenes. After the argument, counsel must remove the exhibits from the courtroom, unless the court directs otherwise. The clerk may destroy or dispose of the exhibits if counsel does not reclaim them within a reasonable time after the clerk gives notice to remove them.

You may file a motion and request to attend oral arguments via telephone, or allow the case to be submitted on the briefs. If you're not confident with your public speaking skills, it is in your best interest to let your case be submitted on the briefs.

EXAMPLE APPELLANT'S BRIEF

IN THE UNITED STATES COURT OF APPEALS
FOR THE EIGHTH CIRCUIT

ZACHARY SMITH	§	
	§	
Plaintiff-Appellant	§	
	§	
v.	§	NO. 08-1901
	§	
MIKE KEMNA et al	§	
	§	
Defendants-Appellees	§	

* * * * * * * * * *

ON APPEAL FROM THE UNITED STATES DISTRICT COURT
FOR THE WESTERN DISTRICT OF MISSOURI
WESTERN DIVISION

* * * * * * * * * *

CIVIL NO. 07-06068-CV-SJ-ODS

* * * * * * * * * *

APPELLANT'S BRIEF

ELIZABETH UNGER CARLYLE
P.O. Box 866
Columbus, MS 39703
(816) 525-6540
FAX (866) 249-8264
Missouri Bar No. 41930
elizcar@bellsouth.net

ATTORNEY FOR APPELLANT

[Note: This cover sheet should be blue in color.]

EXAMPLE APPELLANT'S BRIEF (continued)

SUMMARY AND REQUEST FOR ORAL ARGUMENT

This appeal concerns the issue of whether Mr. Smith, who was convicted of first degree murder and sentenced to life in prison without parole, was denied effective assistance of counsel. Trial counsel, who was subsequently disbarred due to physical and mental difficulties and numerous instances of malpractice, failed to interview and call a witness disclosed to him by Mr. Smith. The witness would have discredited physical evidence against Mr. Smith. Ten minutes of oral argument would assist the court in determining the merits of this issue.

APPELLANT'S BRIEF – Page i

EXAMPLE APPELLANT'S BRIEF (continued)

TABLE OF CONTENTS

APPELLANT'S BRIEF – **Page ii**

EXAMPLE APPELLANT'S BRIEF (continued)

TABLE OF AUTHORITIES

APPELLANT'S BRIEF – Page iii

EXAMPLE APPELLANT'S BRIEF (continued)

IN THE UNITED STATES COURT OF APPEALS
FOR THE EIGHTH CIRCUIT

ZACHARY SMITH	§	
	§	
Plaintiff-Appellant	§	
	§	
v.	§	No. 08-1901
	§	
MIKE KEMNA et al	§	
	§	
Defendants-Appellees	§	

APPELLANT'S BRIEF

JURISDICTIONAL STATEMENT

1. Judgment was entered on January 28, 2008. App. A-118. A timely motion to alter or amend judgment under Fed. R. Civ. P. 59(e) was denied March 18, 2008. App. A-148. Notice of appeal was filed April 14, 2004. App. A-151.

2. The district court's jurisdiction was founded upon 28 U.S.C. §2254, in that appellant was attacking a judgment and sentence imposed by the State of Missouri.

3. This Court's jurisdiction is founded upon 28 U.S.C. §2253 in that appellant is appealing from a final judgment in a habeas corpus case.

APPELLANT'S BRIEF – Page 1

EXAMPLE APPELLANT'S BRIEF (continued)

STATEMENT OF THE ISSUES

GROUND OF ERROR NO. ONE: TRIAL COUNSEL FAILED TO INTERVIEW OR CALL AS A WITNESS ALVINO CARRILLO, WHO WOULD HAVE DISCREDITED PHYSICAL EVIDENCE AGAINST MR. SMITH. A DEFENDANT IS ENTITLED TO HAVE TRIAL COUNSEL INTERVIEW AND CALL AVAILABLE WITNESSES FOR HIS DEFENSE. WAS MR. SMITH DENIED EFFECTIVE ASSISTANCE OF COUNSEL?

White v. Roper, 416 F.3d 728, 732 (8th Cir. 2005)

Stanley v. Bartley, 465 F.3d 810 (7th Cir. 2006)

Anderson v. Johnson, 338 F.3d 382, 393 (5th Cir. 2003)

Smith v. Dretke, 417 F.3d 438 (5th Cir. 2005)

STATEMENT OF THE CASE

This case is before the Court on the petition of Zachary Smith for a writ of habeas corpus under 28 U.S.C. §2254. Mr. Smith's first trial for the murder of Derek Hoskins ended in a mistrial after the jury was unable to reach a verdict. Resp. Ex. 2, p. 23. After a second trial, the conviction was reversed on appeal because of error in the disposition of a motion to suppress evidence. *State v. Smith*, 966 S.W.2d 1 (Mo. App. 1998).

At his third trial, Mr. Smith was convicted of first degree murder and armed criminal action. The death penalty was not sought, and Mr. Smith was

APPELLANT'S BRIEF – **Page 2**

EXAMPLE APPELLANT'S BRIEF (continued)

therefore sentenced to life in prison without parole for murder and 99 years'

imprisonment for armed criminal action. His convictions and sentences were

affirmed on appeal. *State v. Smith,* 90 S.W.3d 132, 141 (Mo. App. 2002).

Mr. Smith timely filed a motion for post-conviction relief under

Missouri Supreme Court Rule 29.15. After a hearing, the motion court denied

relief. The Missouri Court of Appeals affirmed the motion court's judgment.

Smith v. State, 207 S.W.3d 135 (Mo. App. 2006).

On June 18, 2007, Mr. Smith filed his habeas corpus petition and a

request for evidentiary hearing. A-5. The habeas corpus petition included

eight grounds for relief. They were:

1. Violation of Mr. Smith's right to due process of law when the

prosecutor was permitted to testify about an encounter with state's witness

Kevin Glavin outside the courtroom, which the prosecutor suggested was an

attempt by Mr. Smith's brother to intimidate or influence Mr. Glavin.

2. Violation of Mr. Smith's right to due process of law when the jury

was permitted to view the videotaped statement of Kevin Glavin, which had

been presented at trial, for a second time during deliberations.

3. Violation of Mr. Smith's right to effective assistance of counsel when

trial counsel failed to interview and call as a witness Alvino Carrillo.

APPELLANT'S BRIEF – Page 3

EXAMPLE APPELLANT'S BRIEF (continued)

4. Violation of Mr. Smith's right to effective assistance of counsel when trial counsel failed to object to the prosecutor's testimony about the encounter with Kevin Glavin.

5. Violation of Mr. Smith's right to effective assistance of counsel when trial counsel failed to object to the jury's viewing the Glavin statement during deliberations.

6. Violation of Mr. Smith's right to due process of law when the prosecutor made baseless allegations tending to suggest that Mr. Smith's brother had influenced the trial testimony of prosecution witnesses Catherine and Lorie Stone, and threatened Lorie Stone with prosecution if she did not testify as the prosecutor wished.

7. Violation of Mr. Smith's right to effective assistance of counsel when trial counsel failed to impeach prosecution witness Kevin Glavin with the fact that he had previously been convicted of theft, and had lied to officers investigating that offense.

On January 29, 2008, the district court denied both the petition and the request for hearing. AD-1. Mr. Smith's motion pursuant to Rule 59(e) of the Federal Rules of Civil Procedure, (A-143), was denied on March 18, 2008. A-148. On April 16, 2008, the district court granted a certificate of appealability as to Ground 3, the issue raised in this appeal.

APPELLANT'S BRIEF – Page 4

EXAMPLE APPELLANT'S BRIEF (continued)

STATEMENT OF FACTS.

Trial evidence. Because prejudice from trial counsel's failure to call a witness is the major issue in this case, a summary of trial evidence is provided.

At Mr. Smith's trial, the state attempted to present the testimony of an alleged eyewitness, Kevin Glavin. Mr. Glavin, however, informed the court that he was not "mentally capable to go through with this testimony." Resp. Ex. 1b, p. 474.[1] He said that he could not remember the facts of the case. Resp. Ex. 1b, p. 476. He appeared to be shaking and emotionally upset. Resp. Ex. 1b, p. 476. Mr. Glavin testified before the jury that he could not remember any of the circumstances of Derek Hoskins's death. Resp. Ex. 1b, p. 479-557.

The state then elicited from Mr. Glavin that he had previously given a videotaped statement describing the offense. Mr. Glavin was extensively examined about this statement, and the statement itself was offered into evidence. Resp. Ex. 1b, p. 557. In the statement, Mr. Glavin said that he was a passenger with Mr. Smith, Ricky Sosa and Derek Hoskins in a vehicle Mr. Smith had borrowed that evening. At Mr. Glavin's request, Mr. Smith stopped the car to let Mr. Glavin out to urinate. Mr. Hoskins also got out. According to Mr. Glavin, he and Mr. Hoskins walked to the back of the car,

---

[1] The reference is to the respondent's exhibits to the response to order to show cause, which are being forwarded to the Court.

APPELLANT'S BRIEF – Page 5

EXAMPLE APPELLANT'S BRIEF (continued)

turned to the curb, and began to urinate. Mr. Smith came up behind them and stood between them. Mr. Glavin said he saw a flash and heard a shot. He looked up and saw Mr. Smith holding a gun. Mr. Smith lowered his arm, and Mr. Hoskins went limp and fell to the ground. According to Mr. Glavin, he and Mr. Smith got back into the car. Mr. Smith fired another shot at Mr. Hoskins's body as they drove away. Mr. Glavin opined that Mr. Smith killed Mr. Hoskins because Mr. Hoskins had stolen Mr. Smith's lawnmower.

In addition to the fact that Mr. Glavin repudiated his prior statement at trial (Resp. Ex. 1b, p. 597), he admitted that he had prior convictions for tampering and theft, and, on cross-examination, for robbery. Resp. Ex. 1b, p. 477, 575. He also admitted that he had been drinking beer and smoking crack cocaine before the event in question, and that he had used cocaine as many as five times in the 48 hours before the event. Resp. Ex. 1a, p. 486, 518, 568, 577. He had been hospitalized for mental problems, and his memory was not good. Resp. Ex. 1b, p. 563.

Finally, Mr. Glavin had originally been charged with armed criminal action and murder, but the charges were dismissed after he implicated Mr. Smith. He was also rewarded for his testimony with a reduction in a Clay County, Missouri charge from second degree robbery to stealing. Evidence was also presented that Mr. Glavin initially said that Mr. Smith was not

APPELLANT'S BRIEF – Page 6

EXAMPLE APPELLANT'S BRIEF (continued)

involved, and only later, when it was clear that he would receive

consideration, implicated Mr. Smith. Resp. Ex. 1b, p. 850.

Although the murder weapon was not found, the state presented

evidence that shells found at 411 Indiana Street in Kansas City, Missouri

matched the shell that was recovered from the body of Hoskins. Resp. Ex. 1b,

pp. 791, 804, 889-895. The state then presented prior testimony of Cathy and

Lorie Stone. (The witnesses could not be located for the third trial.) In their

prior testimony, the Stones admitted that they had previously told police that

Mr. Smith had fired a weapon at 411 Indiana Street two weeks before the

Hoskins murder. However, they both recanted their prior statements and said

that they were under the influence of crack cocaine when they made them.

They denied seeing Mr. Smith fire a gun. Lorie Stone also testified at the

prior trial that the prosecutor had threatened her if she did not testify as he

wished. Resp. Ex. 1b. p. 638. The Stones's statements that Mr. Smith had

fired a gun were also contradicted by the physical evidence; a Kansas City

detective testified that the shells found at 411 Indiana were not in the

location where Mr. Smith was supposedly seen firing. Resp. Ex. 1b, pp. 788-

789.

Other evidence presented by the state included testimony of Roxanna

Soriano that she saw Mr. Hoskins get into a car driven by Mr. Smith on the

night of the murder. Resp. Ex. 1a, p. 363. Ms. Soriano's identification of Mr.

APPELLANT'S BRIEF – Page 7

EXAMPLE APPELLANT'S BRIEF (continued)

Smith was impeached with inconsistencies in her description of the driver

and Mr. Smith's appearance. Resp. Ex. 1a, pp. 413-414. Rose Sanchez

testified that on the evening of the murder, she saw Mr. Glavin, Mr. Smith,

and Mr. Sosa, but not Mr. Hoskins, in a car together. At trial, she denied

seeing a gun in the car. Jacob Cordry testified that Mr. Smith gave him a

bike, identified as that of Hoskins, after the murder. Resp. Ex. 1b, pp. 758-

759. The bike, which was yellow, had been covered with black tape. Finally,

the state presented evidence that Mr. Smith's fingerprints were found in the

back of the car allegedly involved. Resp. Ex. 1b, p. 918.

Post-conviction evidence. At the post-conviction hearing, Alvino Carrillo

testified that he had been present at the Indiana Street incident referred to

by the Stones. He said that Mr. Smith did not fire a weapon that night.

Instead, Mr. Carrillo testified that the shots were fired at Mr. Smith, among

others. Resp. Ex. 6, p. 43. Mr. Carrillo would have been available to testify at

the time of Mr. Smith's trial, and would have been willing to do so. He was

never interviewed by trial counsel, and was unaware that evidence from the

Indiana Street incident was being used against Mr. Smith. Resp. Ex. 6, pp.

44, 49. Mr. Smith also presented at the post-conviction hearing a letter he

had written to his trial counsel identifying Mr. Carrillo as a witness.

Traverse, Ex. A (App. A-64).

APPELLANT'S BRIEF – Page 8

EXAMPLE APPELLANT'S BRIEF (continued)

Trial counsel did not testify at the post-conviction hearing. Mr. Smith presented evidence that trial counsel had been disbarred, and that he suffered from mental and physical problems and had committed numerous acts of malpractice before he was disbarred. Traverse, Ex. B-D (App. A-67-107). After obtaining a California address, post-conviction counsel hired California counsel to attempt to serve trial counsel with a deposition subpoena in California, but that they were unable to do so. Traverse, Ex. E-H. (App. A-108-115). No evidence was offered as to any attempt by the state to locate trial counsel.

The state post-conviction court rejected Mr. Smith's assertion of ineffective assistance of counsel because of trial counsel's failure to interview and call Alvino Carrillo as a witness for two reasons. First, the court held that Mr. Smith had not disproved the "presumption" that trial counsel had a strategic reason for failing to call Mr. Carrillo because he had not presented the testimony of trial counsel. In so holding, The Missouri Court of Appeals relied on Missouri law construing *Strickland v. Washington*, 466 U.S. 668, 687-88 (1984), to mean that the presumption of trial strategy could only be overcome if the post-conviction movant presents the testimony of trial counsel. See, e.g., *State v. Tokar*, 918 S.W.2d 753, 768 (Mo. banc 1996); *Taylor v. State*, 126 S.W.3d 755, 758 (Mo. banc 2004); and *State v. Booker*, 945 S.W.2d 457, 459 (Mo. App. 1997).

APPELLANT'S BRIEF – Page 9

EXAMPLE APPELLANT'S BRIEF (continued)

Alternatively, the state court held that Mr. Smith had not demonstrated prejudice from the failure to call Mr. Carrillo. The court suggested that the evidence against Mr. Smith was "overwhelming," and therefore Mr. Carrillo's testimony would have made no difference.

Evidence presented at the post-conviction hearing relevant to grounds for relief for which a certificate of appealability was not issued has been omitted from this statement.

SUMMARY OF ARGUMENT

Mr. Smith has demonstrated both ineffective assistance of counsel and prejudice. Trial counsel's "decision" not to call Mr. Carrillo was based on insufficient investigation, since he was informed by Mr. Smith about Mr. Carrillo and failed even to interview him. Thus, particularly in light of trial counsel's disbarment for impairment and professional misconduct and Mr. Smith's unsuccessful attempts to present his testimony, any presumption of trial strategy has been overcome.

Prejudice is shown because the state's case was based almost entirely on the statement of Kevin Glavin, a felon and drug addict who had received consideration for his statement and refused to repeat it under oath. Mr. Carrillo's testimony would have substantially weakened the state's attempt to

EXAMPLE APPELLANT'S BRIEF (continued)

corroborate the statement, resulting in a reasonable probability of a different outcome.

ARGUMENT AND AUTHORITIES

GROUND OF ERROR NO. ONE:

TRIAL COUNSEL FAILED TO CALL AS A WITNESS ALVINO CARRILLO, WHO WOULD HAVE DISCREDITED POWERFUL PHYSICAL EVIDENCE AGAINST THE DEFENDANT. A DEFENDANT IS ENTITLED TO HAVE TRIAL COUNSEL INTERVIEW AND CALL AVAILABLE WITNESSES FOR HIS DEFENSE. WAS MR. SMITH DENIED EFFECTIVE ASSISTANCE OF COUNSEL?

Standard of review. The factual findings of the district court are reviewed for clear error. The legal conclusions of the district court are reviewed *de novo*.

The district court agreed with the Missouri Court of appeals that Mr. Smith had not demonstrated that trial counsel's failure to call Mr. Carrillo was not reasonably effective, the "performance prong" of the *Strickland v. Washington*, 466 U.S. 668, 687-88 (1984), test for ineffective assistance of counsel. In so holding the district court did not comment on the fact that Mr. Smith had tried, but failed, to present his trial counsel's testimony, and that the Missouri Court of Appeals had relied on that failure to find that Mr. Smith had not established the performance prong.

APPELLANT'S BRIEF – Page 11

EXAMPLE APPELLANT'S BRIEF (continued)

The uncontroverted evidence at the post-conviction hearing established that Mr. Smith had informed trial counsel of Alvino Carrillo, how he could be contacted, and what he would say. App. A-64. The evidence also established that trial counsel never contacted Mr. Carrillo. Resp. Ex. 6, pp. 44, 49. Yet, the Missouri courts found that Mr. Smith could not establish that the failure to interview and call Mr. Carrillo was not "reasonable trial strategy" without presenting the testimony of trial counsel.

Of course, *Strickland v. Washington*, 466 U.S. 668, 687-88 (1984) does not so hold. That case merely cautions reviewing courts that they should not attempt to second-guess trial strategy decisions by trial attorneys. At the same time, numerous decisions hold that a decision not to call a particular witness should not generally be sanctioned as reasonable strategy unless trial counsel has adequately investigated the case. *Wiggins v. Smith*, 539 U.S. 510, 525 (2003); *Rompilla v. Beard*, 545 U.S. 374, 383 (2005); *White v. Roper*, 416 F.3d 728, 732 (8th Cir. 2005).

It is not uncommon that a post-conviction litigant will be unable to present testimony from his trial counsel. Trial counsel may be absent, or he may be dead. See, e.g. *White v. Roper*, 416 F.3d 728, 733 (8th Cir. 2005): "White's trial counsel, Robert Duncan, died in 1996, before the district court's evidentiary hearing." A review of the *White* case reveals that the Missouri courts never conducted an evidentiary hearing on Mr. White's allegations of

APPELLANT'S BRIEF – **Page 12**

EXAMPLE APPELLANT'S BRIEF (continued)

ineffective assistance of counsel. See *White v. State*, 939 S.W.2d 887 (Mo. banc 1997). Thus, at the only evidentiary hearing held for Mr. White, his trial counsel was absent. Yet, this Court was able to conclude that Mr. White was denied effective assistance of counsel.

> As in *Anderson v. Johnson*, 338 F.3d 382, 393 (5th Cir. 2003), "There is no evidence that counsel's decision to forego investigation was reasoned at all. . . Counsel's failure to investigate was not 'part of a calculated trial strategy' but is likely the result of either indolence or incompetence." As the court put it in *Bryant v. Scott*, 28 F.3d 1411, 1415 (5th Cir. 1994), "[A]n attorney must engage in a reasonable amount of pretrial investigation and 'at a minimum. . . interview potential witnesses and. . . make an independent investigation of the facts and circumstances in the case'" (quoting *Nealy v. Cabana*, 764 F.2d 1173, 1177 (5th Cir. 1985).) Here, there was no evidence that trial counsel made an adequate investigation before deciding not to interview or call Mr. Carrillo.

The state court's conclusion that Mr. Smith had not shown ineffective assistance of counsel was an unreasonable application of *Strickland v. Washington*, 466 U.S. 668, 687-88 (1984) and its progeny because the court relied on state authority holding that a post-conviction litigant could overcome the presumption of reasonableness *only* through the testimony of his trial counsel. The state court completely ignored the fact that Mr. Smith

APPELLANT'S BRIEF – **Page 13**

EXAMPLE APPELLANT'S BRIEF (continued)

presented evidence that he had attempted to locate and call his trial attorney but that his trial attorney had evaded service of process, and that his attorney had been disbarred for impairments leading to professional misconduct.

The evidence before the post-conviction court showed that Mr. Smith's trial counsel had been disbarred before the post-conviction hearing. Post-conviction counsel had retained a private investigator to locate his former counsel, and had ultimately obtained a California address. At that point, counsel obtained letters rogatory from the Missouri post-conviction court, retained California counsel, and caused a deposition subpoena to be issued in Los Angeles County, California. California counsel attempted to serve the subpoena. According to their affidavits, they located trial counsel's sister and mother, but they were unwilling to disclose trial counsel's whereabouts. They also sent a certified letter to the address, but no response was received. Traverse Ex. E-H, App. A-108-115. The state offered no evidence of any attempts to locate trial counsel.

In this case, it is clear that trial counsel was unavailable not because of circumstances beyond his control, but because he intentionally avoided service of process by Mr. Smith. The state apparently did not expect favorable testimony from trial counsel, because the prosecutors made no effort at all to find him. Moreover, trial counsel was found to have performed incompetently

APPELLANT'S BRIEF – **Page 14**

EXAMPLE APPELLANT'S BRIEF (continued)

as an attorney in numerous instances. This is evidence tending to show that trial counsel was ineffective; it militates against a finding of reasonable trial strategy.

Without the Missouri gloss on the *Strickland v. Washington*, 466 U.S. 668, 687-88 (1984), standard requiring the movant to present evidence *from trial counsel* in order to rebut the presumption of trial strategy, it is clear that trial counsel's failure to interview and call Mr. Carrillo was not reasonably effective assistance of counsel. Because Missouri misinterpreted the *Strickland v. Washington*, 466 U.S. 668, 687-88 (1984), standard to Mr. Smith's detriment, his conviction cannot stand. 28 U.S.C. §2254(d); *Williams (Terry) v. Taylor*, 529 U.S. 362 (2000).

The district court also endorsed the Missouri court's alternative holding that Mr. Smith had not shown prejudice from the failure to call Mr. Carrillo as a witness. In so holding, the district court first noted with approval the Missouri court's observation that Mr. Carrillo's evidentiary hearing testimony might have concerned another incident than that about which Cathy and Lorie Stone testified. This finding was contrary both to the law and to the state court record.

Mr. Carrillo's testimony made it clear that he was talking about the same incident. The time period and location matched that to which the Stones referred. Resp. Ex. 6, p. 42. Resp. Ex. 1b, p. 639, 648, 775. Mr. Carrillo

APPELLANT'S BRIEF – Page 15

EXAMPLE APPELLANT'S BRIEF (continued)

testified, as did the Stones, that Mr. Smith was present. Resp. Ex. 6, p. 42. Resp. Ex. 1b, p. 639. Like the Stones, he described the arrival of a car as the event which precipitated the shooting. Resp. Ex. 6, p. 42. His testimony, unlike that of the Stones, did not contradict the physical evidence seized at the scene. Resp. Ex. 1b, p. 639, 783, 789. The fact that his description of the incident was different was precisely what made his testimony such powerful impeaching evidence. The Stones, who were intoxicated at the time, fabricated their description under pressure from the prosecutor. Mr. Carrillo's, on the other hand, was accurate, and the jury would likely have so found had they heard his testimony.

The district court also agreed with the court of appeals that the evidence of Mr. Smith's guilt was "overwhelming." A-124. This conclusion simply belies the evidence in the case. The evidence against Mr. Smith consisted primarily of the repudiated statement of Kevin Glavin, a convicted felon and crack addict who was present at the scene of the murder and had every motive to conceal his own guilt. Mr. Glavin was the only "eyewitness" who placed the weapon in the hand of Mr. Smith.

Apart from the repudiated statement of Rose Sanchez and the impeached identification of Roxana Soriano, the other evidence against Mr. Smith was extremely thin: the fact that Mr. Smith later gave away Mr. Hoskins's bike, and that he gave inconsistent statements about the offense.

APPELLANT'S BRIEF – Page 16

EXAMPLE APPELLANT'S BRIEF (continued)

Without the ballistics evidence and Mr. Glavin's repudiated statement, this evidence is clearly insufficient to prove guilt.

To support Mr. Glavin's repudiated statement, the state relied heavily on the ballistics evidence—the match between bullets fired at another time on Indiana Street and the bullet that killed the victim here. That evidence, in turn, was based on the testimony of Cathy and Lorie Stone, whose prior testimony was read into evidence, that Mr. Smith had fired shots. They also repudiated their initial statements to the police. Lorie Stone testified that she had been intimidated and coerced into lying by the prosecutor. Both of the Stones testified that they were under the influence of crack cocaine at the time of the incident. And their testimony was further weakened by the fact that the place where the expended shells were found on Indiana Street was inconsistent with their testimony about Mr. Smith's location at the time he supposedly fired into the air. Resp. Ex. 1b, pp. 782-784.

This was hardly "overwhelming evidence" of Mr. Smith's guilt. The first trial of Mr. Smith's case resulted in a mistrial because of a hung jury. During deliberations, the jury sent out a note reading, "Can we find guilty of being present but not actually shooting the gun?" Exhibit, Motion to Alter or Amend Judgment, App. A-142. *These* jurors clearly did not credit either the weak ballistics evidence or the testimony of Kevin Glavin. And one of the jurors at

APPELLANT'S BRIEF – Page 17

EXAMPLE APPELLANT'S BRIEF (continued)

the most recent trial contacted trial counsel and said that he was confused and wished to change his mind. Resp. Ex. 1b, p. 1061.

Finally, the Missouri courts failed to give sufficient weight to Mr. Smith's post-conviction testimony that had Mr. Carrillo testified at trial, he would also have testified. He would have testified not only that he did not fire the shots outside 411 Indiana, but that as far as he knew Kevin Glavin, and not he, had killed Derek Hoskins. Resp. Ex. 6, p. 66, Resp. Ex. 7, pp. 91-97.

Mr. Smith's testimony would also have negated other circumstantial evidence the state contended supported his guilt. He would have explained that the shell casings found in his yard were there because another person, Ricky Sosa (whom Mr. Glavin said was in the car when the shooting occurred) fired shots in his yard the same night of the 411 Indiana incident. Mr. Smith would further have explained the fact that his fingerprints were found in the back seat of a vehicle identified by Mr. Glavin as the car used in the offense (Resp. Ex. 1b p. 918); he would have stated that he was in the vehicle on another occasion and sat in the back seat. Resp. Ex. 6, p. 66, Resp. Ex. 7, pp. 91-97.

Under these facts, the Missouri court's holding that Mr. Smith had not established *Strickland v. Washington*, 466 U.S. 668, 687-88 (1984), prejudice was an unreasonable application of that case. Under *Strickland v. Washington*, 466 U.S. 668, 687-88 (1984), a petitioner must only show a

APPELLANT'S BRIEF – **Page 18**

EXAMPLE APPELLANT'S BRIEF (continued)

"reasonable probability" of a different outcome to obtain relief. *Williams (Terry) v. Taylor*, 529 U.S. 362 (2000). A "reasonable probability" of a different outcome does not mean a certainty that the verdict would have been different, but means that the confidence of the court in the outcome is undermined.

To obtain relief under *Strickland*, the petitioner need not show that the omitted witness, by himself, would have established a defense. For example, in *White v. Roper*, 416 F.3d 728, (8th Cir. 2005), this Court found ineffective assistance for failure to interview and present witnesses who would have testified that the defendant did not commit the crime. This finding was made despite the presentation of other evidence supporting this defense. Similarly, in *Smith v. Dretke*, 417 F.3d 438 (5th Cir. 2005), the court found ineffective assistance of counsel for failing to present evidence of self-defense which would have corroborated the defendant's testimony to that defense.

In the closely analogous case of *Stanley v. Bartley*, 465 F.3d 810 (7th Cir. 2006), the court confronted a situation where the state's "eyewitness", like Mr. Glavin in Mr. Smith's case, could easily have been the murderer himself. At least the witness in Mr. Stanley's case was willing to testify in court; Mr. Glavin refused even to do that. And, in *Stanley*, the state presented evidence that Mr. Stanley had made admissions to his sister. No evidence of any admission by Mr. Smith was presented. Nonetheless, under the Strickland standard, the federal appeals court in *Stanley* found that the failure of trial

APPELLANT'S BRIEF – **Page 19**

EXAMPLE APPELLANT'S BRIEF (continued)

counsel to interview and call witnesses was prejudicial, and that the state

court's contrary conclusion was not reasonable. The conviction was reversed.

See also *Smith v. Dretke*, 417 F.3d 438 (5th Cir. 2005), where the court found

ineffective assistance of counsel for failing to present evidence of self-defense

which would have corroborated the defendant's testimony to that defense.

The state's case against Mr. Smith was sufficiently weak that one jury

failed to reach a verdict. It was based on repudiated statements and

testimony by absent witnesses. The only eyewitness was a convicted felon

who was addicted to cocaine and was intoxicated at the time of the offense.

The evidence presents a significant possibility that he, rather than Mr.

Smith, actually committed the murder. The failure to call Mr. Carrillo not

only deprived Mr. Smith of his refutation of an important part of the state's

evidence, it deprived Mr. Smith of his own testimony.

Under these circumstances, the finding of the state court that there was

not prejudice is both an unreasonable application of *Strickland v.*

Washington, 466 U.S. 668, 687-88 (1984) and an unreasonable interpretation

of the facts. See *Miller-El v. Cockrell*, 537 U.S. 322 (2003) (Miller-El I); *Miller-*

El v. Dretke, 525 U.S. 231 (2005) (Miller-El II). The writ must issue, and relief

is required.

APPELLANT'S BRIEF – **Page 20**

EXAMPLE APPELLANT'S BRIEF (continued)

CONCLUSION

Wherefore, Mr. Smith prays the court to issue the writ of habeas corpus and to vacate his conviction and sentence and direct the State of Missouri either to retry him within a reasonable time or release him.

Respectfully submitted,

Elizabeth Unger Carlyle
P.O. Box 866
Columbus, MS 39703
(816)525-6540
FAX (866) 764-1249
Mo. Bar No. 41930
ATTORNEY FOR APPELLANT

CERTIFICATE OF COMPLIANCE

Pursuant to Fed. R. App. Pro. 32(a)(7)(C), the undersigned attorney certifies that this brief complies with the type-volume limitation in that rule. According to Microsoft Word 2003, the word processing program used to produce this brief, it contains 5,207 words. The disk submitted with this brief has been scanned and is virus-free.

ELIZABETH UNGER CARLYLE

APPELLANT'S BRIEF – Page 21

EXAMPLE APPELLANT'S BRIEF (concluded)

CERTIFICATE OF SERVICE

I certify that a copy of the foregoing brief, along with a copy of the Appellant's Separate Appendix, was served upon opposing counsel Stephen Hawke, Asst. Missouri Attorney Gen., by U.S. Mail on August 11, 2008.

_____
ELIZABETH UNGER CARLYLE

APPELLANT'S BRIEF – *Page 22*

SUMMARIZED ADDENDUM FOR EXAMPLE APPELLANT'S BRIEF

The example appellant's brief included one addendum, which is not included in this book. That addendum is summarized below.

> Order and Opinion Denying Petition for Writ Of Habeas Corpus (14 pages): "Pending is Petitioner's Petition for Writ of Habeas Corpus filed pursuant to 28 U.S.C. §2254. After reviewing the Record and the parties' arguments, the Court concludes the Petition must be denied."

EXAMPLE APPELLEE'S BRIEF

08-1901

IN THE UNITED STATES COURT OF APPEALS
FOR THE EIGHTH CIRCUIT

ZACHARY SMITH,
Petitioner/Appellant,

v.

MIKE KEMNA et al,
Respondent/Appellee.

APPEAL FROM THE UNITED STATES DISTRICT COURT FOR THE
WESTERN DISTRICT OF MISSOURI
THE HONORABLE ORTRIE D. SMITH PRESIDING

APPELLEE'S BRIEF

JEREMIAH W. (JAY) NIXON
ATTORNEY GENERAL

MICHAEL J. SPILLANE
Assistant Attorney General
Missouri Bar No. 40704
P.O. Box 899
Jefferson City, MO 65102
(573) 751-3321
Fax: (573) 751-3825
Attorneys for Respondent/Appellee

[Note: This cover sheet should be red in color]

EXAMPLE APPELLEE'S BRIEF (continued)

TABLE OF CONTENTS

The Missouri courts reasonably applied *Strickland v. Washington*, 466 U.S. 668 (1984) in rejecting a claim that trial counsel was ineffective for not calling Alvino Carrillo, because it was objectively reasonable not to call Carrillo based on Carrillo's history of selling drugs and Smith's concern about that history, and the collateral nature of Carrillo's testimony, and because there is no reasonable probability the outcome of trial was changed.

EXAMPLE APPELLEE'S BRIEF (continued)

TABLE OF AUTHORITIES

Cases

Other Authorities

EXAMPLE APPELLEE'S BRIEF (continued)

ISSUE PRESENTED FOR REVIEW

Whether the Missouri courts reasonably applied *Strickland v. Washington*, 466 U.S. 668 (1984) in rejecting a claim that trial counsel was ineffective in not interviewing and presenting testimony from Alvino Carrillo.

Strickland v. Washington, 466 U.S. 668 (1984); and

28 U.S.C. §2254(d).

3

EXAMPLE APPELLEE'S BRIEF (continued)

STATEMENT OF THE CASE

The sole issue in this case is whether the Missouri courts unreasonably applied *Strickland v. Washington*, 466 U.S. 668 (1984) in rejecting, after an evidentiary hearing, a claim that trial counsel was ineffective for not interviewing and calling Alvino Carrillo, a friend of Smith's since 1984, to testify that on an unknown date approximately two weeks prior to the murder, a drive by shooting occurred near 411 Indiana (Smith's father's home), in which Carrillo, Ricky Sosa, and Smith were the targets, but that only Sosa returned fire, and that Sosa returned fire with a handgun. The testimony allegedly would have been relevant to rebut testimony that the neighbors residing at 409 Indiana told a detective that they saw Smith fire a pistol in the air approximately two weeks prior to the murder, and testimony that shell casings found in the area were from the same weapon that was used in the murder. The facts of the case with transcript references are set out in the State of Missouri's state direct appeal brief, which is Respondent's Exhibit 4 in the federal habeas corpus litigation. These facts are set out below.

> At around 10 o'clock on the evening of June 23, 1995, the appellant left his father's home at 411 Indiana in Kansas City, Missouri, and started "riding around" in a borrowed, maroon Buick with Kevin Glavin and Jose Sosa (Tr. 477-479, 485-486, 501, 551-557, 809-810). The appellant, who was driving the vehicle, was armed with a black .45-caliber handgun (Tr. 486-491, 551-557). Ultimately, the three men stopped at the K.C. Oil Station at 19th and Jackson to buy some cigarettes (Tr. 350-364,

4

EXAMPLE APPELLEE'S BRIEF (continued)

551-557). While they were there, Derek Hoskins rode up on his bicycle (Tr. 360-362, 551-557, 781, 961-962).

Several weeks earlier, Hoskins had confessed to stealing the appellant's lawnmower (Tr. 496-498, 500, 551-557). Hoskins had promised to pay the appellant back for the lawnmower, but never did (Tr. 496-498, 551-557). About a week earlier, the appellant showed Hoskins a pistol he was carrying and warned him, "You better get my money" (Tr. 496-498, 551-557).

When Hoskins rode up to the gas station on his bicycle, the appellant asked if he had the money that he owed him (Tr. 362-363, 492.494, 551-557). Hoskins said that he did not have the money with him, but that he had it "up at [his] house" and he would go and get it (Tr. 362-363, 551-557). When Hoskins suggested that they follow him to the house of his cousin, Tyrone Morgan, the appellant insisted that they put the bike in the trunk and that Hoskins ride with them in the car (Tr. 363, 502-508, 551-557). During this incident, a witness heard what sounded like two guns being cocked (Tr. 366, 389). After placing Hoskins' bicycle in the trunk of the car, they drove to Morgan's home (Tr. 461-462, 508, 556-557). Once there, Hoskins spoke with Tyron's younger brother, Glenn Hemmingway, who told him that Tyrone was not home (Tr. 508).

After Hoskins got back in the Buick, the appellant told him that he could work off the debt by burglarizing a house; Hoskins agreed (TR. 510-513, 551-557). The appellant took Hoskins' bicycle from the trunk and put it in a field near the appellant's house at 1901 Lawn (Tr. 459, 465, 512-513, 551-557). The appellant next drove the group to a house, where Hoskins and Glavin got out of the car (Tr. 510-516, 551-557). Hoskins knocked on the door, and when nobody answered, he kicked the door and entered the house (Tr. 511). Hoskins made two trips into the house taking a television set and a stereo, both of which he placed in the trunk of the Buick (Tr. 510-516, 551-557). The men returned to 1901 Lawn and dropped off the television and stereo (Tr. 515-516, 551-557). The appellant then informed Hoskins that he would have to

EXAMPLE APPELLEE'S BRIEF (continued)

commit another burglary to fully repay the debt (Tr. 516-517, 551-557).

The appellant drove the group to the northeast part of the city, where they stopped to buy some beer (Tr. 320, 517-518, 551-557). After driving around for about half an hour, Glavin told the appellant he needed to urinate in an area called Cliff Drive (Tr. 320, 517-518, 551-557). The appellant stopped the car under a streetlight, but then backed the car out of the light, even though the street was deserted (Tr. 524). When Hoskins asked if he could also get out of the car to urinate, Glavin cautioned him to remain seated in the vehicle because "something did not feel right" (Tr. 522-524, 551-557). Hoskins told Glavin "I got to go pee" and got out of the car anyway (Tr. 525, 551-557).

As Hoskins and Glavin stood by the curb urinating, the appellant got out of the car and stood behind and in between the two (Tr. 526-527, 551-557). Glavin then heard a gunshot, looked up, and saw a bright flash (Tr. 520, 529-530, 551-557). He saw appellant holding a piston about one to two feet away from Hoskins (Tr. 529-530, 551-557). Hoskins went limp and fell to the ground (Tr. 529-530, 551-557). After the appellant and Glavin got back in the car, the appellant muttered something about "[g]ood measure[]," and fired another shot out the window at Hoskins' body (Tr. 320,533).

About sunrise the next day, the three men went to the house of Sosa's girlfriend, Rose Marie Sanchez. Sanchez later told the police that the appellant had arrived in a newer, four-door, burgundy or red car and had a gun tucked into his waistband (Tr. 535-536, 551-557, 706-708, 711-712, 725-726). Later that morning, Catherine Stone looked out her window at 409 Indiana and saw the appellant standing next to the maroon car (Tr. 626-632).

The appellant then drove back to 411 Indiana where he and his girlfriend, Cynthia Frost, had been living for about a month due to plumbing problems in their house at 1901 Lawn (Tr. 538-539, 551-557). The appellant handed his gun to Frost and told her to "put this up" (Tr. 538-539, 551-557).

6

EXAMPLE APPELLEE'S BRIEF (continued)

The following day, the appellant took Glavin to his bedroom and showed him Hoskins' bicycle which was now covered in black tape (Tr. 543-544). The appellant told Glavin that he was going to give the bicycle to "a little kid" (Tr. 543). The appellant later gave the bicycle to 11-year-old Jacob Cordry, who was visiting the house at 411 Indiana (Tr. 754-755).

The appellant sought Glavin's help in disposing of the murder weapon (Tr. 545). He wanted Glavin to accompany him while he drove across the Choteau Bridge and threw in it the river (Tr. 546). Glavin asked the appellant whether Sosa was in on the plan to kill Hoskins (Tr. 547). The appellant told him that "Ricky didn't know anything about it," and that he (the appellant) was the "master mind" (Tr. 547). As he said the words "master mind," the appellant pointed to his head (Tr. 547). The appellant told Glavin that the "last words that nigger said" were "I got to go pee," and that the victim "had it coming for stealing from him" (Tr. 547-549).

Between 3 and 4 o'clock on the morning of June 24, 1995, two security officers patrolling in the area of Cliff Drive heard gunshots (Tr. 321-322). Later, a man reported that he had seen someone lying in the street who appeared to be seriously injured (Tr. 323). The security officers went to the scene, where they found Hoskins' body (Tr. 323-324). When Detective Ron Payne, a crime scene technician, arrived several hours later, he found Hoskins' body lying in the street with his head facing south and the snap of his shorts unfastened (Tr. 851). On the ground, Payne found two spent bullets and two shell casings nearby (Tr. 322-323, 350, 799-804, 843-844).

An autopsy revealed that Hoskins' death was caused by a gunshot would to the right temple region (Tr. 674-677, 679, 681). The bullet entered his head from the front and penetrated his brain at a forty-five degree angle (Tr. 679-681). The bullet exited from the left side of his upper neck (Tr. 679-681). Hoskins was also wounded by a cluster of five superficial, slit-like cuts in the upper left

EXAMPLE APPELLEE'S BRIEF (continued)

chest and an abrasion consistent with a ricochet shot (Tr. 677).

When police learned that the appellant had given Hoskins' yellow bicycle to Jacob Cordry, they went to 411 Indiana to question Jacob and his mother (Tr. 759, 780-781, 961-962). The appellant told the boy that it was "a real expensive bike" that cost around $500 (Tr. 758). When he received the bike, the frame was completely covered by black tape; Jacob removed the tape and discovered that the bike was yellow (Tr. 759). When the detectives realized that it had belonged to Hoskins, they confiscated the bicycle (Tr. 759).

On June 26, 1995, a police detective recovered two shell casings in front of the appellant's house at 1901 Lawn (Tr. 846-848). One of the casings was located on the south side of the sidewalk in front of the steps leading to the house (Tr. 847). The other casing was on the north side of the sidewalk (Tr. 847-848).

On June 27, 1995, a police officer spoke with Lori Stone, who lived next door to 411 Indiana (Tr. 772). She told the officer that two weeks prior to Hoskins' death, she had seen the appellant fire a black .45 caliber handgun into the air twice (Tr. 775-776), The officer then recovered two shell casings from the west side of the street, near the curb in front of Stone's house (Tr. 783-784, 791).

Catherine Stone, Lori's sister, later told officers that she too had seen the appellant go out by the fence, near the alley and shoot his gun in the air (Tr. 634-635, 645-648, 650, 722-726, 781-783). The appellant noticed Stone and told her that if "you guys [are] going to watch all the time, you guys could get hurt if you guys snitch or anything" (Tr. 637).

Police detectives Roger Lewis and Mark Heimer also spoke with Cynthia Frost (Tr. 729). During that interview, Frost told the detectives that she owned the property at 1901 Lawn, which she had purchased with money from her parents (Tr. 729). On June 27, 1995, detectives asked Frost to sign a consent to search form for 1901 Lawn, and she complied (Tr. 826). Frost, who

8

accompanied the detectives to the house, informed them that the front door was partially broken and that she had nailed it shut the previous day (Tr. 827). Frost opened the front door for the detectives by banging her fist against it and kicking it (Tr. 827). The detectives then entered the house and searched it (Tr. 827).

In one of the bedrooms, the detectives found the appellant's driver's license and some personal papers (Tr. 829). They also found a locked safe in the bedroom (Tr. 829). The appellant told the police that the safe was "hers and Zachs" and authorized them to open it (Tr. 61, 74). One of the detectives quoted Frost as stating that "it was her safe and that we could open it" (Tr. 70).

The detectives carried the safe out to the front porch where they forced it open using a hammer, a crowbar, and a heavy-duty screwdriver (Tr. 61, 836). Inside the safe, the detectives found a purple Crown Royal bag containing several live .45 rounds and an empty box of .45-caliber ammunition (Tr. 830-832). The safe also contained a Missouri inmate card in the same name of Jose Sosa and a Missouri Identification card in the name of "Zachary Smith" (Tr. 830-832).

On June 29, 1995, the police found the appellant hiding underneath a bed at 2000 Oakley and arrested him (Tr. 921-923). After receiving and waiving his *Miranda* rights, the appellant told the police that on the evening of June 24, 1995, he had gone bowling with several friends (Tr. 931-932). He said that he and his friends had then gone to his father's house at 411 Indiana, where they remained until 11 o'clock the next morning (Tr. 935). The appellant denied owning a gun, claimed not to know Glavin, and stated that he had not seen Hoskins for a month. He also told police that he did not have Hoskins' bicycle, he had not been in a maroon car, and had not been to Cliff Drive in at least three to four months (Tr. 936-937). He could not explain why shell casings from the crime scene matched casings from outside his house (Tr. 937).

On June 30, 1995, the police examined the Buick for fingerprints (Tr. 813-816). A print taken from the

EXAMPLE APPELLEE'S BRIEF (continued)

interior of the driver's side front door matched the appellant's left middle finger (Tr. 916). In addition, William Newhouse, a firearms and tool mark examiner with the Kansas City Regional Crime Laboratory, examined the shell casings and bullets collected during the investigation of Hoskins' death (Tr. 876-885). After examining the two shell casings found at the crime scene, the two casings found at 1901 Lawn, and the two casings found at 411 Indiana, Newhouse determined that all six casings had been fired from the same .45-caliber pistol (Tr. 876-885). Newhouse also determined that the bullets recovered from the crime scene were fired from the same pistol (Tr. 876-878). One of the bullets was "flattened," which was consistent with a ricochet off the pavement (Tr. 878-879). The recovered bullet fragments also indicated a ricochet (Tr. 878-879).

(Resp. Exh. 4 at 6-12).

Smith alleged in his state post-conviction review motion that trial counsel should have called Alvino Carrillo to testify that approximately two weeks before the murder Jose Sosa, not Smith, fired a weapon at persons in a car, at least one of whom had shot at Smith, Sosa and Carrillo near Smith's father's home at 411 Indiana. The state post-conviction review court held a hearing on Smith's motion (Resp. Exh 6, PCR Hearing Transcript). At the hearing Smith testified that he wrote a letter to counsel concerning the potential testimony of Carrillo, and Smith testified that counsel's failure to call Carillo was the reason Smith decided not to testify (Rep. Exh. 6 at 62-65). The letter to counsel was admitted into evidence (*Id.* at 64). The letter states that Carrillo is in the Western Diagnostic and Correctional Center and twice questions whether counsel would want to use Carrillo as a

EXAMPLE APPELLEE'S BRIEF (continued)

witness (Appendix at 64). The letter states the following concerning Carrillo's potential testimony and his history of drug dealing. "He could testify that it wasn't me doing the shooting it was Jose Sosa in order to refute the Stone girl's statements. However, I could testify to that. Mr. Carrillo has a record of selling drugs so I don't know if you want to use him" (Appendix at A-64).

Alvino Carrillo testified at the post-conviction hearing that he could have testified at trial that on an unknown date about two weeks before the murder, a drive by shooting occurred at 411 Indiana with himself, Smith, and Sosa as the targets but that only Sosa returned the fire from the vehicle (Resp. Exh. 6 PCR Tr. at 42). Carrillo also testified that at the time of Smith's most recent trial Carrillo was imprisoned for two counts of distributing, delivering and manufacturing a controlled substance (*Id.* at 44-50). Trial counsel did not testify at the post-conviction review hearing (Resp. Exh. 6).

The post-conviction review court found the claim to be without legal merit, holding both that Smith had failed to overcome the presumption that the decision not to interview and call Carrillo was reasonable trial strategy, and that there was no reasonable probability the that Carrillo's testimony would have changed the outcome of the proceeding (Resp. Exh. 7, PCR L.F. at 146-148). The Missouri Court of Appeals affirmed the denial of post-conviction relief finding both that Smith failed to prove that the decision not to call Carrillo was unreasonable in light

11

EXAMPLE APPELLEE'S BRIEF (continued)

of Carrillo's history as a drug dealer and his incarceration at the time of trial, and that there was no reasonable probability the outcome of the proceeding was changed as the evidence of guilt was overwhelming, and not only did Carrillo's testimony not pertain to the night of the murder it was not even certain he describing the same incident approximately two weeks before the murder that had been described by Smith's father's neighbors (Resp. Exh. 11, Memorandum of Missouri Court of Appeals at 14-16).

Smith raised the claim in a petition for habeas corpus relief in the States District Court for the Western District of Missouri (Appendix A10-A11). The United States District Court denied relief finding that there is no reasonable probability the outcome of the trial would have been changed had Carrillo testified at trial (Appendix at 123-124).

12

EXAMPLE APPELLEE'S BRIEF (continued)

STANDARD OF REVIEW

Smith's claim alleging ineffective assistance of trial counsel and was presented to, and rejected by, the Missouri courts using the analysis set out in *Strickland v. Washington*, 466 U.S. 668 (1984). Under *Strickland*, analysis of counsel's actions is highly deferential and a reviewing court must indulge a strong presumption that counsel's conduct falls within the wide range of professional competence. *Id.* at 689. Counsel is strongly presumed to have rendered adequate assistance and to have made all significant decision in the exercise of reasonable professional judgment. *Id.* at 690. Strategic choices made after a thorough investigation of the law and facts are virtually unchallengeable. *Id.* at 691. The reasonableness of counsel's actions may be determined or substantially influenced by the defendants own statements or actions. *Id.* at 691 Even if counsel acted unprofessionally, a defendant must show that but for counsel's unprofessional errors, there is a reasonable probability the result of the proceeding would have been different. *Id.* at 694. This Court has held that in analyzing in effective of counsel claims "cumulative error does not call for habeas relief as each claim must stand or fall on its own." *Girtman v. Lockhart*, 942 F.2d 468, 475 (8th Cir. 1994); *see also Pryor v. Norris*, 103 F.3d 710, 714 n.6 (8th Cir. 1997); *Middleton v. Roper*, 455 F.3d 838, 851 (8th Cir. 2006) (rejecting the idea that United States

EXAMPLE APPELLEE'S BRIEF (continued)

Supreme Court precedent calls for the cumulative review of prejudice from separate allegedly ineffective acts or omissions by counsel).

Additionally, federal court review of the analysis of the Missouri courts must be conducted through the highly deferential lens of 28 U.S.C. §2254 (d) and (e). 28 U.S.C. §2254(d) precludes a writ from being granted unless a state court decision was "contrary to" or "involved an unreasonable application of" clearly established United States Supreme Court precedent. 28 U.S.C. §2254(e) provides that factual determinations made by a state court are presumed correct unless refuted by clear and convincing evidence. A federal habeas court, under 28 U.S.C. §2254(d), may not grant a writ of habeas corpus even if it believes a state court erroneously applied clearly established United States Supreme Court precedent, unless that application is both wrong and unreasonable. *Colvin v. Taylor*, 324 F.3d 583, 587 (8th Cir. 2003).

14

EXAMPLE APPELLEE'S BRIEF (continued)

SUMMARY OF ARGUMENT

The Missouri courts rejected Smith's claim that trial counsel was ineffective for not interviewing and calling Alvino Carrillo, in decisions made after an evidentiary hearing. The decisions applied, and were consistent with a reasonable application of, *Strickland v. Washington*, 466 U.S. 668 (1984), the controlling United States Supreme Court precedent on ineffective assistance of counsel claims. Prejudice from each allegedly improper act or omission by counsel must be analyzed individually. *Middleton v. Roper,* 455 F.3d 838, 851 (8th Cir. 2006). A federal habeas court may not grant relief unless it finds not only that a state court misapplied clearly established federal law but also that the decision is both wrong and unreasonable. *Colvin v. Taylor*, 324 F.3d 583, 587 (8th Cir. 2003).

In this case, the Missouri courts reasonably concluded that Smith had failed to rebut the presumption that the decision not to interview and call Carrillo was consistent with reasonable trial strategy in light of Carrillo's history as a drug dealer, his incarceration at the time of trial, Smith's reservations about calling Carrillo, which had been expressed in a letter to counsel, and the collateral nature of Carrillo's proposed testimony. The Missouri courts also reasonably concluded that in light of the strong evidence of guilt and the collateral nature of Carrillo's proposed testimony there is no reasonable probability that the outcome of the proceeding was changed by the absence of Carrillo's testimony.

15

EXAMPLE APPELLEE'S BRIEF (continued)

The district court acted correctly under 28 U.S.C. §2254(d) in leaving undisturbed the reasonable decisions of the Missouri Courts, which found Smith's claim to be without legal merit.

16

EXAMPLE APPELLEE'S BRIEF (continued)

ARGUMENT

The Missouri courts reasonably applied *Strickland v. Washington*, 466 U.S. 668 (1984) in rejecting a claim that trial counsel was ineffective for not calling Alvino Carrillo, because it was objectively reasonable not to call Carrillo based on Carrillo's history of selling drugs and Smith's concern about that history, and the collateral nature of Carrillo's testimony, and because there is no reasonable probability the outcome of trial was changed.

Smith alleges that the district court erred in leaving undisturbed the decision of the Missouri courts that Smith failed to demonstrate that trial counsel was ineffective for not interviewing for declining to interview and call Alvino Carrillo at Smith's trial for the murder of Derek Hoskins, for Carrillo to testify that at an incident approximately two weeks before the murder it was Ricky Sosa not Smith who returned fire when the three were the target of a drive by shooting near Smith's father's home.(Appellant's Brief at 11-20). The district court acted correctly because there is no contention that counsel was unaware of the nature of Carrillo's proposed testimony, and it was objectively reasonable not to present that testimony in light of Carrillo's history of drug dealing, his incarceration at the time of trial, Smith's reservations about calling Carrillo expressed in a letter to counsel, and the collateral nature of Carillo's proposed testimony. There also is no

17

EXAMPLE APPELLEE'S BRIEF (continued)

reasonable probability the outcome of trial would have been changed by calling an incarcerated convicted drug dealer and long time friend of Smith to testify about an incident approximately two weeks before the murder, in which Ricky Sosa, as opposed to Smith, allegedly returned fire during an exchange of gun fire with drive by shooters, because such testimony would have little value in refuting testimony from neighbors that Smith had fired a pistol in the air about two weeks prior to the murder, as Carrillo's testimony apparently describes a different incident, Carrillo would have little credibility, and the matter is collateral to the events on the night of the killing. Under these circumstances the decisions of the Missouri Courts to reject the ineffective assistance of counsel claim was consistent with a reasonable application of *Strickland v. Washington*, 466 U.S. 668 (1984) and should be left undisturbed under 28 U.S.C. §2254(d).

The Circuit Court of Jackson County, Missouri convicted Zachary Smith of first degree murder and armed criminal action following a jury trial for the murder of Derek Hoskins on the night of June 23-24, 1995 and sentenced Smith to concurrent terms of life imprisonment without the possibility of parole and ninety-nine years imprisonment. *State v. Smith*, 90 S.W.3d 132, 135-137 (Mo. App. W.D. 2002). Smith, Sosa and Glavin abducted Hoskins, because Hoskins stole Smith's lawnmower, and had not paid Smith for it despite previously being threatened by Smith at gun point about a week earlier. *Id.* at 135. The group forced Hoskins to

18

EXAMPLE APPELLEE'S BRIEF (continued)

participate in a burglary to work off his debt, took the stolen goods to Smith's home then, then took Hoskins to an isolated area, on the pretext of committing another burglary, where Smith shot Hoskins in the head with a .45 caliber pistol while Hoskins was urinating outside the vehicle. *Id.* at 135.

Roxana Soriano saw the abduction of Hoskins, identified Smith, Sosa and Glavin as the abductors, and testified that she heard guns being cocked before the abductors put Hoskin's bike in the trunk of a maroon car. (Tr.359-366). Glen Hemingway testified that he saw Hoskin's bike in the partially open trunk of a red or burgundy car that was used to drive Hoskins to Hemingway's brother Tyrone's girlfriend's house (Tr. 455-473). Glavin gave a statement under oath identifying Smith as the shooter (Tr. 526-31). Rose Sanchez gave a statement indicating that Smith, Glavin, and Sosa arrived at her home on the morning after the murder and that Smith had a pistol in his waistband (Tr.699-713). Jacob Cowdry a neighbor of Smith's father's testified that Smith gave him a yellow bike that had been covered with black tape and that the police seized this bike from him (Tr. 753-761). Hemingway identified photographs of the seized bike as fairly and accurately representing Hoskin's bike (Tr. 462-463). Two shell casings found near Smith's house at 1901 Lawn, two shell casings near Smith's father's house at 411 Indiana and two shell casings found at the murder scene were all fired from the same .45 caliber pistol (Tr. 876-885). Catherine and Lori Stone, Smith's father's neighbors

19

EXAMPLE APPELLEE'S BRIEF (continued)

told police that they had seen Smith fire a pistol in the air near his father's home at 411 Indiana about two weeks prior to the murder (Tr. 634-650, 772-783). The safe in Smith's home contained identification for Zachary Smith and Sosa, live .45 caliber ammunition, and an empty .45 caliber ammunition box (Tr. 830-832). Zachary Smith's fingerprints was recovered from a burgundy 1985 Buick Park Avenue seized by the police (Tr. 812-816). Smith was arrested as he hid under a bed at 2000 Oakley on June 29, 1995 (Tr.921-925). Smith claimed to have been bowling on the night of the murder, not to have had Hoskin's bicycle, not to have been in a Maroon car, not to own a gun, and not to know Glavin (Tr.935-937).

On April 1, 2000 Smith wrote his attorney stating that Smith had received a letter from Alvino Carrillo who was incarcerated at the Western Reception Diagnostic Correctional Center and that Carillo could testify that it was Jose Sosa not Smith who discharged a weapon outside Smith's father's home at 411 Indiana, to refute testimony from Smith's father's neighbors (Appendix at 64). Smith's letter went on to state that Smith could testify to the same thing and that Carrillo had a record for selling drugs so Smith did not know if counsel would want to use Carrillo. Counsel did not call Carrillo at trial (Resp. Exh. 1 Tr. Index). Smith then alleged in a state post-conviction relief motion that counsel was ineffective for not interviewing Carrillo and calling Carrillo to testify.

EXAMPLE APPELLEE'S BRIEF (continued)

Carillo testified at Smith's post-conviction review hearing that approximately two weeks before the murder, Smith, Sosa and Carrillo were targets of a drive by shooting near Smith's father's home at 411 Indiana but that only Sosa returned fire (Resp. Exh. 6 PCR Tr. at 42). The thrust of this testimony was presumably to provide a possible alternate source for the .45 caliber shells found near Smith's father's home at 411 Indiana, which were fired from the same pistol as the shells found at the murder scene. Carrillo's testimony would not have explained why shell's fired from the same weapon as those found at the crime scene were also found outside Smith's home at 1901 Lawn, or why Smith's locked safe in his home at 1901 Lawn contained .45 caliber ammunition, although Smith claimed not to own a weapon. Carrillo also testified that at the time of Smith's trial Carrillo was imprisoned for two counts of distributing, delivering and manufacturing a controlled substance (*Id.* 44-45). Carrillo testified that he had grown up with Smith and had known Smith and his family since 1984 (*Id.* at 41). Trial counsel did not testify at the post-conviction review hearing (*Id.* Index).

The post-conviction review court found the claim of ineffective assistance of trial counsel to be without merit holding both that Smith failed to overcome the presumption that the decision not to call Carrillo was reasonable trial strategy, and that he failed to show prejudice in that Smith failed to acknowledge "the mountain

21

EXAMPLE APPELLEE'S BRIEF (continued)

of evidence that proved his guilt at trial" in light of which Carrillo's testimony would not have provided a viable defense (Resp Exh. 7 PCR L.F. at 146-147).

The Missouri Court of Appeals affirmed the decision relying on *Strickland v. Washington*, 466 U.S. 668 (1984). (Resp. Exh. 11 Memorandum of Missouri Court of Appeals at 5). The Missouri Court of Appeals found that trial counsel's testimony is not always necessary to rebut *Strickland's* "strong presumption" that counsel's actions were reasonable trial strategy, and then evaluated, based on the record, whether Smith had overcome the presumption (*Id*. at 6-8). The Missouri Court of Appeals found that Smith failed to overcome the presumption that counsel's actions were reasonable trial strategy in that both Smith's reservations in his letter to counsel about calling a convicted drug dealer and the fact that Carrillo was imprisoned at the time of trial support the conclusion that it was a reasonable decision not to call Carrillo (*Id*. at 15). The Court of Appeals also noted that Carrillo testified about an incident in which two groups exchanged gunfire and that this may have been a description of an entirely different incident than the incident described by Smith's father's neighbors in which there were not two groups exchanging fire and Smith fired a weapon in the air (*Id*. at 15). The Missouri Court of Appeals also found that in light of "overwhelming evidence of Smith's guilt it cannot be said that Carrillo's testimony would have had any effect on the outcome of the trial " (*Id*. at15).

22

EXAMPLE APPELLEE'S BRIEF (continued)

The Missouri courts applied the controlling precedent of *Strickland v. Washington.* A federal court may not grant habeas corpus relief to a state prisoner, even if that court would itself decide the case differently, unless the application of *Strickland* by the state courts was both wrong and unreasonable. *Colvin v. Taylor,* 324 F.3d 583, 587 (8th Cir. 2003). The application of *Strickland* by the Missouri courts in this case is firmly within the range of a reasonable application of *Strickland.* It is reasonable to conclude that counsel acted in an objectively reasonable manner in not bringing in a convicted drug dealer from prison to testify on a collateral matter that at best would have provided a possible, but improbable, explanation of why shells matching those at the murder scene were found outside Smith's father's house, without explaining why matching shells were also found outside Smith's own house or why bullets of the same caliber were found in Smith's locked safe, even though he denied owning a gun. It is also reasonable to conclude that Carrillo's testimony would have had no reasonable probability of changing the outcome of the proceeding. The testimony at most provides a possible but improbable explanation for a small part of the "mountain of evidence" pointing to guilt while at the same time tainting Smith as a person who keeps company with drug dealers and is a target for drive by shooting attempts. The district court acted correctly in leaving the reasonable decision of the Missouri Court of Appeals undisturbed as is required by 28 U.S.C. § 2254(d).

23

EXAMPLE APPELLEE'S BRIEF (continued)

Smith argues that the Missouri Court of Appeals unreasonably applied *Strickland* because "the court relied on state authority holding that a post-conviction litigant could overcome the presumption of reasonableness *only* through the testimony of counsel." (Appellants Brief at 13)(emphasis in the original). Smith misreads the opinion of the Missouri Court of Appeals which in fact held that "We do not read any of the mentioned cases, nor the opinion of the motion court, as holding that there is an irrebuttable presumption of reasonableness in the absence of trial counsel's testimony." (Resp. Exh. 11 at 7). Smith argument that the Missouri Court of Appeals unreasonably applied the performance prong of Strickland is an attack on straw man rather than on the actual reasoning of the Missouri Court of Appeals.

Smith next argues that the Missouri Court of Appeals unreasonably applied *Strickland* in finding that Carrillo's testimony would not have created a reasonable probability that the outcome of the proceeding would have changed (Appellant's Brief 15-20). Specifically, Smith argues that Carrillo must have been talking about the same incident as Smith's father's neighbors because the location and time frame were similar, although the details were different, and that the neighbors were "intoxicated at the time and fabricated their description under pressure from the prosecutor" and that the jury would likely have believed Carrillo (Appellants Brief 15-16). Smith dismisses the testimony of the eyewitness Glavin as that of a

24

EXAMPLE APPELLEE'S BRIEF (continued)

"convicted felon and crack addict" two sentences after asserting that the jury would likely have believed Carrillo, a convicted drug dealer (Appellant's Brief at 16). Smith dismisses the statement of Rose Sanchez and the identification by Roxana Soriano, in the same sentence in which he characterizes Smith's possession of Hoskin's bicycle, and his giving away of the victim's bicycle, and Smith's own false statements to the police as "extremely thin" evidence (Appellant's Brief at 16). Smith's analysis on the prejudice prong does not mention or provide an explanation for the shell casings outside Smith's home at 1901 Lawn which were fired from the same .45 caliber pistol as the shells found at the murder scene, nor does Smith explain why he denied owning a pistol but the locked safe in his home contained identification in his name, live .45 caliber ammunition and an empty ammunition box for .45 caliber ammunition (Appellant's Brief 15-20).

In rejecting Smith's motion to alter or amend which challenged the finding of the district court that no *Strickland* prejudice resulted from not calling Carrillo, the district court found that "Petitioner's motion does not include all the evidence presented at Petitioner's trial that supported the jury's verdict." (Appendix at 149). Smith's argument to this Court suffers from the same flaw. Carrillo's attempt to explain away the shell casings at 411 Indiana lacks credibility in light of the shell casings fired from the same weapon outside Smith's home at 1901 Lawn, and the

25

EXAMPLE APPELLEE'S BRIEF (continued)

bullets and empty ammunition box found with Smith's identification in a locked safe found in the home at 1901 Lawn where Smith resided. It was well with the realm of what is reasonable for the Missouri Courts to conclude that there is no reasonable probability that Carrillo's testimony would have changed the outcome of the trial, and that reasonable decision should be left undisturbed

CONCLUSION

The decision of the United States District Court for the Western District of Missouri should be affirmed.

Respectfully submitted,

JEREMIAH W. (JAY) NIXON
Attorney General

MICHAEL J. SPILLANE
Assistant Attorney General
Missouri Bar No. 40704

P.O. Box 899
Jefferson City, MO 65102
(573)751-3321
(573)751-3825 fax
mike.spillane@ago.mo.gov

Attorneys for Respondent/Appellee

26

EXAMPLE APPELLEE'S BRIEF (concluded)

CERTIFICATE OF SERVICE
I hereby certify that two copies of the foregoing were mailed, postage prepaid, this 12th day of September, 2008, to:

Elizibeth Unger Carlyle
P.O. Box 866
Columbus Mississippi 39703

Michael J. Spillane
Michael J. Spillane

CERTIFICATE OF COMPLIANCE

I hereby certify that the foregoing document is printed in 14 point proportionally spaced type (Times New Roman), that it was prepared with Word 2003 software and according to this software the document contains 6,223 words. In addition, I certify that the computer disk submitted with this brief was scanned for viruses and that the disk is virus free.

Michael J. Spillane
MICHAEL J. SPILLANE

27

EXAMPLE APPELLATE'S REPLY BRIEF

IN THE UNITED STATES COURT OF APPEALS
FOR THE EIGHTH CIRCUIT

ZACHARY SMITH	§	
	§	
Plaintiff-Appellant	§	
	§	
v.	§	NO. 08-1901
	§	
MIKE KEMNA et al	§	
	§	
Defendants-Appellees	§	

* * * * * * * * * *

ON APPEAL FROM THE UNITED STATES DISTRICT COURT
FOR THE WESTERN DISTRICT OF MISSOURI
WESTERN DIVISION

* * * * * * * * * *

CIVIL NO. 07-06068-CV-SJ-ODS

* * * * * * * * * *

APPELLANT'S REPLY BRIEF

ELIZABETH UNGER CARLYLE
P.O. Box 866
Columbus, MS 39703
(816) 525-6540
FAX (866) 249-8264
Missouri Bar No. 41930
elizcar@bellsouth.net

ATTORNEY FOR APPELLANT

[Note: This cover sheet should be gray in color.]

EXAMPLE APPELLANT'S REPLY BRIEF (continued)

TABLE OF CONTENTS

APPELLANT'S REPLY BRIEF – Page i

EXAMPLE APPELLANT'S REPLY BRIEF (continued)

TABLE OF AUTHORITIES

EXAMPLE APPELLANT'S REPLY BRIEF (continued)

IN THE UNITED STATES COURT OF APPEALS
FOR THE EIGHTH CIRCUIT

ZACHARY SMITH	§	
	§	
Plaintiff-Appellant	§	
	§	
v.	§	No. 08-1901
	§	
MIKE KEMNA et al	§	
	§	
Defendants-Appellees	§	

APPELLANT'S REPLY BRIEF

Appellant Zachary Smith files this reply brief in response to the brief of the appellee. This brief discusses only those issues raised in the state's brief which, in the belief of appellant, require a response. The failure to re-urge any contention made in the opening brief is not intended as a waiver of that contention, and Mr. Smith relies on each and every point and contention in his opening brief.

APPELLANT'S REPLY BRIEF – Page 1

EXAMPLE APPELLANT'S REPLY BRIEF (continued)

REPLY ARGUMENT AND AUTHORITIES

GROUND OF ERROR NO. ONE:

TRIAL COUNSEL FAILED TO CALL AS A WITNESS ALVINO CARRILLO, WHO WOULD HAVE DISCREDITED POWERFUL PHYSICAL EVIDENCE AGAINST THE DEFENDANT. A DEFENDANT IS ENTITLED TO HAVE TRIAL COUNSEL INTERVIEW AND CALL AVAILABLE WITNESSES FOR HIS DEFENSE. WAS MR. SMITH DENIED EFFECTIVE ASSISTANCE OF COUNSEL?

In its statement of facts in this case, the state quotes extensively from the state's appellate brief in Mr. Smith's direct appeal. In that appeal, of course, the state was entitled to rely on the principle that on direct appeal, the facts are considered in the light most favorable to the verdict. However, in order to determine whether Mr. Smith was denied effective assistance of counsel, the district court and this Court must consider the *whole* record, both evidence that was admitted, and evidence that could have been admitted had trial counsel's performance been within the constitutional standard of *Strickland v. Washington*, 466 U.S. 668, 687-88 (1984). *Rompilla v. Beard*, 545 U.S. 374 (2005); *Wiggins v. Smith*, 539 U.S. 510 (2003); *Williams (Terry) v. Taylor*, 529 U.S. 362 (2000). Thus, Mr. Smith's summary of the evidence in this case, which includes contradictory and impeaching evidence, should provide the proper framework for this Court's analysis.

APPELLANT'S REPLY BRIEF – Page 2

EXAMPLE APPELLANT'S REPLY BRIEF (continued)

Specifically, the state's narrative totally omits the fact that Kevin Glavin refused to testify at trial; the evidence attributed to him came entirely from his pretrial statement. Similarly, the state avers that Rose Sanchez testified that Mr. Smith had arrived at her home the day after the shooting with a gun tucked into his waistband. But that fact came from a statement Ms. Sanchez allegedly made to a detective. At trial, she denied having made the statement, and specifically denied that Mr. Smith had a gun. Trial Tr. pp. 706, 708. Many other witnesses who testified at trial repudiated their pretrial statements. This fact is not evident from the state's narrative, but is highly relevant both to the performance and prejudice prongs of the *Strickland v. Washington*, 466 U.S. 668, 687-88 (1984), standard.

The state argues that trial counsel's decision not to *call* Mr. Carrillo was reasonable because of his record and because of what the state says is the collateral nature of his testimony. But the primary issue here is not whether Mr. Carrillo should have been *called* as a witness. It is whether trial counsel's "decision," if he made one, not to *interview* Mr. Carrillo was reasonable. It is clear that counsel was made aware of Mr. Carrillo. It is equally clear that he never contacted Mr. Carrillo. The fact that Mr. Smith drew counsel's attention to some disadvantages which *might* make calling Mr. Carrillo inadvisable did not excuse trial counsel from interviewing him. In fact, the United States Supreme Court has held that even if a defendant tells an

APPELLANT'S REPLY BRIEF – Page 3

EXAMPLE APPELLANT'S REPLY BRIEF (continued)

attorney NOT to interview a witness, that statement does not necessarily absolve the attorney from the duty to investigate and make an independent professional decision as to whether the witness should be called. *Rompilla v. Beard*, 545 U.S. 374 (2005).

Mr. Glavin's evidence was weak. Even in his statement to police, he failed to acknowledge that he saw Mr. Smith shoot Mr. Hoskins. Then, he refused to repeat his under oath in the courtroom. Trial Tr. p. 479. Moreover, under the circumstances, it was as likely that Mr. Glavin was the shooter and was testifying against Mr. Smith to protect himself as that Mr. Smith was, in fact, the shooter. It was therefore critical for the state to corroborate Mr. Glavin, and the prosecutor chose to do so by emphasizing the match between the bullets which killed Mr. Hoskins and those fired on Indiana street two weeks before. Trial Tr. p. 998. In order to tie those bullets to Mr. Smith, the state relied on the testimony of Cathy and Lorie Stone, who not only were absent from Mr. Smith's final trial but, in their previous testimony, had repudiated their prior statements and accused the prosecutor and law enforcement of misconduct. Trial Tr. pp. 624-649; 771-778. Their statements also contradicted the place where the shell casings were found.

Trial counsel brought out these inconsistencies, but did not present Mr. Carrillo, an available witness who would have come to court and completely eliminated the Stones' testimony by establishing that Mr. Smith was not the

APPELLANT'S REPLY BRIEF – Page 4

EXAMPLE APPELLANT'S REPLY BRIEF (continued)

shooter on Indiana street, and therefore was not the shooter of Hoskins. This testimony was not "collateral." It related to the central issue in the case, the identity of the shooter.

Counsel did not present this testimony because he had not interviewed Mr. Carrillo. Counsel's "strategic" decisions are entitled to much less deference when they are not based on a proper investigation. *Wiggins v. Smith*, 539 U.S. 510, 525 (2003) *Rompilla v. Beard*, 545 U.S. 374, 383 (2005); *White v. Roper*, 416 F.3d 728, 732 (8th Cir. 2005).

In denying post-conviction relief the Missouri Court of Appeals applied a restriction on the *Strickland v. Washington*, 466 U.S. 668, 687-88 (1984), standard, requiring the post-conviction movant to present the testimony of trial counsel in order to show ineffectiveness. As discussed in more detail in the opening brief, this concept is nowhere contained in *Strickland v. Washington*, 466 U.S. 668, 687-88 (1984), and its progeny.

Mr. Smith showed in the post-conviction hearing that he had attempted to obtain the testimony of trial counsel but he had evaded their attempts, and the state offered no evidence that it had made any attempt to contact him. Traverse, Ex. E-H. (App. A-108-115). Mr. Smith also showed that trial counsel had been disbarred for professional misconduct, including neglect of his legal duties to his clients. Traverse, Ex. E-H. (App. A-108-115). This set of facts requires the inference that trial counsel would have testified that, in

APPELLANT'S REPLY BRIEF – Page 5

EXAMPLE APPELLANT'S REPLY BRIEF (continued)

fact, he made no reasonable professional judgment not to interview Mr. Carrillo. Given trial counsel's evasion of Mr. Smith's counsel and disbarment for misconduct, the performance prong of *Strickland v. Washington*, 466 U.S. 668, 687-88 (1984), is clearly established, and the Missouri court's contrary finding is an unreasonable application of *Strickland v. Washington*, 466 U.S. 668, 687-88 (1984).

As to the prejudice prong, the state's brief completely ignores the highly analogous case of *Stanley v. Bartley*, 465 F.3d 810 (7th Cir. 2006). In a very similar factual situation, where the state's evidence rested on testimony of a supposed eyewitness who could have been an accomplice, the Seventh Circuit found ineffectiveness where trial counsel failed to interview and call a witness who would have impeached that account. Like Mr. Glavin, the "eyewitness" in *Stanley* claimed he was standing next to Mr. Stanley when Mr. Stanley committed the murder.

The state suggests that the evidence against Mr. Smith was so strong that calling Mr. Carrillo would not have had a reasonable probability of affecting the outcome. The state conveniently ignores the fact that the case was once tried to a hung jury on substantially similar evidence. And the state court's concept that there is a "mountain of evidence" against Mr. Smith is based entirely on ignoring all evidence which did not support the verdict. That approach is improper where the issue is ineffectiveness of counsel and

APPELLANT'S REPLY BRIEF – Page 6

EXAMPLE APPELLANT'S REPLY BRIEF (continued)

where the petitioner must show only a reasonable probability of a different outcome in order to gain relief. The Missouri courts failed to apply this test properly, and relief is required.

CONCLUSION

Wherefore, for the reasons stated in his opening brief and this reply brief, Mr. Smith prays the court to issue the writ of habeas corpus and to vacate his conviction and sentence and direct the State of Missouri either to retry him within a reasonable time or release him.

Respectfully submitted,

Elizabeth Unger Carlyle
P.O. Box 866
Columbus, MS 39703
(816)525-6540
FAX (866) 764-1249
Mo. Bar No. 41930
ATTORNEY FOR APPELLANT

APPELLANT'S REPLY BRIEF – Page 7

EXAMPLE APPELLANT'S REPLY BRIEF (concluded)

CERTIFICATE OF COMPLIANCE

Pursuant to Fed. R. App. Pro. 32(a)(7)(C), the undersigned attorney certifies that this brief complies with the type-volume limitation in that rule. According to Microsoft Word 2003, the word processing program used to produce this brief, it contains 1,685 words. The disk submitted with this brief has been scanned and is virus-free.

ELIZABETH UNGER CARLYLE

CERTIFICATE OF SERVICE

I certify that a copy of the foregoing brief was served upon opposing counsel Stephen Hawke, Asst. Missouri Attorney Gen., by U.S. Mail on October 17, 2008.

ELIZABETH UNGER CARLYLE

APPELLANT'S REPLY BRIEF – Page 8

9. COURT OF APPEALS DECISION

ENTRY OF JUDGMENT: NOTICE

Federal Rules of Appellate Procedure Rule 36

(a) Entry. A judgment is entered when it is noted on the docket. The court must prepare, sign, and enter the judgment:

(1) after receiving the court's opinion -- but if settlement of the judgment's form is required, after final settlement; or

(2) if a judgment is rendered without an opinion, as the court instructs.

(b) Notice. On the date when judgment is entered, the clerk must serve on all parties a copy of the opinion -- or the judgment, if no opinion was written -- and a notice of the date when the judgment was entered.

If you were denied a certificate of appealability from the district court, the court of appeals will decide whether to issue one. When the court reaches a decision, most often the court denies your request for a COA without an opinion.

If you were granted a COA, and your claims were briefed and argued before the court of appeals, the panel will write an opinion. An example opinion is provided at the end of this chapter.

PETITION FOR PANEL REHEARING

Federal Rules of Appellate Procedure Rule 40

(a) Time to File; Contents; Answer; Action by the Court if Granted.

(1) <u>Time</u>. Unless the time is shortened or extended by order or local rule, a petition for panel rehearing may be filed within 14 days after entry of judgment. But in a civil case, if the United States or its officer or agency is a party, the time within which any party may seek rehearing is 45 days after entry of judgment, unless an order shortens or extends the time.

(2) <u>Contents</u>. The petition must state with particularity each point of law or fact that the petitioner believes the court has overlooked or misapprehended and must argue in support of the petition. Oral argument is not permitted.

(3) <u>Answer</u>. Unless the court requests, no answer to a petition for panel rehearing is permitted. But ordinarily rehearing will not be granted in the absence of such a request.

(4) <u>Action by the Court</u>. If a petition for panel rehearing is granted, the court may do any of the following:

(A) make a final disposition of the case without reargument;

(B) restore the case to the calendar for reargument or resubmission; or

(C) issue any other appropriate order.

(b) <u>Form of Petition; Length</u>. The petition must comply in form with Rule 32. Copies must be served and filed as Rule 31 prescribes. Unless the court permits or a local rule provides otherwise, a petition for panel rehearing must not exceed 15 pages.

EN BANC DETERMINATION

Federal Rules of Appellate Procedure Rule 35

(a) When Hearing or Rehearing En Banc May Be Ordered. A majority of the circuit judges who are in regular active service may order that an appeal or other proceeding be heard or reheard by the court of appeals en banc. An en banc hearing or rehearing is not favored and ordinarily will not be ordered unless:

(1) en banc consideration is necessary to secure or maintain uniformity of the court's decisions; or

(2) the proceeding involves a question of exceptional importance.

(b) Petition for Hearing or Rehearing En Banc. A party may petition for a hearing or rehearing en banc.

(1) The petition must begin with a statement that either:

(A) the panel decision conflicts with a decision of the United States Supreme Court or of the court to which the petition is addressed (with citation to the conflicting case or cases) and consideration by the full court is therefore necessary to secure and maintain uniformity of the court's decisions; or

(B) the proceeding involves one or more questions of exceptional importance, each of which must be concisely stated; for example, a petition may assert that a proceeding presents a question of exceptional importance if it involves an issue on which the panel decision conflicts with the authoritative decisions of other United States Court of Appeals that have addressed the issue.

(2) Except by the court's permission, a petition for an en banc hearing or rehearing must not exceed 15 pages, excluding material not counted under Rule 32.

(3) For purposes of the page limitation in Rule 35(b)(2), if a party files both a petition for panel rehearing and a petition for rehearing en banc, they are considered a single document even if they are filed separately, unless separate filing is required by local rule.

(e) Time for Petition for Hearing or Rehearing En Banc. A petition that an appeal be heard initially en banc must be filed by the date when the appellee's brief is due. A petition for a rehearing en banc must be filed within the time prescribed by Rule 40 for filing a petition for rehearing.

(d) Number of Copies. The number of copies to be filed must be prescribed by local rule and may be altered by order in a particular case.

(e) Response. No response may be filed to a petition for an en banc consideration unless the court orders a response.

(f) Call for a Vote. A vote need not be taken to determine whether the case will be heard or reheard en banc unless a judge calls for a vote.

Examples of a petition for rehearing and a petition for rehearing en banc are provided at the end of this chapter to assist your decision to file one or both, and to aid in their preparation.

When the court of appeals enters a judgment without an opinion, it is usually in a case where a COA is denied. In such a case, you will need to point out the facts and law the court overlooked that entitle you to a COA. Try to find a similar case in which a COA was granted and point it out to the court in your petition. You may even attach a copy of the case, if it is identical to yours.

You'll also find at the end of this chapter an example of a one-page order denying a petition for rehearing, and a petition for rehearing en banc.

MANDATE: CONTENTS; ISSUANCE AND EFFECTIVE DATE; STAY

Federal Rules of Appellate Procedure Rule 41

(a) Contents. Unless the court directs that a formal mandate issue, the mandate consists of a certified copy of the judgment, a copy of the court's opinion, if any, and any direction about costs.

(b) When Issued. The court's mandate must issue 7 calendar days after the time to file a petition for rehearing expires, or 7 calendar days after entry of an order denying a timely petition for rehearing, petition for rehearing en banc, or motion for stay of mandate, whichever is later. The court may shorten or extend the time.

(c) Effective Date. The mandate is effective when issued.

(d) Staying the Mandate.

(1) <u>On Petition for Rehearing or Motion</u>. The timely filing of a petition for panel rehearing, petition for rehearing en banc, or motion for stay of mandate, stays the mandate until disposition of the petition or motion, unless the court orders otherwise.

(2) <u>Pending Petition for Certiorari</u>.

(A) A party may move to stay the mandate pending the filing of a petition for a writ of certiorari in the Supreme Court. The motion must be served on all parties and must show that the certiorari petition would present a substantial question and that there is good cause for a stay.

(B) The stay must not exceed 90 days, unless the period is extended for good cause or unless the party who obtained the stay files a petition for the writ and so notifies the circuit clerk in writing within the period of the stay. In that case, the stay continues until the Supreme Court's final disposition.

(C) The court may require a bond or other security as a condition to granting or continuing a stay of the mandate.

(D) The court of appeals must issue the mandate immediately when a copy of a Supreme Court order denying the petition for writ of certiorari is filed.

An example mandate titled "Judgment" is provided at the end of this chapter.

EXAMPLE COURT OF APPEALS DECISION

United States Court of Appeals
For The Eighth Circuit
Thomas F. Eagleton U.S. Courthouse
111 South 10th Street, Room 24.329
St. Louis, Missouri 63102

Michael E. Gans   VOICE (314) 244-2400
Clerk of Court   FAX (314) 244-2780
                                                   www.ca8.uscourts.gov

February 02, 2009

Ms. Elizabeth Unger Carlyle
P.O. Box 962
Columbus, MS 39703-0000

    RE: 08-1901 Zachary Smith v. Mike Kemna

Dear Counsel:

    The court has issued an opinion in this case. Judgment has been entered in accordance with the opinion. The opinion will be released to the public at 10:00a.m. today. Please hold the opinion in confidence until that time.

    Please review Federal Rules of Appellate Procedure and the Eighth Circuit Rules on post-submission procedure to ensure that any contemplated filing is timely and in compliance with the rules. Note particularly that petitions for rehearing and petitions for rehearing en banc <u>must</u> be received in the clerk's office within 14 days of the date of the entry of judgment. Counsel-filed petitions must be filed electronically in CM/ECF. Paper copies are not required. No grace period for mailing is allowed, and the date of the postmark is irrelevant for pro-se-filed petitions. Any petition for rehearing or petition for rehearing en banc which is not received within the 14 day period for filing permitted by FRAP 40 may be denied as untimely.

                     Michael E. Gans
                     Clerk of Court

CMD

Enclosure(s)

cc: Ms. Patricia L. Brune
       Mr. Zachary Smith
       Mr. Michael Joseph Spillane

       District Court/Agency Case Number(s): 5:07-cv-06068-ODS

EXAMPLE COURT OF APPEALS DECISION (continued)

Case: 08-1901   Page: 1   Date Filed: 02/02/2009 Entry ID: 3512633

United States Court of Appeals
FOR THE EIGHTH CIRCUIT

No. 08-1901

Zachary Smith,	*
	* Appeal from the United States
Plaintiff-Appellant,	* District Court for the
	* Western District of Missouri
v.	*
	* [UNPUBLISHED]
Mike Kemna, Superintendent,	*
Crossroads Correctional Center,	*
	*
Defendants-Appellees.	*

Submitted: December 9, 2008
Filed: February 2, 2009

Before MELLOY, and BENTON, Circuit Judges, and DOTY,[1] District Judge.

PER CURIAM.

Zachary Smith appeals from the district court's[2] denial of his petition for a writ of habeas corpus pursuant to 28 U.S.C. § 2254. We affirm.

---

[1] The Honorable David S. Doty, United States District Court for the District of Minnesota, sitting by designation.

[2] The Honorable Ortrie D. Smith, United States District Judge for the Western District of Missouri.

EXAMPLE COURT OF APPEALS DECISION (continued)

Case: 08-1901   Page: 2   Date Filed: 02/02/2009 Entry ID: 3512633

I.

A jury in Missouri state court convicted Smith of first degree murder and armed criminal action, and he was sentenced to concurrent terms of imprisonment of life without the possibility of parole and ninety-nine years.[3] Smith's conviction and sentence were affirmed on appeal. See State v. Smith, 90 S.W.3d 132, 142 (Mo. Ct. App. 2002). Smith timely petitioned for state post-conviction relief, which the district court denied after an evidentiary hearing. The Missouri court of appeals affirmed. See Smith v. State, 207 S.W.3d 135, 135 (Mo. Ct. App. 2006) (per curiam). Thereafter, Smith filed this § 2254 petition, asserting eight grounds for relief and requesting an evidentiary hearing. The district court denied the petition and request for hearing but granted a certificate of appealability on Smith's claim that his trial counsel was ineffective for failing to interview and call Alvino Carrillo as a witness.

II.

We state the facts as recited by the Missouri court of appeals on direct appeal from Smith's conviction. See Chavez v. Weber, 497 F.3d 796, 799 (8th Cir. 2007).

On June 23, 1995, at around 10:00 p.m., Zachary Smith left his father's home in Kansas City and started driving around in a borrowed, maroon Buick with Kevin Glavin and Jose Sosa. Smith was armed with a black .45-caliber handgun. The men stopped at a gas station to buy some cigarettes. While they were there, Derek Hoskins rode up on his bicycle. Several weeks earlier, Hoskins had confessed to stealing Smith's lawn mower. Hoskins had promised to pay Smith back for the lawn mower, but never did. About a week earlier, Smith had shown Hoskins a pistol he was carrying and warned him, "You better get my money."

---

[3] Smith's conviction followed two prior trials. The jury was unable to reach a verdict in the first proceeding and Smith's conviction in the second trial was reversed on appeal. See State v. Smith, 966 S.W.2d 1, 9 (Mo. Ct. App. 1997).

EXAMPLE COURT OF APPEALS DECISION (continued)

Case: 08-1901   Page: 3   Date Filed: 02/02/2009 Entry ID: 3512633

When Hoskins rode up to the gas station on his bicycle, Smith asked if he had the money he owed him. Hoskins said he did not have the money he owed him, but the money was at his house and he would go and get it. When Hoskins suggested that they follow him to his cousin Tyrone Morgan's house, Smith insisted they put the bike in the trunk and that Hoskins ride with them in the car. During this incident, a witness heard what sounded like two guns being cocked. After placing Hoskins' bicycle in the trunk of the car, they drove to Morgan's home, where Tyrone's younger brother told Hoskins that Tyrone was not home.

After Hoskins got back in the Buick, Smith told him that he could work off the debt by burglarizing a house. Hoskins agreed. Smith took Hoskins' bicycle from the trunk and put it in a field near Smith's house. Smith next drove the group to a house, where Hoskins and Glavin got out of the car. Hoskins knocked on the door, and when nobody answered, he kicked in the door and stole a television set and a stereo, both of which he placed in the trunk of the Buick. The men returned to Smith's house and dropped off the television and the stereo. Smith then informed Hoskins that he would have to commit another burglary to fully repay the debt.

Smith drove the group to the northeast part of the city, where they stopped to buy some beer. After driving around for about half an hour, Glavin told Smith he needed to urinate. They were in an area called Cliff Drive at the time. Smith stopped the car under a streetlight, but then backed the car out of the light, even though the street was deserted. When Hoskins asked if he could get out of the car to urinate, Glavin told him to remain in the vehicle because "something did not feel right." Hoskins told Glavin, "I got to go pee," and got out of the car anyway.

As Hoskins and Glavin stood by the curb urinating, Smith got out of the car and stood behind and in between the two. Glavin then heard a gunshot, looked up, and saw a bright flash. He saw Smith holding a pistol about one to two feet away from Hoskins. Hoskins went limp and fell to the ground. After Smith and Glavin got back in the car, Smith

-3-

EXAMPLE COURT OF APPEALS DECISION (continued)

Case: 08-1901   Page: 4   Date Filed: 02/02/2009 Entry ID: 3512633

muttered something about "good measure" and fired another shot out the window at Hoskins.

About sunrise the next day, the three men went to the house of Sosa's girlfriend, Rose Marie Sanchez. Sanchez later told the police that Smith had arrived in a newer, four-door burgundy or red car and had a gun tucked into his waistband. Later that morning, Catherine Stone looked out her window and saw Smith standing next to the maroon car.

Smith then drove back to his father's house, where he and his girlfriend, Cynthia Frost, had been living for about a month. Smith handed his gun to Frost and told her to put it up.

The following day, Smith took Glavin to his bedroom and showed him Hoskins' bicycle, which was now covered in black tape. Smith told Glavin that he was going to give the bicycle to a little kid. Smith later gave the bicycle to a boy who was visiting Smith's father's house.

Smith sought Glavin's help in disposing of the murder weapon. He wanted Glavin to accompany him while he drove across the Chouteau Bridge and threw it in the river. Glavin asked Smith whether Sosa was in on the plan to kill Hoskins. Smith told him that Sosa did not know anything about it, and that he (Smith) was the "master mind." Smith told Glavin that the last words Hoskins said were "I got to go pee" and that Hoskins "had it coming for stealing from him."

Between 3:00 and 4:00 a.m. on June 24, 1995, two security officers patrolling the Cliff Drive area heard gunshots. Later, a man reported that he had seen someone lying in the street who appeared to be seriously injured. The security officers went to the scene, where they found Hoskins' body. When Detective Ron Payne, a crime scene technician, arrived several hours later, he found Hoskins' body lying in the street with his head facing south and the snap of his shorts unfastened. On the ground, Payne found two spent bullets and two shell casings. . . . Police confiscated the bicycle that had belonged to Hoskins.

-4-

EXAMPLE COURT OF APPEALS DECISION (continued)

Case: 08-1901   Page: 5   Date Filed: 02/02/2009 Entry ID: 3512633

A police officer spoke with Lori Stone, who lived next door to Smith's father's house. She told the officer that two weeks before Hoskins' death, she had seen Smith fire a black .45-caliber handgun into the air twice. Catherine Stone, Lori's sister, later told officers that she had also seen Smith shoot his gun in the air near his father's house.

Police detectives Roger Lewis and Mark Heimer spoke with Cynthia Frost. Frost told the detectives that she co-owned a house with Smith. On June 27, 1995, detectives asked Frost to sign a consent to search form for Smith's house, and she complied. Frost accompanied the detectives to the house. In one of the bedrooms, the detectives found Smith's driver's license and some personal papers. They also found a locked safe in the bedroom. Frost told the police that the safe was "her and Zach's" and authorized them to open it. One of the detectives quoted Frost as stating that "it was her safe and that we could open it."

The detectives carried the safe out to the front porch, where they forced it open using a hammer, a crowbar, and a heavy-duty screwdriver. Inside the safe, the detectives found a purple Crown Royal bag containing several live .45 rounds and an empty box of .45-caliber ammunition. The safe also contained a Missouri inmate card in the name of Jose Sosa and a Missouri identification card in the name of Zachary Smith.

On June 29, 1995, the police found Smith hiding underneath a bed at 2000 Oakley and arrested him. After receiving and waiving his Miranda rights, Smith told the police that on the evening of June 24, 1995, he had gone bowling with several friends. He said that he and his friends had then gone to his father's house, where they remained until 11:00 a.m. the next morning. Smith denied owning a gun, claimed not to know Glavin,

EXAMPLE COURT OF APPEALS DECISION (continued)

Case: 08-1901   Page: 6   Date Filed: 02/02/2009 Entry ID: 3512633

and stated that he had not seen Hoskins for a month. He also told police that he did not have Hoskins' bicycle, he had not been in a maroon car, and he had not been to Cliff Drive in at least three to four months.

On June 30, 1995, the police examined the Buick for fingerprints. A print taken from the interior of the driver's side door matched Smith's left middle finger. In addition, William Newhouse, a firearms and tool mark examiner with the Kansas City Regional Crime Laboratory, examined the shell casings and bullets collected during the investigation of Hoskins' death. After examining the two shell casings found at the crime scene, the two casings found at Smith's house, and the two casings found at Smith's father's house, Newhouse determined that all six casings had been fired from the same .45-caliber pistol. Newhouse also determined that the bullets recovered from the crime scene were fired from the same pistol.

Smith, 90 S.W.3d at 135-38.

III.

Section 2254 provides for habeas relief from a state court judgment if a petitioner establishes that the state court's adjudication "resulted in a decision that was contrary to, or involved an unreasonable application of, clearly established Federal law, as determined by the Supreme Court of the United States." 28 U.S.C. § 2254(d)(1); see also Williams v. Taylor, 529 U.S. 362, 402-3 (2000). A decision is contrary to clearly established federal law if it applies a rule that contradicts Supreme Court precedent. Brown v. Payton, 544 U.S. 133, 141 (2005); Swartz v. Burger, 412 F.3d 1008, 1009-10 (8th Cir. 2005). An unreasonable application of federal law occurs when a state court applies Supreme Court precedent in an "objectively unreasonable manner." Brown, 544 U.S. at 141; Swartz, 412 F.3d at 1009-10. Habeas relief is not warranted when a federal court concludes that a state court erroneously applied federal law. Davis v. Norris, 423 F.3d 868, 875 (8th Cir. 2005) (citing Williams, 529 U.S. at 411). Rather, "the test is whether the state court's

EXAMPLE COURT OF APPEALS DECISION (continued)

Case: 08-1901   Page: 7   Date Filed: 02/02/2009 Entry ID: 3512633

application of the law was unreasonable." Id. We review the district court's findings of fact for clear error and its conclusions of law de novo. Richardson v. Bowersox, 188 F.3d 973, 977 (8th Cir. 1999).

IV.

To prevail on his ineffective assistance of counsel claim, Smith must show that counsel's performance was deficient and that he was prejudiced by that deficient performance. Strickland v. Washington, 466 U.S. 688, 687 (1984). Our review of counsel's efforts is "highly deferential," and "counsel is strongly presumed to have rendered adequate assistance and made all significant decisions in the exercise of reasonable professional judgment." Id. at 689-90. Under Strickland's performance prong, we apply an objective standard and "determine whether, in light of all the circumstances, the identified acts or omissions were outside the wide range of professionally competent assistance." Id. at 690. Strickland's prejudice prong "requires proof 'that there is a reasonable probability that, but for a counsel's unprofessional errors, the result of the proceeding would have been different.'" Lawrence v. Armontrout, 31 F.3d 662, 666 (8th Cir. 1994) (quoting Strickland, 466 U.S. at 694). A reasonable probability is a probability sufficient to undermine confidence in the outcome. See id. In making this determination, a court hearing an ineffectiveness claim must consider the totality of the evidence before the jury. Id. Failure to satisfy both prongs is fatal to the claim. See Pryor v. Norris, 103 F.3d 710, 713 (8th Cir. 1997) (no need to reach performance prong if defendant suffered no prejudice from alleged ineffectiveness). An ineffective assistance of counsel claim is a mixed question of law and fact. Parkus v. Bowersox, 157 F.3d 1136, 1138 (8th Cir. 1998).

The Missouri courts concluded that Smith was not prejudiced by his counsel's failure to interview or call Carrillo. Smith argues that this was an unreasonable application of Strickland. Specifically, Smith maintains that Carrillo would have

-7-

EXAMPLE COURT OF APPEALS DECISION (concluded)

Case: 08-1901   Page: 8   Date Filed: 02/02/2009 Entry ID: 3512633

testified that he was present during the incident at Smith's father's residence and that Smith never fired a gun. Smith argues that this testimony would have undermined Glavin's identification of Smith as the murderer by disproving the link between Smith, the bullets fired at his father's residence and the bullets that killed Hoskins. Moreover, Smith argues that he would have testified if Carrillo had testified. According to Smith, he would have told the jury that Glavin killed Hoskins and that Sosa fired the shots outside of Smith's father's residence. Smith also would have accounted for his fingerprints in the Buick by testifying that he had ridden in the backseat of the car on another occasion.

Even if Carrillo and Smith had testified, there is no reasonable probability that the result of the trial would have been different. Carrillo would have lacked credibility as Smith's longtime friend and a convicted drug dealer who was incarcerated at the time of trial. Further, Carrillo would have testified only to matters collateral to the events on the night of the killing. Moreover, Smith's testimony would not have explained how shell casings matching those found at the murder scene were located inside his house in a locked safe. Nor would Smith's alleged testimony have refuted the testimony of witnesses who saw him with a gun and the victim's property shortly after the murder. Based on the substantial inculpatory evidence presented at trial, we determine that Smith was not prejudiced by his trial counsel's failure to call and interview Carrillo. Accordingly, the Missouri state courts did not unreasonably apply Strickland.

The judgment is affirmed.

———————————————

-8-

EXAMPLE PETITION FOR REHEARING

IN THE UNITED STATES COURT OF APPEALS
EIGHTH CIRCUIT

ZACHARY SMITH,   )
)
                Appellant,   )
)
v.   )   Case No. 08-1901
)
MIKE KEMNA,   )
)
                Appellee.   )

<u>**PETITION FOR REHEARING**</u>

Appellant Zachary Smith prays the court for rehearing of its opinion entered

February 2, 2009, and in support states:

**A. The panel opinion concerning prejudice from trial counsel's failure to call

Alvino Carrillo as a witness contains errors of fact and law.**

1. *Factual errors.* The opinion contains a glaring factual error that clearly

affected the court's consideration of the prejudice issue. On p. 8, the court states,

"Smith's testimony would not have explained how shell casings matching those found at

the murder scene were located inside his house in a locked safe." *No* shell casings, much

less casings which matched the murder scene, were found in the safe. What was found in

the safe was **live ammunition** of the same caliber as the shell casings found at the scene.

There was no testimony that this ammunition was of the same brand or from the same

source as the casings found at the murder scene. See Tr. p. 830.

The significance of this evidence was limited. In its first opinion, the Missouri

Court of Appeals noted,

<u>**PETITION FOR REHEARING**</u> - Page 1

EXAMPLE PETITION FOR REHEARING (continued)

> The probative value of the live ammunition found in Smith's safe was minimal. The most that evidence could have established for the jury was that Smith owned or had access to the same type of ammunition used in the killing, although, from the testimony at trial, it is questionable whether those rounds were even the same type used to kill Hoskins.

State v. Smith, 966 S.W.2d 1, 9 (Mo. App. 1998).[1]

In its brief statement about why Mr. Smith has not demonstrated prejudice, this error is the first "fact" cited by the panel in connection with his testimony. It seems clear that this misstatement affect the judgment of the panel, requiring rehearing.

2. Legal error

The panel opinion is also based on a legal error. While the panel correctly cites "reasonable probability" as the standard for determining prejudice under *Strickland v. Washington*, 466 U.S. 668, 687-88 (1984), its analysis of the evidence shows that it misapplied the *Strickland v. Washington*, 466 U.S. 668, 687-88 (1984), prejudice standard.

The panel began by quoting the facts of the case from the opinion of the Missouri Western District Court of Appeals on direct appeal. That court, which was reviewing the conviction itself, necessarily recited the facts in the light most favorable to the verdict. As authority for relying on the facts of the direct appeal opinion, the panel cited *Chavez v.*

---

[1] There was evidence that shell casings matching those found at the crime scene were located OUTSIDE of Mr. Smith's house. Resp. Ex. 1b p. 884. But Mr. Smith's testimony would have explained that Ricky Sosa had fired shots outside his house on the same night as the Indiana Street incident; he so testified during the pretrial hearing on the motion to suppress evidence. Resp. Ex. 1a, p. 97.

PETITION FOR REHEARING - Page 2

EXAMPLE PETITION FOR REHEARING (continued)

Weber, 497 F.3d 796, 799 (8ᵗʰ Cir. 2007). The *Chavez* court gave no rationale for relying on the facts as stated by the direct review court. It did cite *Bucklew v. Luebbers*, 436 F.3d 1010, 1013 (8ᵗʰ Cir.), *cert. denied*, 549 U.S. 1079 (2006). But that case, while it employed the same procedure, also gave no rationale.

The problem with a court conducting *Strickland* prejudice review relying on a recitation of the facts which ignores all evidence and inferences contrary to the verdict is that *Strickland* requires that the court consider *all* of the evidence admitted at trial, as well as the evidence that could have been admitted had the defendant had effective assistance of counsel, in applying the reasonable probability standard. *Strickland v. Washington*, 466 U.S. 668, 687-88 (1984*). Rompilla v. Beard*, 545 U.S. 374 (2005); *Wiggins v. Smith*, 539 U.S. 510 (2003); *Williams (Terry) v. Taylor*, 529 U.S. 362 (2000).

Because of the failure to consider the entire record, the panel ignored evidence which contradicted the recitation in the opinion of the Missouri Court of Appeals. For example, the opinion refers to the "testimony of witnesses who saw [Mr. Smith] with a gun and the victim's property shortly after the murder." Opinion, p. 8. This is an apparent reference to the statement in the court of appeals opinion, quoted by the panel, "Sanchez told police that Smith. . . had a gun tucked into his waistband." Opinion, p. 4.² The panel ignores, however, the *trial testimony* of Sanchez that it was not true that Mr. Smith had a

---

² The opinion refers to "witnesses" who saw Mr. Smith with a gun after Hoskins's murder, but Sanchez is the only such witness cited in the opinion. Roxana Soriano testified that she heard guns being cocked while Mr. Smith was in the car with Hoskins, Glavin, and Sosa, but that Mr. Smith's hands were on the steering wheel and he could not have cocked a gun. Resp. Ex. 1b, p. 424.

PETITION FOR REHEARING - Page 3

EXAMPLE PETITION FOR REHEARING (continued)

handgun when she saw him, Resp. Ex. 1b, p. 706, and her denial that she had ever said

that Mr. Smith had a gun. Resp. Ex. 1b, p. 708. Ms. Sanchez also testified at trial that Mr.

Glavin had left her home before Mr. Smith and Mr. Sosa, contradicting Mr. Glavin's

testimony that they left together and picked up Mr. Hoskins together. Resp. Ex. 1b, p.

712. In addition to misstating the contents of the safe at Mr. Smith's house, the panel also

apparently ignored the fact that identification belonging to someone other than Mr.

Smith, Jose Sosa, was also found in the safe. Resp. Ex. 1a, p. 63. In light of this

evidence, it is not even clear that Mr. Smith was the person who placed the ammunition

in the safe.

The panel's statement that Mr. Smith's testimony would not have "refuted" the

testimony of witnesses who saw him with Mr. Hoskins's bicycle is technically correct.

But it would have *explained* it; Mr. Smith would have testified that after Mr. Glavin

returned in the car, Ricky Sosa retrieved the bicycle from it and gave it to Mr. Smith.

Resp. Ex. 6, pp. 65-66, Resp. Ex. 7, p. 95.

The panel made reference to the lack of credibility of Mr. Carrillo, who was

described as "Smith's longtime friend and a convicted drug dealer who was incarcerated

at the time of trial." Opinion, p. 8. But the state's witness, Kevin Glavin, claimed at trial

that he was unable to remember the murder. He had been convicted of tampering,

robbery and theft. Resp. Ex. 1b pp. 477, 575. He was under the influence of drugs on the

day of the murder. Resp. Ex. 1b p. 577. He had initially given a statement which did not

PETITION FOR REHEARING - Page 4

EXAMPLE PETITION FOR REHEARING (continued)

implicate Mr. Smith, and only changed that story when he himself was accused of the murder. Resp. Ex. 1a p. 316.

While Mr. Carrillo's credibility was less than optimum, his testimony contradicted that of Lorie and Kathy Stone, who also had credibility problems. They failed to appear for trial, and their prior testimony was read to the jury. This included Lorie Stone's testimony that she and Cathy were both on crack at the time of the Indiana Street incident, and that she (Lorie) smoked crack before giving a statement to the police. Resp Ex. 1b, pp. 773, 777. The Indiana Street incident was "collateral" in that it was not the murder itself, but it was an integral part of the state's attempt to connect Mr. Smith to the murder by physical evidence. Resp. Ex. 1b, p. 998. The panel failed to note that Mr. Carrillo's explanation of that incident fit the physical evidence seized there, while the version of the Stones did not. Resp. Ex. 1b, p. 788. In light of the state's lack of credible evidence about this critical incident, Mr. Carrillo's testimony would, to a reasonable probability, have made a difference.

In finding that because of the "substantial evidence" of Mr. Smith's guilt, he could not show prejudice, the panel apparently also ignored the fact that Mr. Smith's first trial (at which Mr. Glavin actually testified about the murder) ended in a hung jury. Before announcing that it could not arrive at a verdict, the first jury asked the court, "Can we find guilty of being present but not actually shooting the gun?"

PETITION FOR REHEARING - Page 5

EXAMPLE PETITION FOR REHEARING (continued)

The panel failed to cite *Stanley v. Bartley*, 465 F.3d 810, 814 (7th Cir. 2006), which was cited in Mr. Smith's brief and discussed in oral argument. There, the court held that:

> The issue is not whether Stanley is innocent, but whether if he had had a competent lawyer he would have had a reasonable chance (it needn't be a 50 percent or greater chance, *Miller v. Anderson*, 255 F.3d 455, 459 (7th Cir.2001)) of being acquitted; given that guilt must be proved beyond a reasonable doubt, guilty people are often acquitted.

This Court has held that in determining whether a state court has reasonably applied United States constitutional law, cases which have decided "factually similar issues" should be considered. *Copeland v. Washington*, 237 F.3d 969, 974 (8th Cir. 2000). The facts of *Stanley* are highly similar to those here, and the same result should apply.

Had the panel considered *all* of the evidence presented at trial, together with the evidence that would have been presented had Mr. Smith and Mr. Carrillo testified, it is clear that there is at least a reasonable probability of a different outcome to Mr. Smith's trial.

CONCLUSION

For the foregoing reasons, appellant Zachary Smith prays that this court grant rehearing, and that upon rehearing, he be discharged from his unlawful conviction and sentence.

Respectfully submitted,

/S/ ELIZABETH UNGER CARLYLE

PETITION FOR REHEARING - Page 6

EXAMPLE PETITION FOR REHEARING (concluded)

Elizabeth Unger Carlyle
P.O. Box 866
Columbus, MS 39703
Missouri Bar No. 41930
 (816)525-6540
FAX (866) 764-1240
elizcar@bellsouth.net

ATTORNEY FOR APPELLANT

CERTIFICATE REGARDING SERVICE

I hereby certify that it is my belief and
understanding that counsel for respondent,
Stephen D. Hawke, Asst. Atty. Gen., is a
participant in the Court's CM/ECF program and
that separate service of the foregoing document
is not required beyond the Notification of
Electronic Filing to be forwarded on March 4,
2009, upon the filing of the foregoing
document.

/S/ ELIZABETH UNGER CARLYLE

PETITION FOR REHEARING - Page 7

EXAMPLE PETITION FOR REHEARING AND/OR REHEARING EN BANC

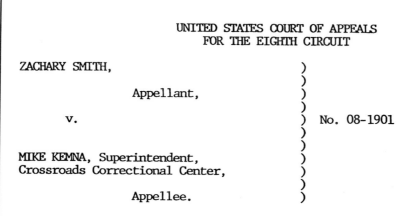

UNITED STATES COURT OF APPEALS
FOR THE EIGHTH CIRCUIT

ZACHARY SMITH,)
)
Appellant,)
)
v.) No. 08-1901
)
)
MIKE KEMNA, Superintendent,)
Crossroads Correctional Center,)
)
Appellee.)

PETITION FOR REHEARING AND/OR REHEARING EN BANC

WITH SUGGESTIONS IN SUPPORT

COMES NOW Appellant, Zachary Smith, and respectfully requests this Court to grant rehearing and/or rehearing en banc, pursuant to FRAP Rules 35(A);(B) and 40. In support of petition, Mr. Smith states the following.

REASONS MERITING REHEARING AND/OR REHEARING EN BANC

1. The panel's decision is in conflict with **Strickland V. Washington**, 466 U.S. 668 (1984); and **Williams (Terry) Taylor**, 529 U.S. 362 (2000), emphasizing that in determining **Strickland** prejudice, the court must examine both the trial testimony and the post-conviction evidence to determine whether, had the omitted evidence been presented, there is a reasonable probability of a different outcome, in that the panel merely examined the opinion of the Missouri Court of Appeals which stated the facts in the light most favorable to the jury's verdict and all contrary evidence ignored. For example, the state court's opinion states; "Sanchez later told the police that Smith had arrived in a newer, four-door burgundy or red car and had a gun tucked into his waistband." The panel completely ignored the fact that Rose Sanchez testified that Smith, Sosa and Glavin had come to her house and Smith was not in possession of a gun. She

1

EXAMPLE PETITION FOR REHEARING AND/OR REHEARING EN BANC (continued)

testified that Smith and Sosa stayed there at her house and Glavin left.
She further testified that she had sex with Smith and he stayed with her
until morning. (Resp. Ex. 1b, pp. 699-718).

The panel further ignored the fact that inside the safe there was
an inmate ID card for Jose Sosa, which jurors could have easily believed
Smith was not the only person that had access to the 45-caliber ammunition.
Furthermore, the state court stated; "The probative value of the live
ammunition found in Smith's safe was minimal. The most that evidence could
have established for the jury was that Smith owned or had access to the
same type of ammunition used in the killing. Although, from the testimony
at trial, it is questionable whether those rounds were even the same type
used to kill Hoskins." State V. Smith, 966 S.W.2d 1, at 8 (Mo.App.1997).
These conclusions are supported by the jury in the first trial when they
sent down a note that read; "can we be a hung jury? We are eight to four
after much discussion. Can we find guilty of being present but not actually
shooting the gun?"

The panel also ignored Smith's post-conviction testimony that Sosa
shot off two rounds at his house on the same night as the Indiana incident.
(Resp. Ex. 6, p. 66, Resp. Ex. 7, pp. 91-97; L.F. 90-91). This is clear
by its conclusion, "Smith's testimony would not have explained how shell
casings matching those found at the murder scene were located inside his
house in a locked safe." (panel's opinion p. 8).

2. The panel's decision is in conflict with Copeland V. Washington,
237 F.3d 969, 974 (8th Cir. 2000); and Stanley V. Bartley, 465 F.3d 810
(7th Cir. 2006), which case is both legally and factually similar that
the same result reached in Stanley is also required here. (See suggestions
in support herein).

2

EXAMPLE PETITION FOR REHEARING AND/OR REHEARING EN BANC (continued)

3. The panel overlooked or misapprehended both matter of material facts and law when it concluded, "Even if Carrillo and Smith had testified, there is no reasonable probability that the result of the trial would have been different. Carrillo would have lacked credibility as Smith's longtime friend and a convicted drug dealer who was incarcerated at the time of trial. Further, Carrillo would have testified only to matters collateral to the events on the night of the killing." The question of Carrillo's credibility are for a jury to decide, not the court. A jury could find him credible simply because his testimony directly refutes Kathy and Lorri Stones' statements that they saw Smith in possession of and firing the weapon used to shot the victim, in that Carrillo's testimony is consistent with the location of where the casings were found. The Stone's statments that were read to the jury were not, they were clearly contradicted by the physical evidence. (Resp. Ex. 1b, pp. 782-784, 787, 797).

Statement of Facts

At a third trial, Zachary Smith was convicted by a jury of first degree murder and armed criminal action and sentenced to life without the possibility of parole and ninety-nine years.

According to the state's key witness, Kevin Glavin, Glavin was a passenger with Smith, Jose "Ricky" Sosa, and Derek Hoskins in a car Smith borrowed on June 23, 1995, cruising around the Northeast area of Kansas City, Missouri. They arrived in an area called Cliff Drive. Glavin told Smith that he needed to urinate, so Smith stopped the car underneath a street light and then backed up the car away from the light. Glavin believed that something was wrong, because there was no need for Smith to back up the car in such an isolated area. Glavin warned Hoskins to stay in the car. Hoskins, however, insisted that he also had to urinate.

3

EXAMPLE PETITION FOR REHEARING AND/OR REHEARING EN BANC (continued)

Glavin walked toward the back of the car, turned to the curb, and began to urinate. Hoskins stood next to him, closer to the driver's side of the car, and also started to urinate. Smith got out of the car, walked behind Glavin and Hoskins, and stood between them. Glavin heard a gunshot, looked up, and saw a bright flash. He saw Smith holding a pistol and lowering his arm, one to three feet away from Hoskins. Hoskins went limp and fell to the ground. Both Smith and Glavin got back in the car. Smith clicked another round into the chamber of the gun. He fired the round out the window towards Hoskins body.

According to Glavin, Smith killed Hoskins because Hoskins stole Smith's lawnmower a week or two prior to the shooting. However, Hoskins allegedly committed a burglary to pay Smith back. The state offered no evidence to support that Hoskins committed a burglary on the night in question.

Although the state of Missouri presented much testimony regarding events preceding and after Hoskins' death, it presented just one eyewitness, Kevin Glavin, to testify regarding the actual shooting. Glavin, however, lacked credibility. Glavin admitted that he had prior convictions for second degree robbery and theft. He also admitted that he smoked crack cocaine and drank beer prior to the events at issue, that he had possibly used cocaine as many as five times that day, and had used cocaine frequently in the 48 hours prior to the shooting. Glavin conceded that he had been charged with murder in the first degree and armed criminal action with regard to Hoskins' death, but the charges were dismissed after he implicated Smith in the crimes. He admitted that his Clay County charge of second degree robbery also was reduced to stealing, which he pled guilty.

Additionally, Glavin changed his version of the events. Initially, Glavin told the police that Smith had no involvement in Hoskins' death.

4

EXAMPLE PETITION FOR REHEARING AND/OR REHEARING EN BANC (continued)

He later changed his account to implicate Smith as the shooter. (Resp. Ex. 1b, pp. 473-601).

The state presented evidence that shells collected at 411 Indiana in Kansas City, Missouri, matched the shells that killed Hoskins. (Weapon itself was not found)(Resp. Ex. 1b, pp 791, 804, 889-895). The state also presented out-of-court statements of witnesses Cathy and Lori Stone that Smith had fired a weapon at 411 Indiana two weeks before Hoskins' death. (Res. Ex. 1b, pp. 625, 675, 782). The testimony of the Stones from Smith's second trial was read to the jury by the state over defense objection; the witnesses could not be located for the third trial. (Resp. Ex. 1b, pp. 615-618). In their testimony, the Stones repudiated their prior statements that they ever actually saw Smith shoot a gun. They testified that they were both under the influence of crack cocaine at the time their statements were made. Moreover, the physical evidence presented at trial contradicted the Stone's account. Detective Beard testified that the shells found at 411 Indiana were not located where they would have been had Smith actually fired from the location specified by the Stones, making their statments that they actually saw Smith shoot a gun questionable. (Resp. Ex. 1b, pp. 782-784, 787, 797. Nonetheless, the state relied heavily on the match between the Indiana Street shells and the shells which killed Hoskins to connect Smith to the murder weapon. The state vehemently argued at trial that this evidence established Smith was the killer because he had possession of and fired the murder weapon two weeks before. (Resp. Ex. 1b, pp. 313-314, 998-999).

Failing to Interview and Call as a Witness Alvino Carrillo

Alvino Carrillo testified at the post-conviction hearing that he had been present at the Indiana Street incident referred to by the Stones.

EXAMPLE PETITION FOR REHEARING AND/OR REHEARING EN BANC (continued)

He said that Smith did not fire a weapon that night. Instead, Carrillo testified that the shots were fired at Smith, among others and Mr. Sosa exchanged fire. (Resp. Ex. 6, pp. 43). Carrillo's testimony would have refuted the Stone's statements that they saw Smith in possession of and firing the weapon that was used to shoot Hoskins. The uncontradicted evidence from the post-conviction hearing was that Smith informed counsel of Carrillo and what he would say, and trial counsel never contacted Carrillo. (Resp. Ex. 6, pp. 44, 49; Exhibit A attached to Petitioner's Traverse). Smith also testified that not only did he not fire the shots outside Indiana, but as far as he knew Kevin Glavin, and not he, had killed Hoskins. (Resp. Ex. 6, p. 66, Resp. Ex. 7, pp. 91-97).

Suggestions in Support of Rehearing and/or Rehearing En Banc

The Missouri Court of Appeals' decsion that Smith could not overcome the presumption that the decision by trial counsel not to interview or call Mr. Carrillo as a witness was trial strategy resulted in both an unreasonable determination of the facts in light of the evidence presented and an unreasonable application of **Strickland V. Washington,** because counsel's failure to even interview Mr. Carrillo was unreasonable and Smith's evidence that he informed counsel of Mr. Carrillo meets the first prong of **Strickland.** As in **Anderson V. Johnson,** 338 F.3d 382, 393 (5th Cir. 2003); "[T]here is no' evidene that counsel's decision to forego investigation was reasoned at all, and it is, in our opinion, far from reasonable. Counsel's failure to investigate was not 'part of a calculated trial strategy' but is likely the result of either indolence or imcompetence. As the court put it in **Bryant V. Scott,** 28 F.3d 1411, 1415 (5th Cir. 1994), "[A]n attorney must engage in a reasonable amount of pretrial investigation and 'at a minimum...interview potential witnesses

EXAMPLE PETITION FOR REHEARING AND/OR REHEARING EN BANC (continued)

and...make an independent investigation of the facts and circumstances

in the case"(quoting **Nealy V. Cabana**, 764 F.2d 1173, 1177 (5th Cir. 1985).

Under the circumstances here, the state had the burden to show a strategy

supporting the failure to interview Mr. Carrillo. Because he failed to

do so, Smith has met the "performance prong" of the **Strickland V.**

Washington, 466 U.S. 668, 687-88 (1984) test. **Riley V. Payne**, 352 F.3d

1313, 1319 (9th Cir. 2003). See also **White V. Roper**, 416 F.3d 728, 732

(8th Cir. 2005). The question for this Court to anwser is whether Smith

was prejudiced by counsel's ineffectiveness.

The state court held that Smith had not demonstrated prejudice from

the failure to call Carrillo. The court suggested that the evidence against

Smith was "overwhelming" and therefore Carrillo would not have made no

difference. This conclusion is likewise an unreasonable interpretation

of **Strickland** and its progeny. **Williams (Terry) Taylor**, 529 U.S. 362 (2000),

emphasizes that in determining **strickland** prejudice, the court must examine

both the trial testimony and the post-conviction evidence to determine

whether, had the omitted evidence been presented, there is a reasonable

probability of a different outcome.

To the extent that inferior federal courts have decided factually

similar cases, reference to those decisions is appropriate in assessing

the reasonableness...of the state court's treatment of the contested issue.

Copeland V. Washington, 237 F.3d 969, 974 (8th Cir. 2000). Smith refers

this Court to **Stanley V. Bartley**, 465 F.3d 810 (7th Cir. 2006)(Smith has

also attached a copy of case to this petition).

As was the case in **Stanley**, the issue is not whether Smith is innocent,

but whether if he had had a competent lawyer he would have had a reasonable

chance (it needn't be a 50 percent or greater chance; **Miller v. Anderson**,

7

EXAMPLE PETITION FOR REHEARING AND/OR REHEARING EN BANC (continued)

255 F.3d 455, 459 (7th Cir. 2001), of being acquitted; given that guilt must be proved beyond a reasonable doubt, guilty people are often acquitted.

Similarly, given Glavin's rampant use of crack cocaine leading up to the shooting, his criminal background, and his self-interest in shifting blame for the shooting away from himself and onto Smith, the jury easily could have disbelieved his account of Hoskins' death. In fact, the first trial of Smith's resulted in a mistrial after the jury sent down a note reading, "can we be a hung jury? We are eight to four after much discussion. Can we find guilty of being present but not actually shooting the gun?" (Appellant's Appendix, A-142). These jurors clearly did not credit either the weak ballistics evidence or the testimony of Kevin Glavin. And one of the jurors at the most recent trial contacted trial counsel and said that he was confused and had serious reservations and reasonable doubt that existed in his mind, as well as in the mind of other jurors, and wished to change his verdict. (Resp. Ex 1b, pp. 112, 1060-1061).

There were other witnesses, but their testimony was distinctly secondary and circumstantial. Smith did not make any admissions to police, and the statements he made, proved nothing. Reasonable jurors could have believed that Smith was merely being uncooperative with the police at the time of his questioning. Smith's possession of the victim's bicycle after the murder is circumstantial and is not conclusive evidence that Smith was the shooter of Hoskins. It was the combination of Glavin's and the Stone's testimony that they saw Smith shoot a gun that matched the shells at the crime scene that convicted Smith of first degree murder. Had Carrillo been called as a witness and testified that Mr. Sosa fired the gun, not Smith, there is a reasonable probability that the jury would have disregarded the Stone's testimony and the shell casing evidence because

8

EXAMPLE PETITION FOR REHEARING AND/OR REHEARING EN BANC (continued)

there was no other witnesses that put the murder weapon in Smith's hands before or after Hoskins' death.

Rose Sanchez testified that Smith, Sosa and Glavin came to her house and Smith was not in possession of a gun. She testified that Smith and Sosa stayed at her house and Glavin left. She further testified that she had sex with Smith and he stayed with her until morning. (Resp. Ex. 1b, pp. 699-718). Inside the safe there was an inmate ID card for Jose Sosa, which jurors could have easily believed Smith was not the only person who had access to the 45-caliber ammunition. And as found by the first trial jurors, they could have easily believed that Smith was never in possession of the gun used to kill Hoskins on the night of the shooting.

The result reached in **Stanley** is also required here. The state's witnesses in this case were highly suspect, not overwhelmingly compelling. Mr. Glavin, a cocaine addict and convicted felon, could have been the murderer. In fact, when defense counsel asked Glavin if he killed Hoskins, Glavin said he couldn't remember whether he had killed Hoskins or not. (Resp. Ex. 1b, pp. 598-600). Kathy and Lori Stone were under the influence of crack cocaine at the time the events they testified about occurred, and their testimony was contradicted by the physical evidence. Nonetheless, the state relied heavily on the match between the casings found at 411 Indiana and the bullet which killed Hoskins to convict Smith. The testimony of Mr. Carrillo would have contradicted their testimony. Moreover, had Mr. Carrillo testified, Smith would have also testified. In his testimony, he would have set out the facts contained in his amended post-conviction motion. (Resp. Ex. 7, pp. 91-97, Resp. Ex. 6, pp. 65-66).

Specifically, Smith would have explained that on the evening of Hoskins' murder, he, Glavin and Sosa were driving around in Mr. Hampton's

9

EXAMPLE PETITION FOR REHEARING AND/OR REHEARING EN BANC (continued)

car looking for cocaine and saw Hoskins. Hoskins and Glavin (who was intoxicated) began arguing about Glavin's alleged theft of cocaine from a friend of Hoskins. Smith intervened and cooled the parties down. Eventually, Hoskins got in the car with them, and Glavin apologized and shook hands with him.

After a fruitless search for drugs, Glavin and Hoskins dropped Smith off at the home of Flo Brown. Later, Glavin returned alone and told Smith, Rose Sanchez, and Sosa that he had an argument with Hoskins and killed him. Glavin brought Hoskins' bike back in the car. Smith took the bike out of the car and returned the car to the owner; he gave the bike to Sandra Cordray in exchange for a power drill she was trying to sell.

Smith would have also explained that he did not fire any shots during the incident at 411 Indiana and the two shells in his yard were there from Sosa shooting a gun off on the same night as the Indiana incident.

Smith never made any admissions to the police. The closest thing to direct evidence connecting him to the crime was Glavin. Had the jury heard the testimony of Carrillo and Smith, there is a reasonable probability of a different outcome.

For the foregoing reasons, Smith prays this Court grant rehearing and/or rehearing En Banc. He further prays for any other and further relief which the Court may deem just and proper under the circumstances.

Respectfully submitted,

ZACHARY SMITH,
Reg. No 521163
CRCC
1115 E. Pence Rd.,
Cameron, MO 64429

Appellant

EXAMPLE PETITION FOR REHEARING AND/OR REHEARING EN BANC (continued)

CERTIFICATE OF SERVICE

The undersigned hereby certifies that a copy of the foregoing was mailed, postage prepaid, this 10th day of February, 2009, to; Michael Spillane, Assistant Attorney General, P.O. Box 899, Jefferson City, Missouri 65102.

_____
Appellant

11

EXAMPLE PETITION FOR REHEARING AND/OR REHEARING EN BANC (concluded)

<u>TABLE OF APPENDIX</u>

1) Panel's decision issued 2/2/09.

2) Copy of Stanley V. Bartley, 465 F.3d 810 (7th Cir. 2006).

EXAMPLE ORDER DENYING PETITION FOR REHEARING

Case: 08-1901   Page: 1   Date Filed: 04/01/2009 Entry ID: 3532811

UNITED STATES COURT OF APPEALS
FOR THE EIGHTH CIRCUIT

No: 08-1901

Zachary A. Smith,

Appellant

v.

Mike Kemna, Superintendent, Crossroads Correctional Center,

Appellee

Appeal from U.S. District Court for the Western District of Missouri - St. Joseph
(5:07-cv-06068-ODS)

ORDER

The pro se petition for rehearing en banc filed by appellant is denied. The petition for rehearing by the panel is also denied.

The petition for rehearing by panel filed by appellant's counsel is also denied.

April 01, 2009

Order Entered at the Direction of the Court:
Clerk, U.S. Court of Appeals, Eighth Circuit.

/s/ Michael E. Gans

EXAMPLE JUDGMENT

UNITED STATES COURT OF APPEALS
FOR THE EIGHTH CIRCUIT

No: 08-1901

Zachary Smith,

Petitioner - Appellant

v.

Mike Kemna, Superintendent, Crossroads Correctional Center,

Respondent - Appellee

Appeal from U.S. District Court for the Western District of Missouri - St. Joseph
(5:07-cv-06068-ODS)

JUDGMENT

This appeal from the United States District Court was submitted on the record of the

district court, briefs of the parties and was argued by counsel.

After consideration, it is hereby ordered and adjudged that the judgment of the district

court in this cause is affirmed in accordance with the opinion of this Court.

February 02, 2009

Order Entered in Accordance with Opinion:
Clerk, U.S. Court of Appeals, Eighth Circuit.

/s/ Michael E. Gans

10. PETITION FOR WRIT OF CERTIORARI FROM U.S. SUPREME COURT

CONSIDERATIONS GOVERNING REVIEW ON CERTIORARI

United States Supreme Court Rule 10. Review on a writ of certiorari is not a matter of right, but of judicial discretion. A petition for a writ of certiorari will be granted only for compelling reasons. The following, although neither controlling nor fully measuring the Court's discretion, indicate the character of the reasons the Court considers.

(a) a United States court of appeals has entered a decision in conflict with the decision of another United States court of appeals on the same important matter; has decided an important federal question in a way that conflicts with a decision by a state court of last resort; or has so far departed from the accepted and usual course of judicial proceedings, or sanctioned such a departure by a lower court, as to call for an exercise of this Court's supervisory power;

(b) a state court of last resort has decided an important federal question in a way that conflicts with the decision of another state court of last resort or of a United States court of appeals;

(c) a state court or a United States court of appeals has decided an important question of federal law that has not been, but should be, settled by this Court, or has decided an important federal question in a way that conflicts with relevant decisions of this Court.

A petition for a writ of certiorari is rarely granted when the asserted error consists of erroneous factual findings or the misapplication of a properly stated rule of law.

PREPARATION OF PETITION

Upon written request, the United States Supreme Court clerk will send you a packet for preparing a petition for a writ of certiorari for indigent petitioners who are proceeding *in forma pauperis* and without the assistance of counsel. I've enclosed an example letter, and a copy of the packet the clerk will send you, at the end of this chapter. I've also enclosed a petition, filed by an attorney, you may refer to when preparing your own petition.

If you were appointed an attorney in the United States court of appeals, he or she is required to file a petition for a writ of certiorari on your behalf, if the attorney believes grounds exist warranting review by the United States Supreme Court.

If you were not granted a certificate of appealability, you'll have to prepare the petition on your own. The packet provided by the clerk of the United States Supreme Court includes step-by-step instructions to guide you.

TIME FOR FILING

You must file your petition within 90 days from the date of the entry of the final judgment in the United States court of appeals from the denial of a timely petition for rehearing, or rehearing en banc. The issuance of a mandate after judgment has been entered has no bearing on the computation of time and does not extend the time for filing. *Supreme Court Rules 13.1 and 13.3.*

Filing in the Supreme Court means the actual receipt of your petition by the clerk; or its deposit in the United States mail, with first-class postage prepaid, on or before the final date allowed for filing. A petition is timely filed if it is deposited in your institution's internal mail system on or before the last day for filing and is accompanied by a notarized statement or declaration, in compliance with 28 U.S.C. 1746, setting out the date of deposit and stating that first-class postage has been prepaid. *Supreme Court Rule 29.2.*

NUMBER OF COPIES TO FILE

When you are an inmate confined in an institution and not represented by counsel, you need only file the original of the motion for leave to proceed *in forma pauperis*, the affidavit or declaration in support of the motion for leave to proceed *in forma pauperis*, the petition for a writ of certiorari, and proof of service. These forms are provided in the packet from the clerk of the Supreme Court.

PAGE LIMITATION

The petition for a writ of certiorari may not exceed 40 pages, excluding the pages that precede Page 1 of the form, such as the cover page, the question[s] presented, the table of contents, and the table of authorities. The documents in the appendix to the petition do not count toward the page limit either. *Supreme Court Rule 33.2(b).* It is best to keep your petition brief, concise, and to the point.

MAILING AND SERVING RESPONDENT

You must mail your petition to:

> The Office of the Clerk
> Supreme Court of the United States
> Washington, DC 20543

It must also be served on the respondent or their counsel in accordance with Rule 29. The respondent is the same party you sent all your pleadings to during litigation in the district court and the United States court of appeals.

DECISION OF THE UNITED STATES SUPREME COURT

Once a decision is made as to whether your case will be heard, the Clerk of the Supreme Court will immediately send you a copy. In my experience, these decisions consist of a single page either granting or denying your petition.

If the Court decides to hear your case, it will immediately appoint counsel to represent you during the Supreme Court's review.

PETITION FOR REHEARING

United States Supreme Court Rule 44. Rehearing.

1. Any petition for the rehearing of any judgment or decision of the Court on the merits shall be filed within 25 days after entry of the judgment or decision, unless the Court or a Justice shortens or extends the time. The petitioner shall file 40 copies of the rehearing petition and shall pay the filing fee prescribed by Rule 38(b), except that a petitioner proceeding *in forma pauperis* under Rule 39, including an inmate of an institution, shall file the number of copies required for a petition by such a person under Rule 12.2. The petition shall be served as required by Rule 29. The petition shall be presented together with certification of counsel (or of a party unrepresented by counsel) that it is presented in good faith and not for delay; one copy of the certificate shall bear the signature of counsel or of a party unrepresented by counsel. A copy of the certificate shall follow and be attached to each copy of the petition. A petition for rehearing is not subject to oral argument and will not be granted except by a majority of the Court, at the instance of a Justice who concurred in the judgment or decision.

2. Any petition for the rehearing of an order denying a petition for a writ of certiorari or extraordinary writ shall be filed within 25 days after the date of the order of denial and shall comply with all the form and filing requirements of paragraph 1 of this Rule, including the payment of the filing fee if required, but its grounds shall be limited to intervening circumstances of a substantial or controlling effect or to other substantial grounds not previously presented. The petition shall be presented together with certification of counsel (or of a party unrepresented by counsel) that it is restricted to the grounds specified in this paragraph and that it is presented in good faith and not for delay; one copy of the certificate shall bear the signature of counsel (or of a party unrepresented by counsel). The certificate shall be bound with each copy of the petition. The Clerk will not file a petition without a certificate. The petition is not subject to oral argument.

3. The Clerk will not file any response to a petition for rehearing unless the Court requests a response. In the absence of extraordinary circumstances, the Court will not grant a petition for rehearing without first requesting a response.

4. The Clerk will not file consecutive petitions and petitions that are out of time under this Rule.

5. The Clerk will not file any brief for an *amicus curiae* in support of, or in opposition to, a petition for rehearing.

6. If the Clerk determines that a petition for rehearing submitted timely and in good faith is in a form that does not comply with this Rule or with Rule 33 or Rule 34, the Clerk will return it with a letter indicating the deficiency. A corrected petition for rehearing submitted in accordance with Rule 29.2 no more than 15 days after the date of the Clerk's letter will be deemed timely.

I've provided an example copy of a petition for rehearing at the end of this chapter that you may refer to should you decide to file one.

EXAMPLE FORM LETTER REQUESTING WRIT OF CERTIORARI PACKET

October 27, 2010

Office of the Clerk

Supreme Court of the United States

Washington, DC 20543

Dear Clerk:

I would like to request a writ of certiorari packet for indigent petitioners please. Thank you for your time and assistance.

Respectfully,

Zachary Smith, #521163/4c-243

Crossroads Corr. Center

1115 E. Pence Road

Cameron, MO 64429

EXAMPLE WRIT OF CERTIORARI PACKET

October 2010

OFFICE OF THE CLERK
SUPREME COURT OF THE UNITED STATES
WASHINGTON, D. C. 20543

GUIDE FOR PROSPECTIVE INDIGENT PETITIONERS FOR WRITS OF CERTIORARI

I. Introduction

These instructions and forms are designed to assist petitioners who are proceeding *in forma pauperis* and without the assistance of counsel. A copy of the Rules of the Supreme Court, which establish the procedures that must be followed, is also enclosed. Be sure to read the following Rules carefully:

Rules 10-14 (Petitioning for certiorari)
Rule 29 (Filing and service on opposing party or counsel)
Rule 30 (Computation and extension of time)
Rules 33.2 and 34 (Preparing pleadings on 8½ x 11 inch paper)
Rule 39 (Proceedings *in forma pauperis*)

II. Nature of Supreme Court Review

It is important to note that review in this Court by means of a writ of certiorari is not a matter of right, but of judicial discretion. The primary concern of the Supreme Court is not to correct errors in lower court decisions, but to decide cases presenting issues of importance beyond the particular facts and parties involved. The Court grants and hears argument in only about 1% of the cases that are filed each Term. The vast majority of petitions are simply denied by the Court without comment or explanation. The denial of a petition for a writ of certiorari signifies only that the Court has chosen not to accept the case for review and does not express the Court's view of the merits of the case.

Every petitioner for a writ of certiorari is advised to read carefully the *Considerations Governing Review on Certiorari* set forth in Rule 10. Important considerations for accepting a case for review include the existence of a conflict between the decision of which review is sought and a decision of another appellate court on the same issue. An important function of the Supreme Court is to resolve disagreements among lower courts about specific legal questions. Another consideration is the importance to the public of the issue.

III. The Time for Filing

You must file your petition for a writ of certiorari within 90 days from the date of the entry of the final judgment in the United States court of appeals or highest state appellate court or 90 days from the denial of a timely filed petition for rehearing. The issuance of a mandate or remittitur after judgment has been entered has no bearing on the computation of time and does not extend the time for filing. See Rules 13.1 and

EXAMPLE WRIT OF CERTIORARI PACKET (continued)

13.3.   Filing in the Supreme Court means the actual receipt of documents by the Clerk; or their deposit in the United States mail, with first-class postage prepaid, on or before the final date allowed for filing; or their delivery to a third-party commercial carrier, on or before the final date allowed for filing, for delivery to the Clerk within 3 calendar days.   See Rule 29.2.

IV.   What To File

Unless you are an inmate confined in an institution and not represented by counsel, file:

—An original and ten copies of a motion for leave to proceed *in forma pauperis* and an original and 10 copies of an affidavit or declaration in support thereof.   See Rule 39.

—An original and 10 copies of a petition for a writ of certiorari with an appendix consisting of a copy of the judgment or decree you are asking this Court to review including any order on rehearing, and copies of any opinions or orders by any courts or administrative agencies that have previously considered your case.   See Rule 14.1(i).

—One affidavit or declaration showing that all opposing parties or their counsel have been served with a copy of the papers filed in this Court.   See Rule 29.

If you are an inmate confined in an institution and not represented by counsel, you need file only the original of the motion for leave to proceed *in forma pauperis*, affidavit or declaration in support of the motion for leave to proceed *in forma pauperis*, the petition for a writ of certiorari, and proof of service.

The attached forms may be used for the original motion, affidavit or declaration, and petition, and should be stapled together in that order.   The proof of service should be included as a detached sheet, and the form provided may be used.

V.   Page Limitation

The petition for a writ of certiorari may not exceed 40 pages excluding the pages that precede Page 1 of the form.   The documents required to be contained in the appendix to the petition do not count toward the page limit.   See Rule 33.2(b).

VI.   Method of Filing

All documents to be filed in this Court must be addressed to the Clerk, Supreme Court of the United States, Washington, D. C. 20543 and must be served on opposing parties or their counsel in accordance with Rule 29.

EXAMPLE WRIT OF CERTIORARI PACKET (continued)

INSTRUCTIONS FOR COMPLETING FORMS

I.   Motion for Leave to Proceed *In Forma Pauperis* - Rule 39

A. On the form provided for the motion for leave to proceed *in forma pauperis*, leave the case number blank. The number will be assigned by the Clerk when the case is docketed.

B. On the line in the case caption for "petitioner", type your name. As a *pro se* petitioner, you may represent only yourself. On the line for "respondent", type the name of the opposing party in the lower court. If there are multiple respondents, enter the first respondent, as the name appeared on the lower court decision, followed by "et al." to indicate that there are other respondents. The additional parties must be listed in the LIST OF PARTIES section of the petition.

C. If the lower courts in your case granted you leave to proceed *in forma pauperis*, check the appropriate space and indicate the court or courts that allowed you to proceed *in forma pauperis*. If none of the lower courts granted you leave to proceed *in forma pauperis*, check the block that so indicates.

D. Sign the motion on the signature line.

II.   Affidavit or Declaration in Support of Motion for Leave to Proceed *In Forma Pauperis*

On the form provided, answer fully each of the questions. If the answer to a question is "0," "none," or "not applicable (N/A)," enter that response. If you need more space to answer a question or to explain your answer, attach a separate sheet of paper, identified with your name and the question number. Unless each question is fully answered, the Clerk will not accept the petition. The form must either be notarized or be in the form of a declaration. See 28 U. S. C. § 1746.

III. Cover Page - Rule 34

When you complete the form for the cover page:

A. Leave case number blank. The number will be assigned by the Clerk when the case is docketed.

B. Complete the case caption as you did on the motion for leave to proceed *in forma pauperis*.

C. List the court from which the action is brought on the line following the words "on petition for a writ of certiorari to." If your case is from a state court, enter the name of the court that last addressed the merits of the case. For example, if the highest state court denied discretionary review, and the state court of appeals affirmed the decision of the trial court, the state court of appeals should be listed. If your case is federal, the United States court of

EXAMPLE WRIT OF CERTIORARI PACKET (continued)

appeals that decided your case will always be listed here.

D. Enter your name, address, and telephone number in the appropriate spaces.

IV. Question(s) Presented

On the page provided, enter the question or questions that you wish the Court to review. The questions must be concise. Questions presented in cases accepted for review are usually no longer than two or three sentences. The purpose of the question presented is to assist the Court in selecting cases. State the issue you wish the Court to decide clearly and without unnecessary detail.

V. List of Parties

On the page provided, check either the box indicating that the names of all parties appear in the caption of the case on the cover page or the box indicating that there are additional parties. If there are additional parties, list them. Rule 12.6 states that all parties to the proceeding whose judgment is sought to be reviewed shall be deemed parties in this Court, and that all parties other than petitioner shall be respondents. The court whose judgment you seek to have this Court review is **not** a party.

VI. Table of Contents

On the page provided, list the page numbers on which the required portions of the petition appear. Number the pages consecutively, beginning with the "Opinions Below" page as page 1.

VII. Index of Appendices

List the description of each document that is included in the appendix beside the appropriate appendix letter. Mark the bottom of the first page of each appendix with the appropriate designation, *e.g.*, "Appendix A." See Rule 14.1 pertaining to the items to be included in the appendix.

A. Federal Courts

If you are asking the Court to review a decision of a federal court, the decision of the United States court of appeals should be designated Appendix A. Appendix A should be followed by the decision of the United States District Court and the findings and recommendations of the United States magistrate judge, if there were any. If the United States court of appeals denied a timely filed petition for rehearing, a copy of that order should be appended next. If you are seeking review of a decision in a habeas corpus case, and the decision of either the United States District Court or the United States Court of Appeals makes reference to a state court decision in which you were a party, a copy of the state court decision must be included in the appendix.

B. State Courts

If you are asking the Court to review a decision of a state court, the decision of which review is sought should be designated Appendix A. Appendix A should be followed by the decision of the lower court or agency that was reviewed in the decision designated Appendix A. If the highest court of the state in which a

EXAMPLE WRIT OF CERTIORARI PACKET (continued)

decision could be had denied discretionary review, a copy of that order should follow. If an order denying a timely filed petition for rehearing starts the running of the time for filing a petition for a writ of certiorari pursuant to Rule 13.3, a copy of the order should be appended next.

As an example, if the state trial court ruled against you, the intermediate court of appeals affirmed the decision of the trial court, the state supreme court denied discretionary review and then denied a timely petition for rehearing, the appendices should appear in the following order:

Appendix A   Decision of State Court of Appeals

Appendix B   Decision of State Trial Court

Appendix C   Decision of State Supreme Court Denying Review

Appendix D   Order of State Supreme Court Denying Rehearing

VIII. Table of Authorities

On the page provided, list the cases, statutes, treatises, and articles that you reference in your petition, and the page number of your petition where each authority appears.

IX. Opinions Below

In the space provided, indicate whether the opinions of the lower courts in your case have been published, and if so, the citation for the opinion below. For example, opinions of the United States courts of appeals are published in the Federal Reporter. If the opinion in your case appears at page 100 of volume 30 of the Federal Reporter, Third Series, indicate that the opinion is reported at 30 F. 3d 100. If the opinion has been designated for publication but has not yet been published, check the appropriate space. Also indicate where in the appendix each decision, reported or unreported, appears.

X. Jurisdiction

The purpose of the jurisdiction section of the petition is to establish the statutory source for the Court's jurisdiction and the dates that determine whether the petition is timely filed. The form sets out the pertinent statutes for federal and state cases. You need provide only the dates of the lower court decisions that establish the timeliness of the petition for a writ of certiorari. If an extension of time within which to file the petition for a writ of certiorari was granted, you must provide the requested information pertaining to the extension. If you seek to have the Court review a decision of a state court, you must provide the date the highest state court decided your case, either by ruling on the merits or denying discretionary review.

EXAMPLE WRIT OF CERTIORARI PACKET (continued)

XI.   Constitutional and Statutory Provisions Involved

Set out verbatim the constitutional provisions, treaties, statutes, ordinances and regulations involved in the case.   If the provisions involved are lengthy, provide their citation and indicate where in the Appendix to the petition the text of the provisions appears.

XII.   Statement of the Case

Provide a **concise** statement of the case containing the facts material to the consideration of the question(s) presented; you should summarize the relevant facts of the case and the proceedings that took place in the lower courts. You may need to attach additional pages, but the statement should be concise and limited to the relevant facts of the case.

XIII.   Reasons for Granting the Petition

The purpose of this section of the petition is to explain to the Court why it should grant certiorari.   It is important to read Rule 10 and address what compelling reasons exist for the exercise of the Court's discretionary jurisdiction.   Try to show not only why the decision of the lower court may be erroneous, but the national importance of having the Supreme Court decide the question involved.   It is important to show whether the decision of the court that decided your case is in conflict with the decisions of another appellate court; the importance of the case not only to you but to others similarly situated; and the ways the decision of the lower court in your case was erroneous.   You will need to attach additional pages, but the reasons should be as concise as possible, consistent with the purpose of this section of the petition.

XIV.   Conclusion

Enter your name and the date that you submit the petition.

XV.   Proof of Service

You must serve a copy of your petition on counsel for respondent(s) as required by Rule 29.   If you serve the petition by first-class mail or by third-party commercial carrier, you may use the enclosed proof of service form.   If the United States or any department, office, agency, officer, or employee thereof is a party, you must serve the Solicitor General of the United States, Room 5614, Department of Justice, 950 Pennsylvania Ave., N.W., Washington, D. C. 20530–0001.   The lower courts that ruled on your case are not parties and need not be served with a copy of the petition.   The proof of service may be in the form of a declaration pursuant to 28 U. S. C. § 1746.

EXAMPLE WRIT OF CERTIORARI PACKET (continued)

No. _____

_____

IN THE

SUPREME COURT OF THE UNITED STATES

_____

_____ — PETITIONER

(Your Name)

VS.

_____ — RESPONDENT(S)

MOTION FOR LEAVE TO PROCEED *IN FORMA PAUPERIS*

The petitioner asks leave to file the attached petition for a writ of certiorari without prepayment of costs and to proceed *in forma pauperis.*

[ ] Petitioner has previously been granted leave to proceed *in forma pauperis* in the following court(s):

_____

_____

[ ] Petitioner has **not** previously been granted leave to proceed *in forma pauperis* in any other court.

Petitioner's affidavit or declaration in support of this motion is attached hereto.

_____

(Signature)

EXAMPLE WRIT OF CERTIORARI PACKET (continued)

**AFFIDAVIT OR DECLARATION
IN SUPPORT OF MOTION FOR LEAVE TO PROCEED *IN FORMA PAUPERIS***

I, _____, am the petitioner in the above-entitled case.   In support of my motion to proceed *in forma pauperis*, I state that because of my poverty I am unable to pay the costs of this case or to give security therefor; and I believe I am entitled to redress.

1. For both you and your spouse estimate the average amount of money received from each of the following sources during the past 12 months.   Adjust any amount that was received weekly, biweekly, quarterly, semiannually, or annually to show the monthly rate.   Use gross amounts, that is, amounts before any deductions for taxes or otherwise.

Income source	Average monthly amount during the past 12 months		Amount expected next month	
	You	Spouse	You	Spouse
Employment	$_____	$_____	$_____	$_____
Self-employment	$_____	$_____	$_____	$_____
Income from real property (such as rental income)	$_____	$_____	$_____	$_____
Interest and dividends	$_____	$_____	$_____	$_____
Gifts	$_____	$_____	$_____	$_____
Alimony	$_____	$_____	$_____	$_____
Child Support	$_____	$_____	$_____	$_____
Retirement (such as social security, pensions, annuities, insurance)	$_____	$_____	$_____	$_____
Disability (such as social security, insurance payments)	$_____	$_____	$_____	$_____
Unemployment payments	$_____	$_____	$_____	$_____
Public-assistance (such as welfare)	$_____	$_____	$_____	$_____
Other (specify): _____	$_____	$_____	$_____	$_____
Total monthly income:	$_____	$_____	$_____	$_____

EXAMPLE WRIT OF CERTIORARI PACKET (continued)

2. List your employment history for the past two years, most recent first.   (Gross monthly pay is before taxes or other deductions.)

Employer	Address	Dates of Employment	Gross monthly pay
_____	_____	_____	$_____
_____	_____	_____	$_____
_____	_____	_____	$_____

3. List your spouse's employment history for the past two years, most recent employer first. (Gross monthly pay is before taxes or other deductions.)

Employer	Address	Dates of Employment	Gross monthly pay
_____	_____	_____	$_____
_____	_____	_____	$_____
_____	_____	_____	$_____

4. How much cash do you and your spouse have? $_____
Below, state any money you or your spouse have in bank accounts or in any other financial institution.

Financial institution	Type of account	Amount you have	Amount your spouse has
_____	_____	$_____	$_____
_____	_____	$_____	$_____
_____	_____	$_____	$_____

5. List the assets, and their values, which you own or your spouse owns. Do not list clothing and ordinary household furnishings.

☐ Home
Value _____

☐ Other real estate
Value _____

☐ Motor Vehicle #1
Year, make & model _____
Value _____

☐ Motor Vehicle #2
Year, make & model _____
Value _____

☐ Other assets
Description _____
Value _____

EXAMPLE WRIT OF CERTIORARI PACKET (continued)

6. State every person, business, or organization owing you or your spouse money, and the amount owed.

Person owing you or your spouse money	Amount owed to you	Amount owed to your spouse
_____	$_____	$_____
_____	$_____	$_____
_____	$_____	$_____

7. State the persons who rely on you or your spouse for support.

Name	Relationship	Age
_____	_____	_____
_____	_____	_____
_____	_____	_____

8. Estimate the average monthly expenses of you and your family. Show separately the amounts paid by your spouse. Adjust any payments that are made weekly, biweekly, quarterly, or annually to show the monthly rate.

	You	Your spouse
Rent or home-mortgage payment (include lot rented for mobile home) Are real estate taxes included? ☐ Yes ☐ No Is property insurance included? ☐ Yes ☐ No	$_____	$_____
Utilities (electricity, heating fuel, water, sewer, and telephone)	$_____	$_____
Home maintenance (repairs and upkeep)	$_____	$_____
Food	$_____	$_____
Clothing	$_____	$_____
Laundry and dry-cleaning	$_____	$_____
Medical and dental expenses	$_____	$_____

EXAMPLE WRIT OF CERTIORARI PACKET (continued)

	You	Your spouse
Transportation (not including motor vehicle payments)	$_____	$_____
Recreation, entertainment, newspapers, magazines, etc.	$_____	$_____
Insurance (not deducted from wages or included in mortgage payments)		
Homeowner's or renter's	$_____	$_____
Life	$_____	$_____
Health	$_____	$_____
Motor Vehicle	$_____	$_____
Other: _____	$_____	$_____
Taxes (not deducted from wages or included in mortgage payments)		
(specify): _____	$_____	$_____
Installment payments		
Motor Vehicle	$_____	$_____
Credit card(s)	$_____	$_____
Department store(s)	$_____	$_____
Other: _____	$_____	$_____
Alimony, maintenance, and support paid to others	$_____	$_____
Regular expenses for operation of business, profession, or farm (attach detailed statement)	$_____	$_____
Other (specify): _____	$_____	$_____
Total monthly expenses:	$_____	$_____

EXAMPLE WRIT OF CERTIORARI PACKET (continued)

9. Do you expect any major changes to your monthly income or expenses or in your assets or liabilities during the next 12 months?

☐ Yes   ☐ No   If yes, describe on an attached sheet.

10. Have you paid – or will you be paying – an attorney any money for services in connection with this case, including the completion of this form?   ☐ Yes   ☐ No

If yes, how much? _____

If yes, state the attorney's name, address, and telephone number:

11. Have you paid—or will you be paying—anyone other than an attorney (such as a paralegal or a typist) any money for services in connection with this case, including the completion of this form?

☐ Yes   ☐ No

If yes, how much? _____

If yes, state the person's name, address, and telephone number:

12. Provide any other information that will help explain why you cannot pay the costs of this case.

I declare under penalty of perjury that the foregoing is true and correct.

Executed on: _____ , 20____

_____
(Signature)

EXAMPLE WRIT OF CERTIORARI PACKET (continued)

No. _____

_____

IN THE

SUPREME COURT OF THE UNITED STATES

_____

_____ — PETITIONER
(Your Name)

vs.

_____ — RESPONDENT(S)

ON PETITION FOR A WRIT OF CERTIORARI TO

_____
(NAME OF COURT THAT LAST RULED ON MERITS OF YOUR CASE)

PETITION FOR WRIT OF CERTIORARI

_____
(Your Name)

_____
(Address)

_____
(City, State, Zip Code)

_____
(Phone Number)

EXAMPLE WRIT OF CERTIORARI PACKET (continued)

QUESTION(S) PRESENTED

EXAMPLE WRIT OF CERTIORARI PACKET (continued)

LIST OF PARTIES

[ ] All parties appear in the caption of the case on the cover page.

[ ] All parties **do not** appear in the caption of the case on the cover page.   A list of all parties to the proceeding in the court whose judgment is the subject of this petition is as follows:

EXAMPLE WRIT OF CERTIORARI PACKET (continued)

TABLE OF CONTENTS

INDEX TO APPENDICES

EXAMPLE WRIT OF CERTIORARI PACKET (continued)

TABLE OF AUTHORITIES CITED

CASES   PAGE NUMBER

STATUTES AND RULES

OTHER

EXAMPLE WRIT OF CERTIORARI PACKET (continued)

IN THE

SUPREME COURT OF THE UNITED STATES

PETITION FOR WRIT OF CERTIORARI

Petitioner respectfully prays that a writ of certiorari issue to review the judgment below.

OPINIONS BELOW

[ ] For cases from **federal courts:**

The opinion of the United States court of appeals appears at Appendix _____ to the petition and is

[ ] reported at _____; or,
[ ] has been designated for publication but is not yet reported; or,
[ ] is unpublished.

The opinion of the United States district court appears at Appendix _____ to the petition and is

[ ] reported at _____; or,
[ ] has been designated for publication but is not yet reported; or,
[ ] is unpublished.

[ ] For cases from **state courts:**

The opinion of the highest state court to review the merits appears at Appendix _____ to the petition and is

[ ] reported at _____; or,
[ ] has been designated for publication but is not yet reported; or,
[ ] is unpublished.

The opinion of the _____ court appears at Appendix _____ to the petition and is

[ ] reported at _____; or,
[ ] has been designated for publication but is not yet reported; or,
[ ] is unpublished.

1.

EXAMPLE WRIT OF CERTIORARI PACKET (continued)

JURISDICTION

[ ] For cases from **federal courts:**

The date on which the United States Court of Appeals decided my case
was _____.

[ ] No petition for rehearing was timely filed in my case.

[ ] A timely petition for rehearing was denied by the United States Court of
Appeals on the following date: _____, and a copy of the
order denying rehearing appears at Appendix _____.

[ ] An extension of time to file the petition for a writ of certiorari was granted
to and including _____ (date) on _____ (date)
in Application No. ___A_____.

The jurisdiction of this Court is invoked under 28 U. S. C. § 1254(1).

[ ] For cases from **state courts:**

The date on which the highest state court decided my case was _____.
A copy of that decision appears at Appendix _____.

[ ] A timely petition for rehearing was thereafter denied on the following date:
_____, and a copy of the order denying rehearing
appears at Appendix _____.

[ ] An extension of time to file the petition for a writ of certiorari was granted
to and including _____ (date) on _____ (date) in
Application No. ___A_____.

The jurisdiction of this Court is invoked under 28 U. S. C. § 1257(a).

EXAMPLE WRIT OF CERTIORARI PACKET (continued)

CONSTITUTIONAL AND STATUTORY PROVISIONS INVOLVED

EXAMPLE WRIT OF CERTIORARI PACKET (continued)

STATEMENT OF THE CASE

EXAMPLE WRIT OF CERTIORARI PACKET (continued)

REASONS FOR GRANTING THE PETITION

EXAMPLE WRIT OF CERTIORARI PACKET (continued)

CONCLUSION

The petition for a writ of certiorari should be granted.

Respectfully submitted,

_____

Date: _____

EXAMPLE WRIT OF CERTIORARI PACKET (concluded)

No. _____

_____

IN THE

SUPREME COURT OF THE UNITED STATES

_____

_____ — **PETITIONER**

(Your Name)

VS.

_____ — **RESPONDENT(S)**

PROOF OF SERVICE

I, _____, do swear or declare that on this date, _____, 20__, as required by Supreme Court Rule 29 I have served the enclosed **MOTION FOR LEAVE TO PROCEED** *IN FORMA PAUPERIS* and **PETITION FOR A WRIT OF CERTIORARI** on each party to the above proceeding or that party's counsel, and on every other person required to be served, by depositing an envelope containing the above documents in the United States mail properly addressed to each of them and with first-class postage prepaid, or by delivery to a third-party commercial carrier for delivery within 3 calendar days.

The names and addresses of those served are as follows:

_____

_____

_____

I declare under penalty of perjury that the foregoing is true and correct.

Executed on _____, 20__

_____

(Signature)

EXAMPLE PETITION FOR WRIT OF CERTIORARI

No._____

IN THE SUPREME COURT OF THE UNITED STATES

ZACHARY SMITH,

Petitioner,

v.

MIKE KEMNA

Respondent.

ON PETITION FOR WRIT OF CERTIORARI TO THE EIGHTH CIRCUIT COURT OF APPEALS

APPLICATION FOR LEAVE TO PROCEED IN FORMA PAUPERIS

COMES NOW the petitioner, by and through counsel, and moves the Court for its order permitting him to file the attached petition for a writ of habeas corpus in forma pauperis. Petitioner proceeded *in forma pauperis* on appeal in the United States Court of Appeals for the Eighth Circuit, and is represented by the undersigned counsel pursuant to an appointment under the Criminal Justice Act.

Respectfully submitted,

Elizabeth Unger Carlyle
*Counsel of Record
P.O. Box 962
Columbus, MS 39703
(816)525-6540
FAX (866) 764-1249

ATTORNEY FOR PETITIONER

EXAMPLE PETITION FOR WRIT OF CERTIORARI (continued)

No._____

IN THE SUPREME COURT OF THE UNITED STATES

* * * * *

ZACHARY SMITH,

Petitioner,

v.

MIKE KEMNA

Respondent.

* * * * *

ON PETITION FOR WRIT OF CERTIORARI TO THE EIGHTH CIRCUIT COURT OF APPEALS

* * * * *

PETITION FOR WRIT OF CERTIORARI

* * * * *

ELIZABETH UNGER CARLYLE
(Counsel of Record)
P.O. Box 866
Columbus, MS 39703
816-525-6540

Counsel for Petitioner

EXAMPLE PETITION FOR WRIT OF CERTIORARI (continued)

QUESTION PRESENTED

Mr. Smith alleged that his trial counsel was ineffective for failing to call a witness of whom Mr. Smith made him aware. Mr. Smith was convicted, in large part, upon evidence that shell casings from another crime scene matched those found at the scene of the charged offense. The omitted witness would have testified that Mr. Smith did not fire shots at the other crime scene. In finding no prejudice, the Eighth Circuit relied upon the state court's statement of the facts on direct appeal, but significantly misstated even that slanted version of the fact. The case thus presents the following question.

Did the Eighth Circuit err in deferring to the state court finding that Mr. Smith was not prejudiced by his trial counsel's failure to call a witness who would have impeached the state's identification evidence when the Eighth Circuit decision was based on a flagrant misreading of the trial record?

EXAMPLE PETITION FOR WRIT OF CERTIORARI (continued)

TABLE OF CONTENTS

EXAMPLE PETITION FOR WRIT OF CERTIORARI (continued)

TABLE OF AUTHORITIES

EXAMPLE PETITION FOR WRIT OF CERTIORARI (continued)

PETITION FOR WRIT OF CERTIORARI TO THE MISSOURI SUPREME COURT

The Petitioner, Zachary Smith, respectfully prays that a Writ of Certiorari issue to review the judgment and opinion of the Eighth Circuit Court of Appeals, rendered in these proceedings on February 2, 2009.

OPINION BELOW

The Eighth Circuit Court of Appeals affirmed petitioner's conviction in its Cause no. 08-1901. The opinion is unpublished, and is reprinted in the appendix to this petition at page 1a, *infra*. The order of the Eighth Circuit Court of Appeals denying rehearing is reprinted in the appendix to this petition at page 68a, *infra*.

JURISDICTION

The original opinion of the Eighth Circuit Court of Appeals was entered February 2, 2009. A timely motion to that court for rehearing was overruled on April 1, 2009.

The jurisdiction of this Court is invoked under 28 U.S.C. §1254.

1

EXAMPLE PETITION FOR WRIT OF CERTIORARI (continued)

STATUTORY AND CONSTITUTIONAL PROVISIONS INVOLVED

The following statutory and constitutional provisions are involved in this case.

U.S. CONST., AMEND. VI

In all criminal prosecutions, the accused shall enjoy the right to a speedy and public trial, by an impartial jury of the State and district wherein the crime shall have been committed, which district shall have been previously ascertained by law, and to be informed of the nature and cause of the accusation; to be confronted with the witnesses against him; to have compulsory process for obtaining witnesses in his favor, and to have the Assistance of Counsel for his defence.

U.S. CONST., AMEND. XIV

Section 1. All persons born or naturalized in the United States, and subject to the jurisdiction thereof, are citizens of the United States and of the State wherein they reside. No State shall make or enforce any law which shall abridge the privileges or immunities of citizens of the United States; nor shall any State deprive any person of life, liberty, or property, without due process of law; nor deny to any person within its jurisdiction the equal protection of the laws.

2

EXAMPLE PETITION FOR WRIT OF CERTIORARI (continued)

28 U.S.C. §2254

(a) The Supreme Court, a Justice thereof, a circuit judge, or a district court shall entertain an application for a writ of habeas corpus in behalf of a person in custody pursuant to the judgment of a State court only on the ground that he is in custody in violation of the Constitution or laws or treaties of the United States.

(b)(1) An application for a writ of habeas corpus on behalf of a person in custody pursuant to the judgment of a State court shall not be granted unless it appears that--

(A) the applicant has exhausted the remedies available in the courts of the State; or

(B)(i) there is an absence of available State corrective process; or

(ii) circumstances exist that render such process ineffective to protect the rights of the applicant.

(2) An application for a writ of habeas corpus may be denied on the merits, notwithstanding the failure of the applicant to exhaust the remedies available in the courts of the State.

3

EXAMPLE PETITION FOR WRIT OF CERTIORARI (continued)

(3) A State shall not be deemed to have waived the exhaustion requirement or be estopped from reliance upon the requirement unless the State, through counsel, expressly waives the requirement.

(c) An applicant shall not be deemed to have exhausted the remedies available in the courts of the State, within the meaning of this section, if he has the right under the law of the State to raise, by any available procedure, the question presented.

(d) An application for a writ of habeas corpus on behalf of a person in custody pursuant to the judgment of a State court shall not be granted with respect to any claim that was adjudicated on the merits in State court proceedings unless the adjudication of the claim--

(1) resulted in a decision that was contrary to, or involved an unreasonable application of, clearly established Federal law, as determined by the Supreme Court of the United States; or

(2) resulted in a decision that was based on an unreasonable determination of the facts in light of the evidence presented in the State court proceeding.

(e)(1) In a proceeding instituted by an application for a writ of habeas corpus by a person in custody pursuant to the judgment of a State court, a determination of a factual issue made by a State court shall be presumed to be correct. The applicant

4

EXAMPLE PETITION FOR WRIT OF CERTIORARI (continued)

shall have the burden of rebutting the presumption of correctness by clear and convincing evidence.

(2) If the applicant has failed to develop the factual basis of a claim in State court proceedings, the court shall not hold an evidentiary hearing on the claim unless the applicant shows that--

(A) the claim relies on--

(i) a new rule of constitutional law, made retroactive to cases on collateral review by the Supreme Court, that was previously unavailable; or

(ii) a factual predicate that could not have been previously discovered through the exercise of due diligence; and

(B) the facts underlying the claim would be sufficient to establish by clear and convincing evidence that but for constitutional error, no reasonable factfinder would have found the applicant guilty of the underlying offense.

(f) If the applicant challenges the sufficiency of the evidence adduced in such State court proceeding to support the State court's determination of a factual issue made therein, the applicant, if able, shall produce that part of the record pertinent to a determination of the sufficiency of the evidence to support such determination. If the applicant, because of indigency or other reason is unable to produce such part of the record, then the State shall produce such part of the record and the Federal court shall direct the State to do so by order directed to an appropriate State

5

EXAMPLE PETITION FOR WRIT OF CERTIORARI (continued)

official. If the State cannot provide such pertinent part of the record, then the court shall determine under the existing facts and circumstances what weight shall be given to the State court's factual determination.

(g) A copy of the official records of the State court, duly certified by the clerk of such court to be a true and correct copy of a finding, judicial opinion, or other reliable written indicia showing such a factual determination by the State court shall be admissible in the Federal court proceeding.

(h) Except as provided in section 408 of the Controlled Substances Act, in all proceedings brought under this section, and any subsequent proceedings on review, the court may appoint counsel for an applicant who is or becomes financially unable to afford counsel, except as provided by a rule promulgated by the Supreme Court pursuant to statutory authority. Appointment of counsel under this section shall be governed by section 3006A of title 18.

(i) The ineffectiveness or incompetence of counsel during Federal or State collateral post-conviction proceedings shall not be a ground for relief in a proceeding arising under section 2254.

6

EXAMPLE PETITION FOR WRIT OF CERTIORARI (continued)

STATEMENT OF THE CASE

Mr. Smith was convicted of the murder of Derek Hoskins. According to Kevin Glavin, a witness who was originally charged with the murder, Mr. Smith accused Mr. Hoskins of stealing, and then shot him while he was urinating at the side of the road. At Mr. Smith's first trial, the jury was unable to reach a verdict. During deliberations, the jury sent out a note reading, "Can we find guilty of being present but not actually shooting the gun?" Mr. Smith was then retried and convicted; his case was reversed for a Fourth Amendment violation. *State v. Smith,* 966 S.W.2d 1 (Mo. App. 1997), App. 25a. At his third trial, he was again convicted of first degree murder and sentenced to life in prison without possibility of parole. His conviction was affirmed on direct appeal. *State v. Smith,* 90 S.W.3d 132 (Mo. App. 2002), App. 34a. State post-conviction proceedings were filed; relief was denied in the motion court and on appeal. *Smith v. State, unpublished,* App. 46a. Mr. Smith then filed a habeas corpus action under 28 U.S.C. §2254. Relief was denied by the district court (App. 9a), but Mr. Smith was granted a certificate of appealability on the issue presented in this petition. App. 22a. However, the Eighth Circuit denied relief. App. 1a.

At Mr. Smith's final trial, Kevin Glavin refused to testify about the incident, saying that he no longer remembered what happened the night of Hoskins's death and was mentally incapable of testifying. The prosecutor was then permitted to

7

EXAMPLE PETITION FOR WRIT OF CERTIORARI (continued)

present a videotaped statement that Mr. Glavin had given which implicated Mr. Smith. On videotape, Mr. Glavin said that he and Mr. Hoskins were standing by the side of the road urinating, and Mr. Smith came up behind Mr. Hoskins. Mr. Glavin did not see Mr. Smith shoot, but heard a shot and saw Mr. Hoskins fall. Mr. Glavin admitted that he had originally been charged with the murder himself, and that he had previously been convicted of theft. Evidence was also presented that Mr. Glavin had used drugs extensively and was intoxicated on the night of the offense. He did not implicate Mr. Smith until he himself was charged, at first denying any knowledge of the incident. On cross-examination, he was asked if he had killed Mr. Hoskins; he said he did not remember.

No murder weapon was ever found. The state presented evidence that shell casings found at the scene matched casings found at 411 Indiana Street in Kansas City. The state then presented the prior testimony of Kathy and Lorie Stone, who were not available at the time of Mr. Smith's trial. The Stones denied that they had ever said that Mr. Smith fired shots at 411 Indiana. The prosecutor was then permitted to impeach them with statements they made to the police which indicated that Mr. Smith *did* fire shots at 411 Indiana at a time before Hoskins's death. However, another detective testified that the Stones' account of what Mr. Smith did was inconsistent with the location of the shell cases at 411 Indiana. Nonetheless, the state argued that the match between the Indiana Street casings and the murder scene casings showed that Mr. Smith was the murderer. Although the jury

8

EXAMPLE PETITION FOR WRIT OF CERTIORARI (continued)

convicted Mr. Smith, one juror later contacted trial counsel and said he wanted to change his verdict.

At his state post-conviction hearing, Mr. Smith testified that he had told his trial counsel about a witness, Alvino Carrillo, who could impeach the testimony of the Stones. He presented a letter to counsel which identified Mr. Carrillo. Mr. Smith further testified that had Mr. Carrillo been called as a witness at trial, he (Mr. Smith) would also have testified. He would have testified that Mr. Glavin left him at the home of Rose Sanchez, and returned without Mr. Hoskins, who had previously been in the car. Mr. Smith's testimony would also have negated other circumstantial evidence the state contended supported his guilt. He would have explained that the shell casings found in his yard were there because another person, Ricky Sosa (who Mr. Glavin said was in the car when the shooting occurred) fired shots in his yard the same night of the 411 Indiana incident. Mr. Smith would further have explained the fact that his fingerprints were found in the back seat of a vehicle identified by Mr. Glavin as the car used in the offense; he would have stated that he was in the vehicle on another occasion and sat in the back seat. He would also have explained his post-offense possession of Mr. Hoskins's bicycle.

Mr. Carrillo also testified at the post-conviction hearing. He said that he recalled the incident at Indiana Street, but that Mr. Smith fired no shots. In fact, other people were shooting at Mr. Smith. Mr. Carrillo further said that trial counsel had never contacted him, although he was available and would have testified. Trial

9

EXAMPLE PETITION FOR WRIT OF CERTIORARI (continued)

counsel did not testify. By the time of the post-conviction hearing, he had been disbarred for professional misconduct stemming from a substance abuse problem. Evidence was presented that post-conviction counsel attempted to have him served with a deposition subpoena in California, but was unable to do so.

The post-conviction court denied relief on this claim on two grounds. First, the court cited Missouri authority that a post-conviction litigant could never meet the "performance prong" of the *Strickland v. Washington*, 466 U.S. 668, 687-88 (1984), test by showing that trial counsel had no reasonable strategic reason for failing to call a witness unless trial counsel testified. Alternatively, the court found that Mr. Smith had not shown prejudice. The Missouri Court affirmed. In so holding, the court found that Mr. Carrillo's testimony would have affected only a collateral issue. It largely ignored Mr. Smith's post-conviction testimony that he would have testified at trial had Mr. Carrillo been called.

Reviewing the denial of habeas corpus relief by the district court, the Eighth Circuit Court of Appeals found that the holding of the Missouri Court of Appeals that Mr. Smith had not shown prejudice was a reasonable application of *Strickland v. Washington*, 466 U.S. 668, 687-88 (1984). In so holding, the Court said, "Smith's testimony would not have explained hcw shell casings matching those found at the murder scene were located inside his house in a locked safe." App. 8a. But NO shell casings, much less casings which matched the murder scene, were found in the safe. What was found in the safe was live ammunition of the same caliber as the shell

10

EXAMPLE PETITION FOR WRIT OF CERTIORARI (continued)

casings found at the scene. There was no testimony that this ammunition was of the same brand or from the same source as the casings found at the murder scene, and there was no finding by *any* Missouri court that casings matching the murder scene were found in Mr. Smith's safe. In fact, the Missouri Court of Appeals found on direct appeal that the evidence in the safe was largely irrelevant to Mr. Smith's guilt.

> The probative value of the live ammunition found in Smith's safe was minimal. The most that evidence could have established for the jury was that Smith owned or had access to the same type of ammunition used in the killing, although, from the testimony at trial, it is questionable whether those rounds were even the same type used to kill Hoskins.

State v. Smith, 966 S.W.2d 1, 9 (Mo. App. 1998).[1]

To determine the facts of the case for the purpose of making the prejudice analysis, the Court of Appeals relied on, and quoted, the statement of facts from the Missouri Court of Appeals opinion on direct appeal. App. 2a-6a. Based on that statement, the Eighth Circuit found the evidence against Mr. Smith so strong that neither his testimony nor that of Mr. Carrillo had a reasonable probability of affecting the outcome.

---

[1] Shell casings matching those found at the crime scene were located OUTSIDE of Mr. Smith's house. But Mr. Smith would have explained that Ricky Sosa (who was with Kevin Glavin the night of the murder) had fired shots outside his house on the same night as the Indiana Street incident. Mr. Smith so testified during a pretrial hearing.

11

EXAMPLE PETITION FOR WRIT OF CERTIORARI (continued)

REASONS FOR GRANTING THE WRIT

I. THE EIGHTH CIRCUIT'S MISAPPLICATION OF THE PREJUDICE STANDARD OF *STRICKLAND* WARRANTS THIS COURT'S ATTENTION.

The Eighth Circuit's opinion misapplied the *Strickland v. Washington*, 466 U.S. 668, 687-88 (1984), test for prejudice in two important ways. First, the Court flagrantly misstated the record. It stated that evidence in Mr. Smith's safe included shell casings matching the murder scene. Such evidence would, indeed, have been strong evidence of Mr. Smith's guilt. But it did not exist. Instead, in order to connect Mr. Smith with the shell casings found at the scene, the state relied on the recanted testimony of the Stones. Evidence which impeached that testimony, such as the omitted testimony of Mr. Carrillo, would have dealt a serious blow to the state's case.

This Court requires, in making the prejudice analysis under *Strickland*, that the reviewing court consider all of the evidence in the record, both that which was admitted at the trial and that which is developed at the post-conviction stage. *Strickland v. Washington*, 466 U.S. 668, 687-88 (1984*). Rompilla v. Beard*, 545 U.S. 374 (2005); *Wiggins v. Smith*, 539 U.S. 510 (2003); *Williams (Terry) v. Taylor*, 529 U.S. 362 (2000). Under this test, it is inappropriate to consider the evidence in the light most favorable to the verdict. It is clear that the Court of Appeals here disregarded this principle. As it has in several other cases, the court began its analysis by setting out the version of the facts given by the Missouri Court of

12

EXAMPLE PETITION FOR WRIT OF CERTIORARI (continued)

Appeals in its direct appeal opinion. See *Chavez v. Weber*, 497 F.3d 796, 799 (8th Cir. 2007). *Bucklew v. Luebbers*, 436 F.3d 1010, 1013 (8th Cir.), *cert. denied*, 549 U.S. 1079 (2006); *Middleton v. Roper*, 455 F.3d 838, 843 (8th Cir. 2006); *Middleton v. Roper*, 498 F.3d 812, 813 (8th Cir. 2007); *Gingras v. Weber*, 543 F.3d 1001, 1002 (8th Cir. 2008).

The Court then went on to hold, based on this recitation and its factual error discussed above, "Based on the substantial inculpatory evidence presented at trial, we determine that Smith was not prejudiced by his trial counsel's failure to call and interview Carrillo." App. 8a. But this analysis ignored *conflicting* evidence that was presented at trial but not recited by the Missouri Court of Appeals.

For example, the opinion refers to the "testimony of witnesses who saw [Mr. Smith] with a gun and the victim's property shortly after the murder." App. 8a. This is an apparent reference to the statement in the court of appeals opinion, quoted by the panel, "Sanchez told police that Smith. . . had a gun tucked into his waistband." App. 4a.[2] The opinion ignores, however, the *trial testimony* of Sanchez that it was not true that Mr. Smith had a handgun when she saw him, and her denial that she had ever said that Mr. Smith had a gun. Ms. Sanchez also testified at trial that Mr. Glavin had left her home before Mr. Smith and Mr. Sosa, contradicting Mr. Glavin's testimony that they left together and picked up Mr. Hoskins together. In addition to

---

[2] The opinion refers to "witnesses" who saw Mr. Smith with a gun after Hoskins's murder, but Sanchez is the only such witness cited in the opinion. Roxana Soriano testified that she heard guns being cocked while Mr. Smith was in the car with Hoskins, Glavin, and Sosa, but that Mr. Smith's hands were on the steering wheel and he could not have cocked a gun.

EXAMPLE PETITION FOR WRIT OF CERTIORARI (continued)

misstating the contents of the safe at Mr. Smith's house, the opinion also ignored

the fact that identification belonging to someone other than Mr. Smith, Jose Sosa,

was also found in the safe. In light of this evidence, it is not even clear that Mr.

Smith was the person who placed the ammunition in the safe.

These factual issues do not require the attention of this Court. What does

merit review is the emerging practice of the Eighth Circuit of ignoring evidence

while performing prejudice analysis. This was precisely the type of review that this

Court condemned in *Williams (Terry) v. Taylor*, 529 U.S. 362, 397-398 (2000).

> [T]he State Supreme Court's prejudice determination was
> unreasonable insofar as it failed to evaluate the totality of
> the available mitigation evidence—both that adduced at
> trial, and the evidence adduced in the habeas proceeding
> in reweighing it against the evidence in aggravation.
> [Citation omitted]. This error is apparent in its
> consideration of the additional mitigation evidence
> developed in the postconviction proceedings. . .
>
> [T]he state court failed even to mention the sole argument
> in mitigation that trial counsel did advance—Williams
> turned himself in, alerting police to a crime they
> otherwise would never have discovered, expressing
> remorse for his actions, and cooperating with the police
> after that. While this, coupled with the prison records
> and guard testimony, may not have overcome a finding of
> future dangerousness, the graphic description of Williams'
> childhood, filled with abuse and privation, or the reality
> that he was "borderline mentally retarded," might well
> have influenced the jury's appraisal of his moral
> culpability. . . .

Because the Eighth Circuit Court of Appeals has truncated the scope of *Strickland v.*

Washington, 466 U.S. 668, 687-88 (1984), prejudice review, this Court must grant certiorari.

14

EXAMPLE PETITION FOR WRIT OF CERTIORARI (continued)

II. THE DECISION OF THE EIGHTH CIRCUIT IS IN CONFLICT WITH THE DECISIONS OF OTHER CIRCUITS.

In the closely analogous case of *Stanley v. Bartley*, 465 F.3d 810 (7th Cir. 2006), the court confronted a situation where the state's "eyewitness", like Mr. Glavin in Mr. Smith's case, could easily have been the murderer himself. At least the witness in Mr. Stanley's case was willing to testify in court; Mr. Glavin refused even to do that. And, in *Stanley*, the state presented evidence that Mr. Stanley had made admissions to his sister. No evidence of any admission by Mr. Smith was presented. Nonetheless, under the *Strickland* standard, the federal appeals court in *Stanley* found that the failure of trial counsel to interview and call witnesses was prejudicial, and that the state court's contrary conclusion was not reasonable. The conviction was reversed. See also *Smith v. Dretke*, 417 F.3d 438 (5th Cir. 2005), where the court found ineffective assistance of counsel for failing to present evidence of self-defense which would have corroborated the defendant's testimony to that defense.

These cases illustrate the fact that the Eighth Circuit Court of Appeals is out of step with this Court and with other circuits in its consideration of the *Strickland v. Washington*, 466 U.S. 668, 687-88 (1984), prejudice prong. Certiorari should be granted to correct this error.

15

EXAMPLE PETITION FOR WRIT OF CERTIORARI (concluded)

CONCLUSION

For these reasons, a Writ of Certiorari should issue to review the judgment and opinion of the Eighth Circuit Court of Appeals.

Respectfully submitted,

ELIZABETH UNGER CARLYLE
P.O. Box 866
Columbus, MS 39703

(816) 525-6540

16

SUMMARIZED APPENDICES FOR EXAMPLE PETITION FOR WRIT OF CERTIORARI

The example petition for writ of certiorari included 7 appendices, none of which are included in this book. Those appendices are summarized below.

1. Decision of the Eighth Circuit Court of Appeals (8 pages): "Zachary Smith appeals from the district court's denial of his petition for a writ of habeas corpus pursuant to 28 U.S.C. §2254. We affirm."

2. Memorandum and Order of the District Court (14 pages): "Pending is Petitioner's Petition for Writ of Habeas Corpus filed pursuant to 28 U.S.C. §2254. After reviewing the Record and the parties' arguments, the Court concludes the Petition must be denied."

3. Order granting certificate of appealability (2 pages): "Upon de novo review of the record and Petitioner's motion, the Court grants a Certificate of Appealability as to the issue of whether Petitioner received ineffective assistance of counsel due to his counsel's failure to interview and call as a witness Alvino Carrillo."

4. State v. Smith, 966 S.W.2d 1 (Mo. App. 1997) (9 pages): "Defendant was convicted in the Circuit Court of Jackson County ... of first degree murder and armed criminal action, and he appealed. The Court of Appeals ... held that: (1) defendant was entitled to instruction on lesser included offense of second degree murder; (2) search of house was lawful; and (3) search of locked safe found in house was unlawful. ... Reversed and remanded."

5. State v. Smith, 90 S.W.3D 132 (Mo. App. 2002) (12 pages): "Defendant was convicted by a jury in the Circuit Court, Jackson County ... or murder in the first degree and armed criminal action. Defendant appealed. The Court of Appeals ... reversed and remanded. On remand, the Circuit Court convicted defendant of first degree murder and armed criminal action. Defendant appealed. The Court of Appeals ... held that: (1) evidence supported finding that defendant's girlfriend had authority to consent to the search of a safe found in their house, and (2) act of the trial court in allow the jury to view the videotaped statement of a witness during jury deliberations did not constitute plain error. ... The judgment of the trial court is affirmed."

6. Smith v. State, unpublished decision Sept. 19, 2006 (22 pages): "Zachary Smith appeals the denial, following an evidentiary hearing, of his Rule 29.15 motion for post-conviction relief, in which he raised claims of ineffective assistance of trial counsel and prosecutorial misconduct. Having carefully considered the contentions on appeal, we find no grounds for reversing the decision. ... Affirmed."

7. Order denying rehearing April 1, 2009 (1 page): "The pro se petition for rehearing en banc by appellant is denied. The petition for rehearing by the panel is also denied. ... The petition for rehearing by panel filed by appellant's counsel is also denied."

EXAMPLE PETITION FOR REHEARING

No. 09-5086

IN THE SUPREME COURT OF THE UNITED STATES

ZACHARY SMITH,

Petitioner,

V.

MIKE KEMNA,

Respondent.

CERTIFICATE OF GOOD FAITH

COMES NOW Petitioner, Zachary Smith, and makes certification that his petition for rehearing is presented to this Court in good faith pursuant to Rule 44. Mr. Smith further states the following:

1. This Court entered its judgment denying petitioner a Writ of Certiorari on October 5, 2009. Petitioner believes that he presents this Court with adequate grounds to justify the granting of rehearing in this case and said petition is brought in good faith and not for delay. Furthermore, petitioner believes that based upon the law of this Court and facts of this case, Smith is entitled to relief which has been unjustly denied him. He further believes that if the Eighth Circuit Court of Appeals are continually allowed to apply the Strickland standard improperly, a number of people will be denied their constitutional right to due process.

I declare under the penalty of perjury that the foregoing is true and correct.

Executed on this 15th day of October, 2009.

Z.A. Smith

EXAMPLE PETITION FOR REHEARING (continued)

No. 09–5086

IN THE SUPREME COURT OF THE UNITED STATES

ZACHARY SMITH,

Petitioner,

V.

MIKE KEMNA,

Respondent.

ON PETITION FOR WRIT OF CERTIORARI TO
THE EIGHTH CIRCUIT COURT OF APPEALS

_____

PETITION FOR REHEARING

_____

ZACHARY SMITH
Reg. No. 521163
Crossroads Corr. Center
1115 E. Pence Road
Cameron, MO 64429

Petitioner Pro Se

EXAMPLE PETITION FOR REHEARING (continued)

TABLE OF CONTENTS

EXAMPLE PETITION FOR REHEARING (continued)

<u>**TABLE OF AUTHORITIES**</u>

Anderson V. Johnson, 338 F.3d 392 (5th Cir. 2003)................6

Bryant V. Scott, 28 F.3d 1411 (5th Cir. 1994)....................6

Miller V. Anderson, 255 F.3d 455 (7th Cir. 2001)................7

Nealy V. Cabana, 764 F.2d 1173 (5th Cir. 1985)..................6

Stanley V. Bartley, 465 F.3d 810 (7th Cir. 2006)..............5, 7

State V. Smith, 966 S.W.2d 1 (Mo.App. 1997)......................4

Strickland V. Washington, 466 U.S. 668 (1984)..................4, 6

Williams (Terry) V. Taylor, 529 U.S. 362 (2000)................4, 6

RULES

Supreme Court Rule 44..1

ii

EXAMPLE PETITION FOR REHEARING (continued)

<h3 style="text-align:center">PETITION FOR REHEARING AND SUGGESTIONS IN SUPPORT</h3>

COMES NOW Petitioner, Zachary Smith, Pro Se, and prays this Court to grant Rehearing pursuant to Rule 44, and thereafter, grant him a Writ of Certiorari to review the opinion of the Eighth Circuit Court of Appeals. In support of petition, Mr. Smith states the following.

STATEMENT OF FACTS

At a third trial, Zachary Smith was convicted by a jury of first degree murder and armed criminal action and sentenced to life without the possibility of probation or parole and ninety-nine years.

According to the State's key witness, Kevin Glavin was a passenger with Smith, Jose Sosa, and Derek Hoskins in a car Smith borrowed on June 23, 1995, cruising around the Northeast area of Kansas City, Missouri. They arrived in an area called Cliff Drive. Glavin told Smith that he needed to urinate, so Smith stopped the car underneath a street light and then backed up the car away from the light. Glavin believed that something was wrong, because there was no need from Smith to back up the car in such an isolated area. Also, there was a black pistol under the armrest. Glavin warned Hoskins to stay in the car. Hoskins, however, insisted that he also had to urinate.

Glavin walked toward the back of the car, turned to the curb, and began to urinate. Hoskins stood next to him and also started to urinate. Smith got out of the car, walked behind Glavin and Hoskins, and stood between them. Glavin heard a gunshot, looked up, and saw a bright flash. He saw Smith holding a pistol and lowing his arm, one to three feet away from Hoskins. Hoskins went limp and fell to the ground. Both Smith and Glavin got back into the car. Smith clicked another round into the chamber of the gun. He fired the round out the window towards Hoskins' body.

1

EXAMPLE PETITION FOR REHEARING (continued)

According to Glavin, Smith killed Hoskins because he stole Smith's lawnmower a week or two prior to the shooting. However, Hoskins allegedly committed a burglary to pay Smith back. The State offered no evidence to support that Hoskins actually committed a burglary on the night in question as Glavin testified.

Although the State of Missouri presented much testimony regarding events preceding and after Hoskins' death, it presented just one eyewitness, Kevin Glavin, to testify regarding the actual shooting. Glavin, however, lacked credibility. Glavin admitted that he had prior convictions for second degree robbery and theft. He also admitted that he smoked crack cocaine and drank beer prior to the events at issue, that he had possibly used cocaine as many as five times that day, and had used cocaine frequently in the 48 hours prior to the shooting. Glavin conceded that he had been charged with murder in the first degree and armed criminal action with regard to Hoskins' death, but the charges were dismissed after he implicated Smith in the crimes. He admitted that his Clay County charge of second degree robbery also was reduced to stealing, which he pled guilty.

Additionally, Glavin changed his version of the events. Initially, Glavin told the police that Smith had no involvement in Hoskins' death. He later changed his account to implicate Smith as the shooter.

The State presented evidence that shells collected at 411 Indiana in Kansas City, Missouri, matched the shells that killed Hoskins. (Weapon itself was never found). The State also presented out-of-court statements of witnesses Cathy and Lori Stone that Smith had fired a weapon at 411 Indiana two weeks before Hoskins' death. The testimony of the Stones from Smith's second trial was read to the jury by the State over objection; the witnesses could not be located for the third trial. In their testimony,

2

EXAMPLE PETITION FOR REHEARING (continued)

the Stones repudiated their prior statements that they ever actually saw Smith shoot a gun. They testified that they were both under the influence of crack cocaine at the time their statements were made. Moreover, the physical evidence presented at trial contradicted the Stones' account. Detective Beard testified that the shells found at 411 Indiana were not located where they would have been had Smith actually fired from the location specified by the Stones, making their statements that they saw Smith shoot a gun questionable. Nonetheless, the State relied heavily on the match between the Indiana Street shells and the shells which killed Hoskins to connect Smith to the murder weapon. The State vehemently argued at trial that this evidence established that Smith, and not Glavin, was the killer because Smith had possession of and fired the murder weapon two weeks before.

Failing to Interview and Call Alvino Carrillo as a Witness

Alvino Carillo testified that the post-conviction hearing that he had been present at the Indiana Street incident referred to by the Stones. He said that Smith did not fire a weapon that night. Instead, Carillo testified that shots were fired at Smith, among others and Mr. Sosa exchanged gunfire. Carillo's testimony would have refuted the Stones' statements that they saw Smith in possession of and firing the weapon that was used to shoot Hoskins. The uncontradicted evidence from the post-conviction hearing was that Smith informed counsel of Carillo and what he would say, and trial counsel never contacted Carillo. Smith also testified that not only did he not fire the shots outside Indiana, but as far as he knew Kevin Glavin, and not he, had killed Hoskins.

REASONS MERITING REHEARING

1. The Eighth Circuit's decision is clearly in conflict with **Strickland**

3

EXAMPLE PETITION FOR REHEARING (continued)

V. Washington, 466 U.S. 668 (19984); and **Williams (Terry) Taylor**, 529 U.S. 362 (2000), emphasizing that in determining Strickland prejudice, the court must examine both the trial testimony and the post-conviction evidence to determine whether, had the omitted evidence been presented, there is a reasonable probability of a different outcome, in that the Eighth Circuit merely examined the opinions of the Missouri Court of Appeals which stated the facts in the light most favorable to the jury's verdict and all contrary evidence ignored. For example, the state court's opinion states; "Sanchez later told the police that Smith had arrived in a newer, four-door burgundy or red car and had a gun tucked into his waistband." The Eighth Circuit completely ignored the fact that Rose Sanchez testified that Smith, Sosa, and Glavin had come to her house and Smith was not in possession of a gun. She testified that Smith and Sosa stayed there at her house and Glavin left. She further testified that she had sex with Smith and he stayed with her until morning.

The Eighth Circuit further ignored the fact that inside the safe there was an inmate Id card for Jose Sosa, which jurors could have easily believed Smith was not the only person that had access to the 45-caliber ammunition. Furthermore, the State court stated; "The probative value of the live ammunition found in Smith's safe was minimal. The most that evidence could have established for the jury was that Smith owned or had access to the same type of ammunition used in the killing. Although, from the testimony at trial, it is questionable whether those rounds were even the same type used to kill Hoskins." **State V. Smith**, 966 S.W.2d 1, at 8 (Mo.App.1997). These conclusions are supported by the jury in the first trial when they sent down a note that read; **"Can we be a hung jury? We are eight to four after much discussion. Can we find guilty of being present but not actually**

4

EXAMPLE PETITION FOR REHEARING (continued)

shooting the gun?"

The panel also ignored Smith's post-conviction testimony that Sosa shot off two rounds at his house on the same night as the Indiana incident. This is clear by the Eighth Circuit's conclusion, "Smith's testimony would not have explained how shell casings matching those found at the murder scene were located inside his house in a locked safe." (panel's opinion p. 8).

2. The Eighth Circuit's decision is clearly in direct conflict with **Stanley V. Bartley**, 465 F.3d 810 (7th Cir. 2006), which case is so strikingly similar, both legally and factually, that the same result reached in **Stanley** must also be reached in this case. This Court **MUST** grant Rehearing and issue a Writ of Certiorari because the failure to do so would allow the Eighth Circuit to continue to apply the wrong standard in deciding the prejudice prong of ineffective assistance claims, and deny justice to those it is entitled to.

3. This Court has an ethical duty by the United States Constitution to establish the law of the land and to assure the Citizens of the United States of America that the lower courts apply that law. When they do not, **it is this Court's obligation to HOLD THAT COURT ACCOUNTABLE and see to it that justice is administered fairly.** This Court **MUST** hear this case and hold the Eighth Circuit accountable for failing to properly apply the law of this Court and relief where relief is do.

SUGGESTIONS IN SUPPORT OF REHEARING

The Missouri Court of Appeals' decision that Smith could not overcome the presumption that the decision by trial counsel not to interview or call Mr. Carillo as a witness was trial strategy resulted in both an unreasonable determination of the facts in light of the evidence presented

5

EXAMPLE PETITION FOR REHEARING (continued)

and an unreasonable application of **Strickland V. Washington**, because counsel's failure to even interview Mr. Carillo was unreasonable and Smith's evidence that he informed counsel of Carillo met the first prong of **Strickland**. As in **Anderson V. Johnson**, 338 F.3d 392 (5th Cir. 2003); "[T]here is no' evidence that counsel's decision to forego investigation was reasoned at all, and it is, in out opinion, far from reasonable. Counsel's failure to investigation was not 'part of a calculated trial strategy' but is likely the result of either indolence or incompetence." As the court put it in **Bryant V. Scott**, 28 F.3d 1411, 1415 (5th Cir. 1994), "[A]n attorney must engage in a reasonable amount of pretrial investigation and 'at a minimum...interview potential witnesses and...make an independent investigation of the facts and circumstances in the case" (quoting **Nealy V. Cabana**, 764 F.2d 1173, 1177 (5th Cir. 1985). Under the circumstances here, the State had the burden to show a strategy supporting the failure to interview Mr. Carillo. Because it failed to do so, Smith has clearly met the "performance prong" of the **Strickland V. Washington**, 466 U.S. 668, 687-88 (1984) test. The question for this Court to answer is whether Smith was prejudiced by counsel's ineffectiveness.

The State court held that Smith had not demonstrated prejudice from the failure to call Carillo. The court suggested that the evidence against Smith was "overwhelming" and therefore Carillo would not have made no difference. This conclusion is likewise an unreasonable interpretation of **Strickland** and its progeny. **Williams (Terry) Taylor**, 529 U.S. 362 (2000), emphasizes that in determining Strickland prejudice, the court **MUST EXAMINE** both the trial testimony and the postconviction evidence to determine whether, had the omitted evidence been presented, there is a reasonable probability of a different outcome.

6

EXAMPLE PETITION FOR REHEARING (continued)

To the extent that inferior federal courts have decided factually similar cases, reference to those decisions is appropriate in assessing the reasonableness...of the state court's treatment of the contested issue. **Copeland V. Washington**, 237 F.3d 969, 974 (8th Cir. 2000). Smith refers this Court to **Stanley V. Bartley**, 465 F.3d 810 (7th Cir. 2006)(Smith has attached a copy of case to this petition).

As was the case in **Stanley**, the issue is not whether Smith is innocent, but whether if he had had a competent lawyer he would have had a reasonable chance (it needn't be a 50 percent or greater chance; **Miller V. Anderson**, 255 F.3d 455, 459 (7th Cir. 2001), of being acquitted; given that guilt must be proved beyond a reasonable doubt, guilty people are often acquitted.

Similarly, given Glavin's rampant use of crack cocaine leading up to the shooting, his criminal background, and his self-interest in shifting blame for the shooting away from himself and onto Mr. Smith, the jury easily could have disbelieved his account of Hoskins' death. In fact, the first trial of Smith's resulted in a mistrial after the jury sent down a note reading, **"Can we be a hung jury? We are eight to four after much discussion. Can we find guilty of being present but not actually shooting the gun?"** These jurors clearly did not credit either the weak ballistics evidence or the testimony of Kevin Glavin. And one juror from the most recent trial contacted trial counsel two days after the trial and said that he was confused and had serious reservations and reasonable doubt that existed in his mind, as well as in the mind of other jurors, and wished to change his verdict.

There were other witnesses, but their testimony was distinctly secondary and circumstantial. Smith did not make any admissions to police, and the statements he made, proved nothing. Reasonable jurors could have

7

EXAMPLE PETITION FOR REHEARING (continued)

believed that Smith was merely being uncooperative with the police at the time of his questioning. Smith's possession of the victim's bicycle after the murder is circumstantial and is not conclusive evidence that Smith was the shooter of Hoskins. It was the combination of Glavin's and the Stone's testimony that they saw Smith shoot a gun that matched the shells at the crime scene that convicted Smith of first degree murder. Had Carillo been called as a witness and testified that Sosa fired the gun, not Smith, there is a reasonable probability that the jury would have completely disregarded the Stone's testimony and the shell casing evidence because there was no other witnesses that put the murder weapon in Smith's hands before or after Hoskins' death. Roxana Soriano testified that she heard what she thought to be guns being cocked while Hoskins was in the car with Hoskins, Glavin, and Sosa, but that Smith's hands were on the steering wheel and he could not have cocked a gun.

Rose Sanchez testified that Smith, Sosa, and Glavin came to her house and Smith was not in possession of a gun. She testified that Smith and Sosa stayed there and Glavin left. She further testified that Smith stayed with her until the next morning. Inside the safe there was an inmate Id card for Jose Sosa, which jurors could have easily believed Smith was not the only person who had access to the 45-caliber ammunition. And as found by the first trial jurors, they could have easily believed that Smith was never in possession of the gun used to kill Hoskins on the night in question.

The result reached in **Stanley** is also required here. The State's witnesses in this case were highly suspect, not overwhelmingly compelling. Mr. Glavin, a cocaine addict and convicted felon, could have been the murderer. In fact, when defense counsel asked Glavin if he had killed

8

EXAMPLE PETITION FOR REHEARING (continued)

Hoskins, Glavin said he couldn't remember whether he had killed Hoskins or not. Kathy and Lori Stone were under the influence of crack cocaine at the time the events they testified about occurred, and their testimony was contradicted by the physical evidence. nonetheless, the State relied heavily on the match between the casings found at 411 Indiana and the bullet which killed Hoskins to convict Smith. The testimony of Mr. Carrillo would have contradicted their testimony. Moreover, had Carrillo testified, Smith would have also testified.

Specifically, Smith would have explained that on the evening of Hoskins' murder, he, Glavin, and Sosa were driving around in Mr. Hampton's car looking for cocaine and saw Hoskins. Hoskins and Glavin (who was intoxicated) began arguing about Glavin's allege theft of cocaine from a friend of Hoskins. Smith intervened and cooled the parties down. Eventually, Hoskins got in the car with them, and Glavin apologized and shook hands with him.

After a fruitless search for drugs, Glavin and Hoskins dropped Smith off at the home of Flo Brown. Later, Glavin returned alone and told Smith, Rose Sanchez, and Sosa that he had an argument with Hoskins and killed him. Glavin brought Hoskins' bike back in the car. Smith took the bike out of the car and returned the car to the owner; her gave the bike to Sandra Cordray in exchange for a power drill she was trying to sell.

Smith would have also explained that he did not fire any shots during the incident at 411 Indiana and the two shells in his yard were there from Sosa shooting a gun off on the same night as the Indiana incident.

Smith never made any admissions to the police. The closest thing to direct evidence connecting him to the crime was Glavin. Had the jury heard the testimony of Carrillo and Smith, there is a reasonable probability

9

EXAMPLE PETITION FOR REHEARING (concluded)

of a different outcome.

CONCLUSION

For the reasons stated, this Court MUST grant Rehearing of its judgment entered on October 5, 2009, and issue a Writ of Certiorari to hold the Eighth Circuit accountable for failing to properly apply the law of this Court and grant Mr. Smith relief. Should Smith's cry for justice not be heard and denied relief; may this Court also cry and not be heard **"For whoever shut their ears to the cry of the poor will also cry themselves and not be heard."** Proverbs 21:13.

Respectfully submitted,

Zachary Smith
ZACHARY SMITH,
Reg. No. 521163
CRCC
1115 E. Pence Rd.,
Cameron, MO 64429

Petitioner

CERTIFICATE OF SERVICE

The undersigned hereby certifies that a copy of the foregoing was mailed, postage prepaid, this _15th_ day of _October_, 2009, to; Michael Spillane, Assistant Attorney General, P.O. Box 899, Jefferson City, Missouri 65102.

Z.A. Smith
Petitioner

10

11. BEYOND THE UNITED STATES SUPREME COURT

PETITION FOR CLEMENCY

After a petition for rehearing is decided, there are no other petitions that can be filed in your case. At this point, you may want to consider preparing a petition for clemency. Clemency, however, is a subject for another book and is not addressed further herein.

LaVergne, TN USA
18 March 2011
220637LV00002B/2/P